The Palace Inns

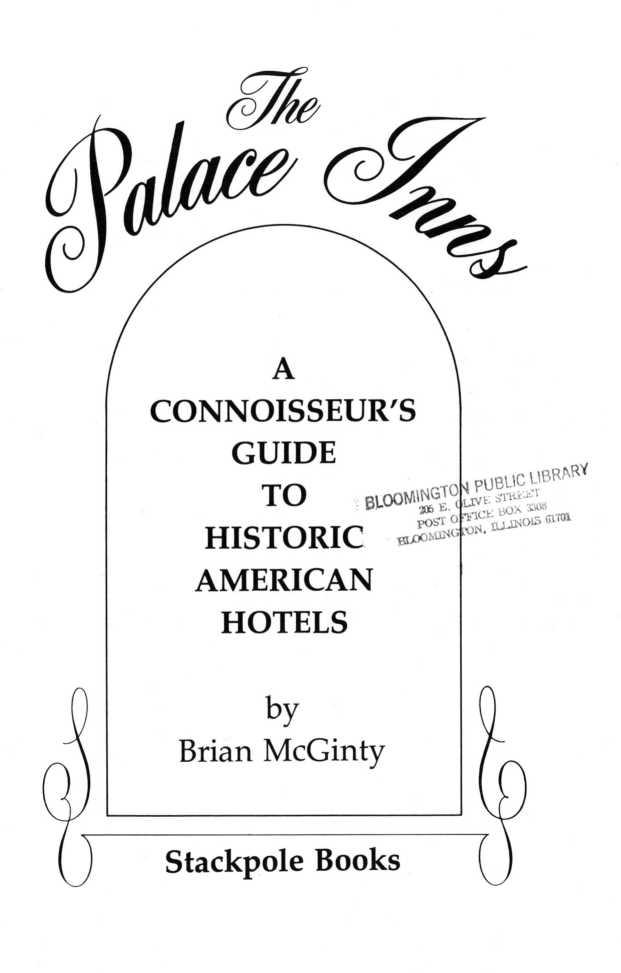

The Palace Inns

A
CONNOISSEUR'S
GUIDE
TO
HISTORIC
AMERICAN
HOTELS

by

Brian McGinty

Stackpole Books

THE PALACE INNS
Copyright © 1978 by
Brian McGinty

Cameron House is an imprint
published by
STACKPOLE BOOKS
Cameron and Kelker Streets
P.O. Box 1831
Harrisburg, Pa. 17105

Published simultaneously in Don Mills, Ontario, Canada
by Thomas Nelson & Sons, Ltd.

Printed in the U.S.A.

Jacket Photograph: Main lobby of the new Breakers Hotel, Palm Beach, Florida (Courtesy of the Breakers Hotel)

Library of Congress Cataloging in Publication Data

McGinty, Brian.
   The palace inns.

   Bibliography: p.
   1. Hotels, taverns, etc.—United States—History.
I. Title
TX909.M29 1978   647'.9473   78-73
ISBN 0-8117-1166-8

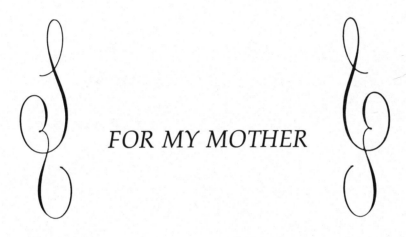

FOR MY MOTHER

The Story of Greece is in its temples,
that of America is in its hotels.

GENE FOWLER

Contents

PREFACE

The process of selection inevitably requires a balance of judgment and discretion. Selecting the hotels whose histories are recounted in this book has not been an easy task. It was necessary in advance to lay down certain criteria for their selection.

First, it was my feeling that the book should be limited to hotels still in existence and still operating as hotels—not as convalescent hospitals, converted office complexes, or college campuses. Two or three interesting histories of hotels that once existed but have since disappeared have been written and published. While valuable as records of a bygone day, they lack the sense of immediacy and tangibility I wished to convey in *The Palace Inns*. By limiting the book to hotels still in operation, readers who like to see and feel history as well as read about it could visit the included hotels, relax in their lobbies, stroll in their corridors, take meals in their dining rooms, dance in their ballrooms.

Second, the hotels should be large and luxurious—what nineteenth-century Americans called "swagger hotels" and contemporary travelers most often think of as "grand hotels." Probably no state in the Union is without at least one inn or hotel that can claim a history of sorts. If George Washington did not sleep there, if Longfellow did not write a poem there, the house may have been a haunt of rebels (vintage 1776 or 1861), a rendezvous of Indian fighters, a retreat for sweat-soaked buffalo hunters, a trysting place for star-crossed lovers. Any attempt to include all such inns and hotels in a single volume would be self-defeating. Readers would find the resulting profusion of histories at best repetitious, at worst bewildering.

Third, the hotels should have played a prominent role in the history of their regions or of the United States. Their histories should have some significance beyond the communities in which they are located. If the present hotel structures were not erected in the nineteenth century, they should perpetuate traditions that began before 1900. Their builders and operators should have been men and women of stature; their most celebrated guests persons of achievement or renown.

Fourth, the hotels should, as far as possible, be fairly representative of different sections of the country. At least two New York City hotels, the Chelsea and the Algonquin, might have been included but, because they seemed generally less historic than the Plaza or the Waldorf-Astoria, which had to be included, they were passed over, albeit reluctantly. San Francisco's Fairmont and St. Francis are hotels of note in California, but their histories do not rival that of the older and more celebrated Palace and, since the stories of three other California hotels would be included, the Fairmont and St. Francis were, again reluctantly, excluded. A surprisingly large number of major American cities—Philadelphia, Atlanta, New Orleans, St. Louis, Los Angeles, Portland, Seattle, among them—are without any hotels that, properly speaking, satisfy the criteria essential for inclusion.

Finally—and most importantly—I believed it imperative that the histories of the hotels should make good reading. They should contain the elements found in any good story: aspiration, disappointment, achievement, hope, suspense, pathos, humor.

There exist, of course, American hotels that are notable but do not satisfy the criteria laid down for the book because they are not, properly speaking, "grand hotels," because their histories do not transcend the confines of a limited locality, because they are not rooted in the nineteenth century, or because the stories of their builders, operators, and guests do not contain the elements of a rousing "good story."

The hotels chosen for inclusion in *The Palace Inns* are, I think, America's most notable surviving historic hotels. Each in its own way satisfies the criteria for selection outlined above. If the present Waldorf-Astoria was built within the lifetimes of

many Americans now living, it is the scion of one of the world's oldest and most celebrated hotel traditions. If Mackinac Island's Grand Hotel is little known beyond the Great Lakes region, it is one of the country's best surviving examples of late nineteenth-century resort architecture. If Del Monte Lodge is today looked upon primarily as a seaside retreat for rich and fashionable Californians, it preserves the tradition of the old Hotel Del Monte and its nineteenth-century builders, the "Big Four" of the Central and Southern Pacific railroads.

These hotels are more than architectural curiosities, more than musty relics of a bygone age. Hotels and their peculiarly twentieth-century progeny, motels, motor-hotels, and franchise-inns, are still very much a part of American life. The palace inns which survive today are the ancestors of all the Hiltons, Hyatt Houses, and Holiday Inns which today dot America and many foreign lands. It is appropriate that their histories be recorded and that they be accorded the recognition they so richly deserve.

ACKNOWLEDGMENTS

The histories of the hotels which appear in this book have, in many cases, proven to be maddeningly elusive. That they have been rescued from the dustbin of historical obscurity is due in large measure to the help I have received from enthusiastic and energetic librarians, historical researchers, and hotel officials throughout the country. Hundreds of preliminary inquiries were directed to chambers of commerce, historical societies, and hotel owners and managers. The answers received did not in all instances lead to material which could be included in the book, but all were informative, and all were appreciated. In collecting the information from which the histories were written and in assembling the photographs, drawings, prints, and engravings which illustrate them, I have received help from many persons, among whom I wish particularly to thank: Samantha Brown, Director of Publicity, the Greenbrier, White Sulphur Springs; Charles B. Simmons, Executive Director, the Henry Morrison Flagler Museum, Palm Beach; John S. Clifford, Vice President and General Manager, the Breakers, Palm Beach; Thomas S. Kenan III, of Chapel Hill, North Carolina; Marcie Buckley, Historian of Hotel del Coronado and author of *The Crown City's Brightest Gem, A History of the Hotel del Coronado*; Sylvia Arden of the research staff of the San Diego Historical Society; Thomas R. De Angelo, General Manager of the Sheraton-Palace Hotel, San Francisco; Potter Palmer of Chicago; B. J. Bradley of the staff of the Art Institute of Chicago; Miriam Blazowski and other staff members of the Chicago Historical Society; Thomas O. Miller, Executive Assistant Manager of the Palmer House; Paul Robbins, formerly Vice President and Director of Public Relations for Sheraton Hotels in the Pacific; Agnes C. Conrad, State Archivist, Honolulu, Hawaii; Patti Felt, Joan L. Swearman, and Jackie Stanley of the public relations staff of Sheraton Hotels in the Pacific; Tom Noel of the Media Library and Catherine T. Engel of the Reference Department of the State Historical Society of Colorado, Denver; Eleanor M. Gehres of the Western History Department of the Denver Public Library; Karl W. Mehlmann, President and General Manager of the Brown Palace Hotel; Smiley Brothers, Inc., and Carolyn Fiske, Director of Public Relations, Mohonk Mountain House; Lt. Cdr. S. L. Snodderly, U.S.N., Public Affairs Officer of the Naval Postgraduate School, Monterey, California; Robert W. Campbell, Director of Advertising and Public Relations, Pebble Beach Corporation, Pebble Beach; Janet L. Altrichter and Scott M. Cornwell of the publicity department of the Broadmoor, Colorado Springs; Joseph M. Grantham, Jr., Vice President and Manager, Grand Hotel, Mackinac Island; Keith R. Widder, Park Interpreter, Mackinac Island State Park Commission; Dr. Eugene T. Petersen, Superintendent, Mackinac Island State Park Commission and author of several historical guides to Mackinac Island, including *Mackinac Island, Its History in Pictures*; Janet Luoma, Public Relations Manager of the Plaza, New York City; Wendy Shadwell, Curator of Prints, New York Historical Society; Esther Brumberg and other staff members of the Museum of the City of New York; W. Dan Reichartz, Executive Assistant Manager, and Edward W. Moles, Director of Public Relations, The Waldorf-Astoria; Olive M. Wakeman, Administrative Assistant to Conrad N. Hilton, Los Angeles; Elaine F. Lavoie, Director of Communications for the Dunfey Family's Hotels and Motor Inns, Boston, Mary Leen of the Bostonian Society; Karen A. Maguire of the Library of the Boston *Globe*; Elvira Lavorgna, Reference Librarian in the Fine Arts Department of the Boston Public Library; Elizabeth T. Durfee, Editorial Assistant, and Elizabeth Reed Amadon, Executive Director, of the Massachusetts Historical Commission, Boston;

Pamela Hoyle and Ann L. Wadsworth of the Library of the Boston Athenaeum; Andrea Schulman, Reference Librarian, Harvard College Library, Cambridge; Roger H. Hall of San Francisco. Additional help was received from staff members of the Bancroft Library of the University of California, Berkeley; the San Francisco Public Library; the Library of the California Historical Society, San Francisco; the Monterey Public Library; and the Library of Congress. Special thanks are due the staff of the National Historical Society and the editors of AMERICAN HISTORY *Illustrated* for permission to reprint a portion of my article, "The Splendid Caravansary" (copyright © 1974 by the National Historical Society), which appeared in AMERICAN HISTORY *Illustrated*, October 1974.

1

America Invents the Hotel

America has always been a nation of travelers—but travel in America has not always been a comfortable exercise. Humble village inns were common in colonial America, and in Revolutionary days few well-traveled roads were without at least one lodging house or wayside tavern. The first American "hotel" did not appear until 1794, when a rambling lodging house arose on the site of the old Burns Coffee House on "The Broad-Way" in New York and its proprietor hung a sign over the door proudly proclaiming it THE CITY HOTEL.

The hotel known to Americans of the late nineteenth and early twentieth centuries was a uniquely American institution. Large, elegantly fitted houses of commercial hospitality, where the best in food, drink, and comfortable lodgings were available to the general public, were unknown before the 1830s, when a succession of dazzling "swagger hotels" was erected in Boston, New York, Baltimore, Philadelphia, and New Orleans. Long after the splendid openings of Boston's Tremont House, New York's Astor House, and New Orleans' St. Charles and St. Louis hotels, European capitals remained without comparable palaces of commercial hospitality.

The blossoming of America's nineteenth-century hotels was the result of many things: the rapidly increasing wealth of the mercantile and industrial classes of American society; the traditional restlessness of the American population (the same restlessness which impelled the pioneers to cross

the continent); the phenomenal growth of the railroads, which vastly increased the total volume of American travel and for the first time made travel a leisurely, even luxurious, undertaking; and the mushrooming of the great industrial and urban centers. During the thirty years preceding the Civil War, hotels finer and grander than any the world had ever seen were built in large cities throughout the United States. These palaces soon became centers of social life—favored locations for banquets, receptions, balls, and cotillions; dens of political intrigue; and the permanent domiciles of growing numbers of Americans, who found the conveniences and amenities of life in large hotels preferable to any of the homier comforts of their own homes and hearths.

That there were no "hotels" in the times of Washington and Franklin, or in the days when red-coated minions of George III swaggered through the Boston Common and along the Bouwerie in old Manhattan, is difficult for many twentieth-century Americans to conceive. Of course most villages and all the larger towns had their inns and taverns (in America, the words "inn" and "tavern" were synonymous, though in England taverns provided only food and drink). But the colonial inns were as different from nineteenth- and twentieth-century hotels as horse-drawn jitneys from steam-propelled Pullmans.

The inns and taverns of the colonial era were typically private residences whose owners had

City Hotel, Broadway, New York City, 1812 (Harper's Weekly)

hung swinging signs over the doors and installed barrooms on the ground floors. Colonial laws required all inns and taverns to have signs. As in the mother country, the signs of American taverns and inns were always pictorial. Many people could not read, but all knew that a sign emblazoned with a white swan, a red horse, or a boar's head marked the door of an inn.

There were no private baths in the old inns, nor water closets "down the hall." A few tavern-keepers kept supplies of bowls and pitchers that they sent to guest rooms on request, but most lodgers washed themselves before breakfast in the kitchen or at a back-yard pump. Meals were taken at appointed hours in a corner of the barroom with the tavern-keeper and his family. Meat-carving duties were delegated to the bartenders, who also acted as room clerks. Private bedrooms were nearly unknown, and even private beds were rare.

Sharing beds with strangers was a familiar necessity in old England, though a preference for nocturnal privacy developed in Britain some time before it did in America. As late as 1823 an Englishman named Edward Allen Talbot discovered that private sleeping facilities could not be depended upon in the inns and taverns of the smaller

American villages. Talbot wrote:

> **On entering one of these taverns and asking for a bed, you are told that your chance of getting one depends entirely on the number of travelers who may want accommodations for the night; and if you obtain possession of a bed by promising to receive a companion when required, it is impossible to say what sort of companion may come; so that instead of hoping for the best, one is led into the commission of a sort of practical bull—to which, however, all who regard their own personal convenience are equally liable, whether they be English or Irish—by keeping awake for the purpose of receiving an intruder while no intruder comes to be received; and thus we are sometimes deprived of a night's rest, without any advantage.**

It made no difference if the guests thrown together were of different sexes. Moral sensibilities were not offended by men and women sleeping in the same room—or even in the same bed—proprieties being sufficiently satisfied by the innkeepers' refusal to accommodate unaccompanied women. A man traveling in Connecticut in about 1820 was reproached by a matron of his acquaintance who accused him of living a dissipated life. The man protested that he was not so different from anyone else, that most people would act as he did when put in similar circumstances. The matron asked him to name one situation in which she would act as he did. "Suppose, then, madam," the man said, "that in traveling you came to an inn, where all of the beds were full except two, and in one of these was a man, and in the other a woman, which would you take?" "Why, the woman's to be sure," the matron answered. "Well, madam," said the man, "so would I."

Despite their many inconveniences, colonial inns and taverns were indispensable social, political, and business institutions. Typically, they stood next to village churches or meeting houses, thus affording townspeople opportunity to drift into their barrooms an hour or so before prayers began or the chairman of a town meeting sounded his gavel. Gathered around the keeper's table, travelers and townspeople alike wet their whistles and warmed their blood. In the inns, letters were posted, village news exchanged, business transactions negotiated, friendships made and renewed. Without the inns and taverns travel in the colonies would have been much more hazardous than it was. From an early date the restlessness of the American spirit manifested itself in a large body of men who were more or less constantly on the move—whether for business, for pleasure, or

merely because they were uneasy when they remained too long in one place. The inns were like manna in the wilderness to these early-day American nomads.

The inns of the larger towns differed little from their country counterparts. They were, in the beginning, converted private residences, though toward the end of the eighteenth century some were built specially for the accommodation of travelers. Swinging signboards hung over their doors; their ground floors were typically occupied by barrooms; and the rooms and beds on the upper floors were shared by a motley throng of men, women, and children. The inns of the cities differed from those of the villages principally in size. Lodging houses which boasted a dozen or more rooms were built in New York City in the 1790s and in other large towns a few years later.

Following close on the heels of the French Revolution, a wave of Francophilia swept through the United States. The Bastille had been stormed in July 1789 by anti-royalist revolutionaries who proclaimed the ideals of *liberté, egalité, fraternité.* Convinced that the French political experience presaged the future of their own, many patriotic Americans sought to imitate French manners, French clothes, French modes of address—and to introduce French words into the common vocabulary. The word *hôtel,* meaning large house or mansion, had been applied in France to private palaces and to public buildings such as town halls. In America a profusion of names had been applied to inns—tavern, caravansary, ale house, porter house, punch house, coffee house.

Probably the first inn or tavern in America to adopt the French word *hôtel* was Corre's Hotel, opened in 1790 at 24 "The Broad-Way" in New York. Corre, who had previously run the City Tavern, was a pastry cook who gave lessons to the servants of private families. His signboard innovation, though scorned by many as "highfalutin'," was imitated by other tavern-keepers and by the company of stockholders who in 1794 opened the City Hotel below Trinity Church on "The Broad-Way."

The builders of the City claimed it was the first structure erected solely for "hotel purposes" in America. The claim was not seriously disputed. New York was a boom town of about thirty thousand inhabitants in the fall of 1794, not far removed from the Iroquois warriors who still scalped white men on their upstate hunting grounds. But the City Hotel seemed far removed from the frontier. With its seventy-three rooms (enough to

Tremont House, Boston (Courtesy of the Bostonian Society, Old State House)

cause visiting Europeans to call it "an immense establishment"), it quickly won the favor of Knickerbocker society. Copying French dance styles, New Yorkers gathered in the new hotel to dance the *rigaudon*, cotillion, and *allemande*, to address each other in the latest French style as "Citizen," and to display their fine gowns, knee-breeches, white dancing gloves, and dress swords.

The City Hotel gave a new meaning to the old French word. No longer was a hotel a public building or elegant private mansion. It was now a large structure built to afford comfortable lodgings to travelers and to serve the best in food and drink—in other words, a superior inn. From New York the word and the concept quickly spread to other Eastern cities. Boston's first real hotel (though it did not carry the name) was the Exchange Coffee House, which opened in 1804. Philadelphia's Mansion House (opened in 1807 as the Exchange Coffee House) was that city's first hotel built as a

hotel. Baltimore's first was the City Hotel, opened in 1826 and operated by David Barnum, formerly the proprietor of Boston's Exchange Coffee House.

The era of "grand hotels" did not begin until 1829, when the first of America's great palace inns was opened on Tremont Street in Boston. Called the Tremont House, it occupied an entire city block adjoining the historic Granary Burying Ground. Designed by the pioneering architect Isaiah Rogers, it was three and a half stories high with four-story wings on either end. Its central façade was faced with white Quincy granite; its massive front entrance was marked by a striking Greek portico.

Inside, the ceilings were high, the floors of marble mosaic, the halls and guest rooms carpeted, and the windows hung with curtains. The Tremont's cavernous public rooms were larger than those of any other hotel—perhaps any other building—in the country. The total number of its guest rooms, 173, nearly defied the imagination. Its "office" (the word "lobby" was not generally used in hotels until the 1850s) was the first entrance room in an American hotel that was not also a barroom. Correspondingly, the Tremont was the first hotel with room clerks who did not double as bartenders and meat-carvers. The main dining room, seventy feet long and thirty-one feet wide, could accommodate the then-amazing number of two hundred diners at a single sitting. The hotel was the first inn of any sort in America that did not have a swinging signboard—or, indeed, any sign—above its door: Its builders were confident that a building as large and grand as the Tremont needed no legend to identify it.

The Tremont's decision to specialize in double and single rooms marked a great advance in hotel-keeping practice. There were "emergency rooms," each furnished with two or three beds, in which new arrivals were temporarily lodged with other new arrivals until they could be transferred to private chambers, but most of the guest rooms were designed to accommodate couples or individuals. Locks, another innovation of the Tre-

mont, were affixed to every door, and no two could be opened with the same key. Every room was equipped with a bowl, a pitcher, and a bar of soap (replaced when succeeding guests had used it up).

Lodgers marveled at the hotel's eight basement water closets and "bathing rooms" (plumbing could not be installed above the first floor). Most wonderful of all were the gaslights—first to be installed in any American hotel—that illuminated all the public rooms (traditional whale-oil lamps were still used in the guest rooms). Bostonians were inordinately proud of the Tremont. When visitors arrived in town to "see the sights," they were first shown the magnificent, late eighteenth-century State House designed by Charles Bulfinch, then taken on a tour of the Tremont, which residents of the city praised as "one of the proudest achievements of American genius."

The Tremont inspired entrepreneurs in other American cities to plan similarly large and lavish hotels. Holt's Hotel was opened at Fulton, Water, and Pearl streets in Manhattan on January 3, 1833. Despite its imposing size—six stories tall, 225

Astor House, New York City. This engraving was published by Herman J. Meyer. (Courtesy of the New-York Historical Society)

ST. CHARLES EXCHANGE HOTEL, NEW ORLEANS, Lᵃ
LESSEES — MUDGE & WILSON — 1845.

St. Charles Hotel, New Orleans (Courtesy of the Louisiana State Museum)

rooms—Holt's bore little resemblance to the Boston palace. It was, as one writer noted, "a perfectly plain building, without the slightest pretension to architectural beauty," and its location far from the fashionable sidewalks of Broadway made it an uninviting rendezvous for men of means and women of taste.

A worthier New York rival to the Tremont was the magnificent Astor House, which the redoubtable fur-trader and real-estate magnate, the original John Jacob Astor, built on Broadway between Barclay and Vesey streets between 1834 and 1836. There was no doubt in anyone's mind that the Astor was modeled after the Tremont. It was, like the Boston hotel, designed by Isaiah Rogers. Like the Tremont, it was built near a cemetery (St. Paul's Churchyard was across the street from the Astor). Like that of the Tremont, the Astor's main entrance was ornamented with a massive Greek portico. But the New York hotel was larger and grander than its Boston prototype. It was two stories taller, had nearly twice as many rooms, and cost considerably more—four hundred thousand dollars—to build. Its reception rooms and dining halls were large and elegantly furnished. According to a New York magazine writer, the guest rooms were "fitted up and furnished in a style of unostentatious richness and severe simplicity, the sofas, bureaus, tables and chairs, from basement to attic, being uniformly of a beautiful black walnut, while the floors are as regularly overlaid with superior oilcloth of various tasteful patterns." The distinguished ex-Mayor of New York, Philip Hone, praised the Astor House as a *palais royal* that "for centuries to come will serve, as it is probably intended, as a monument of its wealthy proprietor."

In faraway New Orleans, a roistering boom town only recently wrested from French control, newer American residents were vying with older

ST. LOUIS HOTEL.

St. Louis Hotel, New Orleans (Courtesy of the Louisiana State Museum)

and more established French Creoles to see who could build the biggest and grandest hotel. The Yankees moved first, opening the splendid St. Charles Hotel in February 1837. Built at a cost of eight hundred thousand dollars, the St. Charles had a soaring dome that made it the most prominent feature of the New Orleans skyline. Almost immediately the Creoles announced plans for an even more lavish hotel to cost $1,500,000. But the nation was beleaguered by one of its periodic financial crises in 1837, and scarcity of money forced the Creoles to scale down their plans. The St. Louis Hotel, which they opened in the summer of 1838, was palatial enough, with a vestibule forty feet wide and 126 feet long, a cavernous rotunda, and a grand ballroom. But its total cost was only five hundred thousand dollars. Even the French agreed that it was a poor imitation of the glorious St. Charles.

Grandeur and cost of construction were not the only attributes with which hotel builders competed. Innovations in plumbing, lighting, and a host of other technological advances improved the quality of service and the comfort of guests, offering seemingly inexhaustible opportunities for one-upmanship.

Throughout the 1820s and 1830s the development of gaslight was proceeding apace. The country's first gas plant had been built in Baltimore in 1817, and Baltimore's City Hotel may have had gaslight when it opened in 1826. The Tremont was the first large hotel to light its public rooms with gas. New York's American Hotel, opened in 1835, was the first to have gaslight throughout the house. The Astor House had its own gas plant in 1836, though the supply was subject to interruptions (newspapers reported on more than one occasion that the glow dimmed "in the midst of a cotillion"). Guests who checked in to the palatial hotels, particularly those from the country, were often ill-prepared to handle the newfangled lamps. When some unfortunate tenants were found dead in their beds, hôteliers posted signs solemnly warning: "This is NOT a kerosene lamp and must NOT be BLOWN OUT unless you COURT DEATH." That some guests did court death was the opinion of one New York hotel-keeper, who wrote:

> **We have never written letters to prospective suicides at other hotels inviting them to come with us at reduced rates, and yet, when a man feels it is time for him to shuffle off this mortal coil, it seems perfectly natural for him to drift into our hotel, unostentatious though it may be. It is a comparatively easy class of trade to satisfy. They do not stop to inquire whether the plumbing is modern or antique. They do not ask whether their rooms are decorated in the style of the First Empire or the Seventh Ward. Give them a good six-foot burner, about fifteen hundred feet of illuminating gas at $1 a thousand, and a few uninterrupted moments and they are content.**

Innovations in plumbing were as marvelous as the development of gaslight, and even more assiduously sought after by many travelers. The Tremont's eight basement water closets and "bathing rooms" had been a great advance for 1829. By 1836, when the Astor House opened, plumbers had devised steam-powered pumps capable of raising water above the ground floor. Though the Astor boasted of its seventeen basement "bathing rooms" and two showers, it was even prouder of the water closets and cold-water taps installed on the upper levels. The first hotel to have private baths connected with bedrooms was probably the New York Hotel, which opened in 1844.

Many years passed before a hotel could boast of "every room with bath." The first to offer this luxury was probably the Victoria Hotel, which opened in Kansas City in 1888. Not even the glamorous Waldorf-Astoria, New York's preeminent "swagger hotel" of the 1890s, had private baths in every room. The first large hotel to be so equipped was the original Hotel Statler, which opened in Buffalo, New York in 1907. Despite the slowness with which private baths came to hotels, the great inns were consistently ahead of most private homes in the quantity and quality of their plumbing, and many Americans first scraped an acquaintance with such inventions as bathtubs, water closets, hot and cold running water, and steam heat in hotels.

As hotels became larger, communication between the desk or office and guest rooms became increasingly difficult. Some inns and taverns hung hand-bells in the bedrooms for guests to use to summon help in emergencies, but the bells did little to enhance the quiet demanded by sleeping guests. In 1829 the Tremont installed a system of "electro-magnetic annunciators," or push-button buzzers. "One ring for ice-water, two for bellboy,

three for porter, four for chambermaid, and not a darned one of them will come," quipped a wit of the day. Various types of annunciators were invented after 1830, and they soon became general in all of the luxury hotels. When the Holland House opened in New York in 1889, each room had a buzzer button with a dial on which 140 different articles and services were listed. Guests turned their dials to any article or service desired and pressed the button.

Although annunciators were used in New York's Grand Union Hotel as late as 1914, telephones had by that time become universal in nearly all palace inns. The first commercial telephone switchboard in the United States began operation in New Haven, Connecticut in 1878. New York's first exchange was opened in 1879. The numbers of several Manhattan hotels appeared in the first exchange directory, but they were office, not room, connections. In 1894 the Hotel Netherland became the first hotel to install a switchboard for room phones. Other grand hotels soon followed the Netherland's lead, and in 1902 the Waldorf-Astoria replaced its annunciators with telephones.

Moving around in the large hotels was even more difficult than attempting to communicate with the management. Owners of multi-story inns found that rooms on the upper floors were less desirable than those on the lower levels and thus commanded lower rents. As early as 1833 Holt's Hotel had been equipped with a crude steam-powered hoist used to raise baggage from the ground to upper floors. The hoist may occasionally have transported humans though, if it did, the practice was not regular. As late as 1852 the New York *Tribune* complained that in hotels "baggage is hauled up, but the guest must trudge up the stairways." When the six-story St. Nicholas Hotel opened the same year, the *Tribune* noted that there were "five weary flights of stairs to the top. This is an awful toll for human legs, and unnecessary. There is steam power at hand and there are ingenious brains enough to invent an elegant and convenient apparatus to convey skyward the upward-bound and earthward the descending, without such excessive labor of mortal muscle."

When the luxurious Fifth Avenue Hotel opened in 1859, it was equipped with three "perpendicular railways" that were powered by steam and furnished with plush-covered seats. The cars were heavy, slow-moving affairs, but guests who were assigned rooms on the fifth and sixth floors welcomed them enthusiastically. The perfection of

Fifth Avenue Hotel, New York City (Courtesy of the New-York Historical Society)

hotel elevators coupled with the introduction of steel and concrete construction in the 1890s permitted America's hotels to grow upward as rapidly as they grew outward. Although six stories was about the maximum possible height in the 1850s, New York's Waldorf-Astoria, finished in 1897, rose a breathtaking seventeen floors above Fifth Avenue. Such a building would have been unthinkable without "perpendicular railways."

The development of electric light wrought a dazzling change in the appearance of hotels. Gas, though more convenient than whale oil, coal oil, or kerosene, produced a flickering, uneven light. It was often treacherous and always odoriferous. When in 1879 Thomas A. Edison pronounced his incandescent light bulb commercially feasible, hôteliers throughout the country made plans to adopt it. The first hotel lighted by electricity was New York's Hotel Everett on Park Row, which early in 1882 blazed forth with 101 incandescent lamps in its dining rooms, lobby, reading room, and parlors. A house organ published by Edison's company noted that "the chandeliers for the lights

are unusually expensive and present a beautiful appearance." A larger electrical plant was installed a few months later in another hotel on New York's Vesey Street. The Palmer House in Chicago became the third hotel with electric lights in the spring of 1882; the Vendome in Boston the fourth in June of the same year. The first hotel with electric lights in all of its rooms was the Sagamore Hotel at Green Island, Lake George, New York. It began its 1883 season with a 350-light-capacity plant that powered lamps in all of its public rooms and at least one in each of its 172 bedrooms. By the end of the 1880s electric lights had become general in fine hotels throughout the country.

Dining service also underwent a striking transformation. In the early days of hotels meals were served in much the same way they had been served in colonial inns and taverns. Guests ate whatever the hotel-keeper and his family were having for breakfast, dinner, or supper, and the quality and quantity of the food depended on how well the hotel larder was stocked. As inns grew larger, "pot luck" gave way to a more definite cuisine, but meals were still served at specified hours, and there was still no opportunity for selection. Venison, wild turkey, pigeon, beef, pork, lamb—whatever was available at meal time was set on the table, and diners helped themselves from the dishes and platters. It was impossible for lodgers to secure rooms without also paying for meals (what later came to be known as the "American plan" was then universal), although townspeople, stage passengers, and casual passers-by could usually secure meals at the tables.

In most establishments male and female diners were rigidly segregated. The guest of a Connecticut inn in the early years of the nineteenth century described the practice of segregating the sexes in a single room:

All of the women sat together, beginning at the lower end of the table; and all of the men sat together, toward the upper; and the only communication between them resulted from the necessity under which the men appeared to labor to be helped by the women.

In larger hotels separate dining rooms called the "men's ordinary" and the "ladies' ordinary" were provided for men and women.

The Tremont House was responsible for the first radical innovation in hotel food service. Doing away with the traditional practice of putting all food on the table (*table d'hôte*), the Tremont adopted the more stylish French practice of bringing each diner only the food that he ordered (*à la carte*). The new service method required a large corps of waiters and the adoption of the previously unheard-of practice of issuing menu cards. At first written in pen and ink, the menu cards were soon printed, then decorated with fancy print and engravings.

About 1835 a second significant innovation—adoption of the so-called "European plan" of hotel operation—was made. For the first time guests were permitted to pay for their rooms and to take their meals wherever they pleased. The "American Plan" died slowly. As late as 1870 many hotels still operated exclusively in the old style, though others offered arriving guests a choice of taking their rooms with or without prepaid meals. Arriving at the desk, a traveler would be asked, "American or European?" It is recorded that one foreign visitor 'replied to the unexpected inquiry by saying, "I'm European, but I don't see what business it is of yours."

The development of railroads did much to in-

crease the size and number of American hotels. Rail travel permitted hundreds of thousands of Americans to make their first visits to large cities and to indulge in the previously unthinkable luxury of vacationing in remote mountain or seaside resorts. While palace inns proliferated in all of the major cities, great resort hotels mushroomed. Fashionable health spas like White Sulphur Springs in Virginia (West Virginia after the Civil War) were popular rendezvous for aristocratic families even before the Iron Horse reached them, but the country's growing network of fast and dependable rail lines did much to make them accessible to middle-class Americans. Hotels that rivaled the swagger-inns of New York, Boston, and San Francisco were built at White Sulphur; at Saratoga Springs, New York; at Cape May and Long Branch, New Jersey; at Newport, Rhode Island; and at choice points along the seacoasts of California and Florida. Though hotels were originally an urban invention, they adapted readily to the atmosphere of posh resorts and soon began to flourish there.

In cities large hotels catered as often to commercial trade as to casual travelers or wide-eyed, sight-seeing vacationers. Before the era of large chain stores "commercial travelers" were frequently encountered in metropolitan hotels. First called "bagmen" (from their habit of carrying their wares in carpetbags), they later became known as "drummers." In 1860 there were about sixty thousand commercial travelers in the country. In 1883 the *Hotel Gazette* estimated their number at more than two hundred thousand. Typically dressed in flashy clothes, colorful neckties, jewelry, and gold watches, they were picturesque characters on all of the railroads and a mainstay of the business of many hotels.

Troupes of traveling actors and actresses were nearly as ubiquitous as the commercial travelers and, if anything, even more colorful. Keeping irregular hours, rehearsing in hotel hallways or on balconies, often cooking their own meals in their rooms, sometimes "skipping" without paying for lodgings or food, they were the bane of many hôteliers. But their numbers—perhaps as many as eight thousand in the 1890s—made them impossible to ignore.

Permanent guests were another important class of hotel patrons. All fine hotels from the time of the Tremont House had parlor-and-bedroom suites that were occupied by bachelors or married couples. Shortly before the opening of the Astor House, a New York newspaper reported that half of the new hotel's rooms were "already engaged by families who give up housekeeping on account of the present enormous rents in the city." In 1857 *Harper's Weekly* commented that there would be less resort to permanent hotel living if

> **the tastes of our people were better regulated, and mere show was not preferred to substance. . . . If gingerbread furniture, damask curtains, tapestry carpets, and a French cook are essential to happiness, there is no doubt they can be secured in greater perfection and at a less price by the gregarious hotel system than by individual effort. Such luxuries, however, as we all know, are not essential to happiness, and however permissible as superfluous enjoyments, they are certainly too dearly paid for when at the expense of domestic virtue and happiness.**

The English journalist George Augustus Sala thought that many Americans lived permanently in hotels because of "restless vanity and ambition," but thought the tendency was inevitable because the American was "emphatically a gregarious animal."

Hotel-keepers welcomed permanent tenants. Indeed, many houses, called "family hotels" by their proprietors, catered specially or even exclusively to nontransient guests. Rents paid weekly or monthly were a dependable source of income and did much to ease the vicissitudes of the country's periodic financial panics, which often struck savagely at hotels.

Although hotel-keeping, like acting, was looked down upon by the "better classes" of professional men, bankers, industrialists, and "gentleman farmers," the business was so profitable that many of the country's wealthiest men were ineluctably drawn to it. Others who started their careers in humble positions as hotel bellboys, waiters, or clerks made great fortunes in hotels. Abraham Lincoln, who operated a village tavern at New Salem, Illinois in the early 1830s (he charged 12½ cents per night for lodging, 25 cents for keeping a horse, and 37½ cents per meal for stage passengers) was the most celebrated of the nation's innkeepers, though he attained his fame in other pursuits. John Jacob Astor was probably the country's wealthiest man when he opened the Astor House. When his great-grandsons built the vastly more luxurious Waldorf-Astoria in the 1890s, the Astor fortune was still counted among the largest in the United States.

Potter Palmer, proprietor of Chicago's great Palmer House, was the most respected businessman of the prairie city, and his wife was its undisputed social queen. William C. Ralston, who built the Palace Hotel in San Francisco in the early 1870s, was California's most prominent citizen, and his partner, William C. Sharon, was a United States Senator. Henry Morrison Flagler, the "Father of Modern Florida," who built a chain of palace inns along that state's palmy east coast, was one of John D. Rockefeller's original partners and himself one of the richest men in the United States.

Because they were palaces of luxury and citadels of financial power, it was inevitable that the grand hotels should become intimately involved in the political life of the nation. Before the Civil War numerous hotels, advertising themselves as "Democratic," "Whig," or "Republican houses," catered more or less exclusively to political partisans. Abraham Lincoln was a frequent guest at Chicago's Briggs House in the 1850s, and he made the hotel his presidential campaign headquarters in 1860. New York's Republican party boss Thomas C. Platt presided for many years in the famous (or infamous) "Amen Corner" of the Fifth Avenue Hotel, while Thurlow Weed made his headquarters in the Astor House. Levi P. Morton, Vice President under President Benjamin Harrison, built the Shoreham Hotel, which was for many years a center of political intrigue in Washington, D. C.

Presidents from the time of Martin Van Buren regularly frequented the hotel at White Sulphur Springs. President Ulysses S. Grant lived at Cape May's Congress Hall during the summers of 1874 and 1875 and held regular cabinet meetings throughout his stay. Potter Palmer of Chicago's Palmer House declined a cabinet appointment in the Grant Administration, but he maintained close political ties with Washington after his sister-in-law married General Grant's son in 1874.

The ties between politics and hotels continued well into the twentieth century. Warren G. Harding was nominated for the presidency in a "smoke-filled room" at Chicago's Blackstone Hotel in 1920, and he died in a suite at San Francisco's Palace in 1923. President Dwight D. Eisenhower vacationed frequently in Denver's Brown Palace Hotel in the 1950s, making it the nation's more or less regular "Summer White House."

Hotels were inextricably intertwined with American life, manners, customs, and aspirations throughout most of the nineteenth century. Following the example of the palace inns of America, large and luxurious hostelries were built in European cities in the second half of the century. They were, however, more exclusive and less egalitarian than their American models. American hotels were unmercifully ostentatious, but they were not palaces set apart from the great mass of the people. Any man walking on Broadway in New York in the 1850s could wander through the lobby of the marvelous St. Nicholas Hotel, if only to admire its lavish mirrors, paneled walls, and acres of carpet. The humblest traveler in San Francisco in the 1880s could pull up to the fabled bar of the Palace Hotel and order a tumblerful of whiskey or a draught of brandy punch.

Americans loved swagger and show, even as they professed to despise the aristocratic airs and habits of Old World society. If there was no royalty in America, there were palaces that dazzled the eyes of every beholder and let humble men and women bask in the reflected glory of home-grown opulence and splendor. The hotels were "palaces of the people," America's answer to the extravagances of Versailles, Blenheim, and the Schönbrunn, glittering monuments to Yankee ingenuity, invention, and daring. As Jefferson Williamson wrote nearly half a century ago, hotels were perhaps "the most distinctively American of all our institutions, for they were nourished and brought to flower solely in American soil and borrowed practically nothing from abroad."

Splendid though they were, the great nineteenth-century hotels proved to be fragile palaces. Philip Hone thought the Astor House would stand as a monument "for centuries to come." In a less dynamic society the hotel probably would have endured for several hundred years while gathering about its stony walls a patina of age and hoary romance like that which envelops English manor houses and French châteaux. But technological advancements were so rapid in nineteenth-century America, and innovations in service, comfort, and design so numerous and quick-paced, that the grand hotels rapidly became outmoded. If hotels were public monuments, they were also private, profitmaking enterprises. It consoled the owners of the Tremont House not at all to recall the splendid press notices of 1829 and 1830 when they saw travelers of the 1860s and 1870s flocking to the more modern Parker House.

Cities grew rapidly throughout the century. Neighborhoods that were once paragons of style quickly became backwaters or, worse, skid rows. Hotels built of stone, brick, steel, or concrete—as opposed to those fashioned of more malleable wood—could not readily be adapted to the needs of succeeding generations of comfort-demanding

travelers. The land on which many hotels were built, particularly in the larger cities, grew rapidly in value, forcing owners to raze them and put up larger structures in their places. Fire, a constant scourge of nineteenth-century cities, leveled many hotels. Although some were rebuilt, others were abandoned as theaters, office buildings, or more modern hotels were built on their sites.

Thirty years after its grand opening, the Astor House was relegated to the dismal status of a second-rate hotel. It was closed for remodeling in 1875, when it got its first private bathrooms, then limped along for another generation. It finally closed in 1913, a score of years short of its hundredth anniversary. Other grand hotels had even shorter lives. The Tremont survived only until 1894. New York's St. Nicholas Hotel, the first inn in America to be built at a cost of more than one million dollars, lasted a little more than thirty years and closed in 1884. The splendid Gilsey House on Broadway survived about forty years. The Fifth Avenue Hotel, originator of the "perpendicular railway," closed in 1908 at the age of forty-nine. The lordly Buckingham, immortalized by Edith Wharton in her *Age of Innocence,* was forty-six years old when it closed in 1922. Philadelphia's finest hotel, the Continental, closed in 1923, sixty-three years after its 1860 opening. The original Waldorf-Astoria, the grandest of all nineteenth-century hotels, lived thirty-two years before it fell to wreckers' balls in 1929.

Hotels that were not demolished were often converted to other uses. The Prescott House at Broadway and Spring streets in New York was made over into a factory. Henry Flagler's splendid Ponce de Leon Hotel in St. Augustine, Florida became a municipal office building. The sprawling Tampa Bay Hotel was transformed into the University of Tampa. The Hotel Del Monte in Monterey, California became the campus of the United States Naval Postgraduate School.

Despite the fragility of the nineteenth-century hotels, some were able to survive the multiple hazards of the age of internal combustion, supersonic speed, and atomic fission. Others that did not survive in their original buildings were replaced by newer structures that perpetuated their names and carried on their traditions.

"If these walls could speak, what stories they would tell. . . ." The time-worn expression is peculiarly applicable to the old hotels. In their heydays they were backdrops for much of the ongoing epic of American history—the homes of heroes and scoundrels, the playgrounds of paupers and millionaires, the scenes of mingled triumph, disappointment, and despair. The cast of characters who thronged their halls and lobbies—frontiersmen and adventurers, poets and philosophers, actors and actresses, railroad barons and oil magnates, kings, queens, and presidents—was as rich and varied as the buildings themselves. Without them the epic of nineteenth-century America would have been much poorer than it was.

This book was inspired by America's surviving palace inns. It is their histories that fill the following pages.

2

The White Façade that Gleams Across the Way

THE PARKER HOUSE, BOSTON

The hotel tradition came early to Boston. There were taverns and inns in the bayside city from colonial days—wayside lodging houses, dram shops with sleeping rooms attached, public houses and restaurants where New England travelers could wet their whistles, fill their bellies, and sleep in warmth and comfort, if not in luxury. Ten years after the City Hotel opened on "The Broad-Way" in New York, Boston's first hotel, the Exchange Coffee House, began business. Though the Massachusetts city was only about half the size of New York, it was the center of the country's most densely populated and heavily industrialized urban area. Throngs of coaches lined its cobbled streets, and straining, masted ships crowded its wharves. Because strangers were seen so frequently on Boston's streets, the demand for inns, restaurants, and hotels was great. By the end of the 1820s, when the luxurious Tremont House was built at the eastern edge of Beacon Hill, Boston was acknowledged as America's hotel capital.

Fast on the heels of the Tremont came the American House, opened in 1835, the Shawmut, opened in 1837 (it boasted that it was the first European-plan hotel in the country), the Adams House, and in 1847 the handsome, porticoed Revere House. When in 1854 Harvey D. Parker opened his "New Marble Building" on School Street, around the corner and down the hill from the Tremont House, *Ballou's Pictorial Drawing-Room Companion* hailed it as "the most costly and extensive" structure ever erected in Boston for "restaurant purposes." Unaware that it was also intended as a hotel, *Ballou's* predicted that the new structure would become "as celebrated in our gastronomical annals as the Trois Freres Provençaux at Paris, to dine at which is—to have lived." Parker's new restaurant was, indeed, well-received, but the hotel he opened in the same building achieved greater fame and, in the end, it was the hotel that made the Parker name immortal.

Harvey Parker's origins were humble enough, and he was born far enough from the staid reserves of Beacon Hill to confound any who might predict his name would one day be a household word in Boston. He was born in the village of Temple, Maine in 1805 (before that state was sliced from the Commonwealth of Massachusetts) and raised in the nearby village of Paris. He was twenty years old when he left home for Boston, with only a few articles of clothing and less than a dollar in his pocket. He found a job in the Boston suburb of Watertown, where he earned eight dollars a month as a stable boy and later worked as a coachman.

Industrious, dependable, and ambitious, the boy from Maine was given the honor of driving his employer, a lady of circumstance, into Boston on shopping trips. His topper set bravely over one ear, his boots planted firmly against the dash, he braved the back roads and crowded city streets to deliver his mistress to smart shops along Tremont and State streets. While in Boston Parker liked to

Parker's "New Marble Building," Boston (Ballou's Pictorial Drawing-Room Companion, February 1855)

dine at a restaurant on Court Square run by John E. Hunt. Set in a shadowy basement at the corner of Court Street, it was not an imposing place, but it was thronged with midday diners, and Parker could see it was making money. Back in Watertown, he saved his money religiously. By 1832, when he was twenty-seven, he had accumulated the grand sum of $432, enough to persuade Hunt to part with his downtown eating house and to permit the coachman to hang a sign over the sidewalk which read "Parker's Restaurant."

Harvey Parker prospered, as did his restaurant. In 1845 he employed John F. Mills as his steward, and two years later the business had grown sufficiently to permit Mills to join him as a partner. That Parker's Court Square restaurant was a dining room of some distinction, and not a blue-plate beanery, is evident from an examination of one of its 1850 menus. Sitting down to a table in Parker's, a diner could select from an impressive array of viands: turkey and chicken with oyster sauce; roasts of beef, pork, mutton, and goose; canvasback, venison, partridge, quail, spring chicken, and squab; tenderloin steaks with truffles, olives and tomato sauce; oysters broiled, fried, roasted, stewed, and on the half-shell; and a complete selection of fine sherries, Madeiras, ports, sauternes, champagnes, clarets, hocks, porters, and cider. As Parker's business increased and his bank balance swelled, he began to look about Boston for a suitable site for a new and grander location. The Tremont and Revere houses had demonstrated that hotel dining rooms were as popular with residents of the city as with travelers, and Parker reckoned he might build a hotel to house his new restaurant.

Menu describing the bill of fare at Harvey Parker's first restaurant

A lot on the south side of School Street attracted the restauranteur's attention. It was a site of some historic importance in Boston, a plot that had been occupied more or less continuously for more than two hundred years. As early as 1654 the land had been purchased by a Sergeant (later Captain) Thomas Clarke. In 1704 it was acquired by John Mico, a wealthy Boston merchant, who built on it a handsome, three-story brick mansion. When Mico died in 1718, the house became the property of his friend and sometime apprentice, Jacob Wendell, father of Oliver Wendell, and great-grandfather of Dr. Oliver Wendell Holmes, who more than a century later would spend much time on the same property.

Nicholas Boylston acquired the house after Jacob Wendell's death, using it to entertain the great and near-great of his day, including his cousin, John Adams. After 1805 the mansion was converted into a boarding house and, in 1829, it became known as the Boylston Hotel. The house was old and creaking in 1854 when Harvey Parker acquired it and began to level its walls. The gleaming "New Marble Building" that arose on the site was not destined to stand as long as the Mico mansion, but it was to achieve greater fame.

It belonged to a distinguished neighborhood in 1854. Across School Street, at the northeast corner of Tremont Street, stood the heavy stone walls of King's Chapel, built in the 1750s, and next to it the chapel burying ground, Boston's oldest cemetery. Beside the chapel was a lot on which the town fathers would raise Boston's City Hall in 1865. A block down the street, at the corner of School and Washington, was the Old Corner Book Store, established in 1828—a gathering place for poets and philosophers famous throughout New England as "Parnassus Corner." Adjoining Parker's on the east was the columned façade of Horticultural Hall, built in 1844 on the site of the former Boston Latin School, from which School Street had derived its name. "Parker's New Marble Building" had handsome neighbors, but its white façade overshadowed them all.

It was built in a modified Italianate style—five stories of brick and stone faced with white marble. The windows on the ground and second floors were gracefully arched, while those above were surmounted with cornices. A low flight of marble steps led from the sidewalk to a broad foyer, paved with marble. Above the door was a sign engraved with the single word, "Parker's"—notice to the world that Harvey Parker's palace required no further identification.

On Monday, October 8, 1855, the Boston *Transcript* announced the hotel's opening:

> **THE PARKER HOUSE.** This elegant new hotel, on School Street, was opened on Saturday for the inspection of the public. Several thousands of our citizens, ladies as well as gentlemen, availed themselves of the invitation, and for many hours the splendid building was literally thronged. All were surprised and delighted at the convenient arrangement of the whole establishment—the gorgeous furniture of the parlors, the extent and beauty of the dining hall, the number and different styles of the lodging rooms—and, in fact, the richness, lavish expenditure and excellent taste which abounded in every department. The house was universally adjudged to be a model one. It opened for business this morning, to be conducted on the European plan, and under the personal supervision of its enterprising, experienced and popular proprietor, its success cannot be doubted.

From the outset the new hotel enjoyed a brisk patronage. The gleaming white façade, the marble foyers, the thick carpets and horse-hair divans presented an aura of elegant comfort. The reputation of Parker's Court Square restaurant was perpetuated in the dining room, which was as crowded as the old basement hall had ever been. The hotel's cuisine was as responsible for its cheery reception by Bostonians as any of its other attractions. The European plan afforded guests flexibility in planning their meals. They could as easily wander into the dining room of the nearby Tremont House or some oyster bar on State Street as pull up to one of Parker's tables. They enjoyed the freedom, though few of them strayed far from the hotel. A further innovation, even more popular than the European plan, was Parker's practice of serving meals continuously, rather than at fixed hours, as had been the universal custom in other hotels. Whenever guests were attacked by pangs of hunger, they hurried into the dining room, where warm meals were ready to placate them.

Exclamations of astonishment greeted the news, whispered in the dining rooms and adjacent lobbies, that Parker's French chef, Sanzian, was receiving the astounding salary of five thousand dollars a year for his services. It was well known that a good chef in Boston could be hired for eight dollars a week, but all who tasted the products of Sanzian's kitchen were sure his money was well earned. The menu of a typical Parker House banquet hints at the Frenchman's versatility:

Oysters on Shell
SOUP
Green Turtle   Tomato

Harvey D. Parker, from 1875 carte de visite (Courtesy of the Bostonian Society)

FISH
Boiled Bass, Egg Sauce   Baked Cod, Claret Sauce

BOILED
Leg Mutton,   Capons and Pork
   Caper Sauce
Ham, Champagne Sauce   Turkey and Oyster Sauce

COLD ORNAMENTED DISHES
Mayonaise of Chicken   Boned Turkey, Decorated
Aspic of Oysters   Lobster Salad
   Partridges, with Truffles and Jelly

ENTREES
Sweet Bread,   Fricand eau Veal,
   Green Peas   Tomato Sauce
Compot of Pigeons   Fillet of Beef with
                         Mushrooms
Oyster Pattie   Maccaroni au
                         Permesan

ROAST
Mongrel Goose   Turkey
     Leg Mutton   Chickens

GAME

Black Ducks	Snipe	Black-breast Plover
Partridges	Grass Birds	Yellow Leg Plover
Woodcock	Widgeon	Peep
	Quail	

PASTRY

Birds Nest Pudding	Cup Custards	Lemon Pie
Apple Pie	Calf's Foot Jelly	Charlotte Russe
Squash Pie	Sago Pudding	Madeira Jelly
	Mince Pie	

FRUIT

Apples, Pears, Oranges, Walnuts, Peaches, Grapes, Almonds, Raisins

Vanilla Ice Cream, Pine Apple Ice Cream, Roman Punch.

Coffee and Olives

Sanzian's specialties were a delicate mayonnaise, a venison-chop sauce, and tomato soup. All were consumed in great quantities by diners in the hotel. Bottled and canned, they were also shipped to fancy food dealers in Eastern cities. Under the chef's direction, beef and large fowl were roasted over a charcoal-burning grate on a revolving spit. When British visitor William Makepeace Thackeray essayed a plump Wellfleet oyster at Parker's, he said it made him feel as if he were swallowing a baby. The comment may be considered a compliment. Boston cream and lemon meringue pies, little known before they were served at the Parker House, became epicurean delights under Sanzian's skilled hands. The Frenchman was unquestionably brilliant, but the Parker House's most enduring contribution to gastronomy was not his work, but that of a German baker named Ward who, shortly after the hotel opened, produced the first of what were later to become known throughout the world as Parker House rolls. Light, yeasty, formed of circles of dough folded in half, the rolls were among Parker's favorite delicacies. Besides great quantities served in the hotel, hundreds of dozens were regularly shipped to hotels and stores in such distant cities as Philadelphia, Cincinnati, and Chicago.

There was a sprinkling of Englishmen and Scots among the corps of uniformed waiters who hurried from kitchen to table at Parker's, as well as Germans, Italians, and Portuguese, but the majority of the hotel's waiters were Irish. "They made the service at Parker's the best possible," explained the Boston *Globe*, "and knew the tastes of their patrons from various sections of the Nation,

patrons who often said they found a more agreeable home at Parker's than at any other hotel. The head waiters were invariably Irish."

The hotel bar was a popular gathering place for single gentlemen on the town. Heady draughts of rum, gin, and whiskey were available in abundance, as were a variety of such exotic concoctions as Gin Sling, "Cocktail," Sangaree, Mint Julep, Sherry Cobbler, and Timber Doodle. There were tipplers and tosspots among the company who regularly thronged the barroom, but their numbers were few compared with the greater complement of shippers, merchants, and traders who came to the sanctum to raise their glasses. Poets, essayists, and philosophers, of which Boston had an embarrassment of riches, occasionally wandered in to appraise the wonders of Sherry Cobbler or, beset by worries, to lift their spirits with discreet draughts of rum or gin. The ivied halls of Harvard College, scarcely five miles distant from the hotel, supplied their share of bibbers—so many that humorist Artemus Ward at one time swore that "Harvard University was pleasantly and conveniently situated in the barroom of Parker's in School Street."

That the Parker House was more than a fine restaurant, more than a convivial bar, more than a handsome hotel with comfortable rooms was evident to all who came in contact with it. From its early days, the inn seemed to capture a large part of the special essence of Boston, reflecting its solemnity, its dignity, its punctilious regard for form and manners, but also its grace and good taste. "Proper Bostonians" were at home there, prim in their morning coats and boiled shirts. Long-whiskered "outlanders" from Maine, Vermont, and New Hampshire were welcomed, too, as were mutton-chopped bankers from far-away New York. Harvard blades arrived and departed in the main lobby, State Street merchants had their first Scotch grouse of the season in the dining rooms, and drummers on wintry afternoons warmed their frosty lips in the bar.

Visiting celebrities found the hotel as much to their liking as the Brahmins of Beacon Hill. Actors and actresses were often in residence, as were stars of the operatic stage—Charlotte Cushman, Edwin Booth, Henry Irving, Ellen Terry, Sarah Bernhardt, Adelina Patti, Lester Wallach, Augustin Daly, and Richard Mansfield. Edwin Booth's younger brother, John Wilkes, was a guest of the hotel in April 1865, though Harvey Parker did not often speak of the visit. Only eight days after the younger Booth left Parker's, he made his unexpected appearance on the stage of Ford's Theatre in Washington, D.C. and in a single, tragic moment changed the history of the nation.

Among the hotel's most notable regular visitors were a group of poets, novelists, and philosophers—probably the most eminent ever to make regular calls at an American hotel. The occasion for their visits was the monthly meeting of a literary club organized in the summer of 1855 for the purpose of exchanging views on philosophy, science, and letters, and to promote the organization of a literary magazine for Boston. The prime mover of the club was a lawyer and publishing agent named Horatio Woodman, and its first meetings were held in the Albion Hotel on Tremont Street. But the roster of members soon included many names more famous than Woodman's, and the meetings were shortly moved from the Albion to Parker's.

There were originally two clubs, though they had the same members. One, dedicated to friendship and conviviality, was called the Literary Club—later, the Saturday Club, from its practice of holding meetings on the last Saturday of each month at Parker's. The second, formed to organize a magazine that would be the equal of any in the United States, was called the Magazine, or Atlantic Club. After 1857, when the first issue of the distinguished *Atlantic Monthly* came off the press, the Magazine Club, its purpose achieved, melted into the Saturday Club.

The first roster of Saturday Club members included the names of Swiss-born scientist Louis Agassiz, lawyer and essayist Richard Henry Dana, Jr., music critic and editor John Sullivan Dwight, philosopher Ralph Waldo Emerson, and poet and *Atlantic* editor James Russell Lowell. They were soon joined by the genial physician-poet, Dr. Oliver Wendell Holmes, novelist Nathaniel Hawthorne, poets Henry Wadsworth Longfellow and John Greenleaf Whittier, and diplomat and son and grandson of presidents, Charles Francis Adams.

Meetings of the club were held in a private dining room on the second floor of the Parker House. The walls of the meeting room were decorated with paintings of Harvey Parker and Charles L. Flint, President of the State Agricultural Society. Long draperies hung at the windows, a thick carpet warmed the floor, and a log fire crackled beneath a marble mantel. Meetings customarily began at three in the afternoon. Agassiz, a large man with a hearty laugh, sat at the head of the table, while Longfellow, handsome with silver hair

and beard, held forth at the foot. Emerson sat near Longfellow, puffing slowly on his stub of a cigar, while Lowell, Whittier, Hawthorne, Holmes, and Adams crossed the table with philosophical comments and bon mots. Poems were read, stories recounted, gossip exchanged, and books criticized, while Harvey Parker's corps of Irish waiters flitted unobtrusively in and among the bards, filling glasses, exchanging plates, lighting cigars. Bills for the club dinners were shared by the members in attendance, and they were rarely modest. Seven courses was the rule for a typical meal, with generous draughts of sherry, sauternes, and claret to wash down the fish, fowl, game, and beef. Any member who wished to toast another in champagne could quickly summon a magnum of Moët, confident that the elixir would speedily and effectively "cheer the heart of man."

All but the Concord members (Emerson and Hawthorne lived in the village west of Boston) made their homes within five miles of the hotel, and members rarely left the club table before nine o'clock in the evening. When they did, they were invariably satisfied that their six hours at Parker's had been well spent.

The hotel's proximity to government offices—the City Hall erected in 1865 across School Street and the State House on nearby Beacon Hill—attracted politicians in large numbers to its halls and dining rooms. Mayors, aldermen, senators, and governors found the good food and stout liquor of the hotel an enhancement to their political intrigues. For years the governor of the commonwealth and his council of advisors met once a week in Room 118 at Parker's (they drank more frequently in its downstairs bar). On election nights, lamps burned late in the hotel as candidates met milling crowds of supporters and returns were tallied, victors congratulated, and losers consoled.

The success of the Parker House led Harvey Parker to begin a program of improvement and enlargement. He acquired the adjoining Horticultural Hall in 1860, demolished it, and in its place built a six-story addition to the hotel. Stepped forward of the old marble façade, the new building was faced with bay windows and topped with a stylish mansard roof. Three years later Parker acquired the land behind the new wing and again expanded the hotel. In 1866 he bought a narrow lot at 66 Tremont Street, a few doors from the corner of School. On this property, which adjoined the rear of his hotel buildings, he built a third hotel extension, closely modeled on the School Street annex, with bay

The Parker House in the 1860s (King's Handbook of Boston)

windows and steep mansard roof. At the same time a roof and two floors of rooms were added to the original School Street building, increasing its height to seven stories. Atop the whole was a profusion of gratings, fences, and iron railings that added an elegant Second Empire note to the gleaming white façade.

The hotel was a curious mixture of styles and heights when Charles Dickens returned to Boston for his second visit in 1867. The Tremont House, where Dickens had stayed in 1842, was still in operation, but the popular writer preferred the more luxurious surroundings of Parker's. Dickens had come to America for another of his popular and highly lucrative lecture tours, and he found the Parker House a comfortable place in which to plan his itinerary, rehearse his readings, and rest between performances. Whisked from his steamer at the wharf, he was delivered by friends and admirers to the lobby of the School Street inn, where Harvey Parker and his partner John Mills showed him to a comfortable, flower-decorated suite on the third floor of the School Street annex. The novelist enjoyed the fine meal served in his room, though he was annoyed when waiters left the door open and curious passers-by peeped in. Two days after his arrival, the visitor set pen to paper to describe the hotel to his daughter:

This is an immense hotel, with all manner of white marble public passages and public rooms. I live in a corner, high up, and have a hot and cold bath in my bedroom (connecting with the sitting room) and comforts not in existence when I was here before. The cost of living is enormous, but happily we can afford it. I dine to-day with Longfellow, Emerson, Holmes, and Agassiz. Longfellow was here yesterday. Perfectly white in hair and beard, but a remarkably handsome and notable-looking man.

Crowds anxious to catch a glimpse of the novelist thronged the lobbies and corridors, prompting Parker to post a guard at Dickens' door to keep out strangers. The novelist spent much of his time writing and rehearsing his lecture programs. To perfect gestures and expressions, he spent hours in front of a large mirror in the hotel sitting room, alternately smiling and frowning, scowling and grimacing, repeating lines from *David Copperfield, The Pickwick Papers,* and the beloved *Christmas Carol.* Each day about noon, he sallied forth from Parker's for his daily walk, a vig-

orous exertion which took him through much of downtown Boston, over Beacon Hill, and even into neighboring Cambridge. On his walks townspeople had a chance to observe the writer's flamboyant dress—bright coats and vests, striped cravats, polished boots, fine hats, and gloves. Leaving the city after a few weeks to fulfill theater engagements in New York, Baltimore, Washington, and Philadelphia, Dickens returned at intervals to Parker's, which was his American home-away-from-home during the whole of his five-month stay in the United States.

The bards of Boston and Cambridge entertained the Englishman in their homes, and he was an honored guest at a meeting of the Saturday Club in Parker's, where he sat between Holmes and Longfellow and delighted all members by serving his own liquid refreshment—gin punch made from a private stock brought over from England. At the end of February 1868 Dickens and his Boston publisher, James T. Fields, staged a "Great Interna-

Cartoon showing author Charles Dickens and his guard attempting to fend off a growing crowd outside his door (*Harper's Weekly, December 1867)*

The Parker House, a conglomeration of architectural styles and periods (Courtesy of the Fine Arts Department, Boston Public Library)

tional Walking Match" of twelve miles in length, after which the novelist was host to a lavish dinner in the Crystal Room of the Parker House. More of Dickens' gin punch must have flowed at the dinner than at the earlier Saturday Club banquet for, some time after the last course was finished, Dickens, clowning in his room with his agent and Fields' partner, fell into the tub—"fully arrayed," according to the witnesses, "with all his boutonnières, gold chains, and brilliantined earlocks."

The splash amused the writer greatly, though it alarmed his companions a little.

The Dickens dinner was remembered as one of the most sumptuous in the history of the Parker House, and it must have been expensive. But the bill did not trouble the novelist. Leaving Boston for the last time at the end of April 1868, he calculated he had taken in something over three hundred thousand dollars on his speaking tour. After deducting all expenses, fees, commissions, hall rentals, and even the bill for the Crystal Room banquet, his net was close to one hundred thousand dollars, a tidy sum in 1868 dollars.

For years Harvey Parker yearned to expand his hotel to the corner of School and Tremont, thus uniting the original marble building with the Tremont Street annex. But the lot's owners, who maintained a book shop and dwelling house on the property, refused to sell. The property passed through various generations of the Burnham family before O. H. P. Burnham acquired it in the early eighties. Burnham was willing to sell his plot to Parker, but only at a stiff price. The hotel owner, nearing the age of eighty, valued the land more dearly than the money and in 1883 agreed to pay Burnham one hundred fifty thousand dollars for his land. Construction of a new hotel section, taller and more elaborate than any that had preceded it, was well under way in May 1884 when Harvey Parker died.

Construction went forward under the auspices of the hotel's new lessees, Edward Punchard and Joseph Beckman. The new wing was an imposing structure of nine stories, surmounted with gables, dormers, and chimneys. At the corner of Tremont and School a tier of circular bay windows ascended from the street to the sixth floor. The walls, gables, and dormers were covered with elaborate stone sculptures—images of gods and goddesses, fruit, cornucopias, chevrons, and leopards (the latter the heraldic symbol of the Parker family in England). In 1886 an eight-story annex was built behind the corner wing, thus completing the vast Parker House complex.

Built in fits and starts over more than thirty years, the hotel did not present a harmonious appearance, but it was, in its own way, amazing. Parts of its exterior suggested a Georgian mansion; others a townhouse in the Paris of Louis Napoleon; still others the fantastical ramparts of the Château of Chambord. Lucius Beebe, who knew the building in his youth, remembered that its corridors were like "gas-lit catacombs carpeted in Turkey red and full of improbable angles, turns and levels. The chances were heavily against a late diner's ever getting to his own apartment, even if the lift deposited him in its approximate vicinage, and one gay old dog used to recall that he slept more frequently in linen closets than in his own bed.''

With all its peculiarities, the hotel was a Boston institution as familiar as Longfellow and Holmes, as widely admired as the Athenaeum or Old State House, as beloved among Bostonians—indeed, among all New Englanders—as baked beans, brown bread, and codfish.

Dr. Oliver Wendell Holmes, the amiable ''Autocrat of the Breakfast Table,'' who was a mainstay of early meetings of the Saturday Club and who outlived his great contemporaries Agassiz, Hawthorne, Longfellow, and Emerson, continued to attend meetings of the club at Parker's until his death in 1894. In a verse entitled ''At the Saturday Club,'' penned a few years before his passing, Holmes recorded his recollections of departed members and of the hotel which had so long sheltered their meetings. One passage, inspired by a view of the building from across School Street, was quoted many times in succeeding years and became a kind of literary hallmark for the hotel:

> **Turn half-way round, and let your look survey**
> **The white façade that gleams across the way,—**
> **The many-windowed building, tall and wide,**
> **The palace-inn that shows its northern side**
> **In grateful shadow when the sunbeams beat**
> **The granite wall in summer's scorching heat.**
> **This is the place; whether its name you spell**
> **Tavern, or caravanserai, or hotel.**
> **Would I could steal its echoes! you should find**
> **Such store of vanished pleasures brought to mind:**
> **Such feasts! the laughs of many a jocund hour**
> **That shook the mortar from King George's tower;**
> **Such guests! What famous names its record boasts,**
> **Whose owners wander in the mob of ghosts!**

That Boston had been good to Harvey Parker was evident from even a cursory examination of his sprawling hotel. That he was also good to Boston became apparent when his will was made public. Disposing of an estate worth more than a million dollars, the testament made generous charitable bequests, including a gift of one hundred thousand dollars to the Museum of Fine Arts.

Because he died without issue, operation of Parker's hotel was delegated to lessees. Punchard and Beckman managed it until Joseph R. Whipple took over in the 1890s. The Whipple Company, organized in 1906, operated the building under lease until 1925, when the fee was sold to Whipple by trustees of the Parker Estate.

The old building was still a center of hotel life in Boston—the scene of banquets, the rendezvous of politicians and visiting performers, the occasional retreat of poets and philosophers. Conventions made the hotel their Boston headquarters, and discriminating diners still frequented the dining rooms, though after World War I increasing numbers of travelers were stopping at the hotel's more modern rivals, the Ritz Carlton and Copley Plaza.

Executives of the Whipple Company were beginning to learn that an historic hotel in a modern American city is something of an anomaly. If the Parker House had been a public building—a town hall, a state house, a museum, or a library—it could not have meant more to the people of Boston or, indeed, to the people of New England. As a

School Street in the 1890s. The Parker House is shown on the left; the courtyard of Old City Hall (foreground) and King's Chapel (partially hidden by trees) on the right. (Courtesy of the Bostonian Society)

public property, it could have looked to the government of the city or state for protection and support. Because it was not a public asset, because it was a private, profit-making enterprise, its future depended wholly on its balance sheet.

Corridors that resembled "gas-lit catacombs" were historical curiosities of interest to wide-eyed tourists, but not comfortable halls through which to tread regularly to sleep. The property on which the Parker House stood was one of Boston's most valuable plots, heavily taxed by local authorities. As more and more hotel business drifted to the city's modern, high-rise hotels, executives of the Whipple Company contemplated modernizing the old hotel. The "New Marble Building" built in 1855 was gray now, the annexes streaked with soot and grime. The soaring stone walls of the nine-story wing at the corner of School and Tremont streets, though unmarked by age, seemed strangely out of place in the company of the large, new buildings that now lined Tremont Street. Rehabilitation of the old structures would be costly. Nothing less than demolition and building anew would effect a complete rejuvenation and firmly restore the Parker House to the front rank of Boston's hotels.

Wreckers attacked the old walls in 1925—sparing only the annex built in 1886—and construction of the new Parker House promptly began. Designed by the architectural firm of Desmond and Lord, the new building was a sleek, modern structure of steel and granite, but one that recaptured at least part of the style of its predecessor.

It rose fourteen stories above the corner of School and Tremont streets. The first floor was faced with black Quincy marble, the floors above with limestone and buff brick. At the corner of School and Tremont a tier of circular bay windows, like those which graced the old building, rose from the fifth to eleventh floors. Bronze marquises overhung the School and Tremont Street entrances, which led to lobbies of paneled oak. Limestone floors covered with thick carpets, sofas and chairs upholstered with Spanish leather, sculptured plaster ceilings, crystal chandeliers, colorful oil paintings all lent an atmosphere of old Boston to the hotel's public rooms and corridors. The main banquet room on the second floor was covered from floor to ceiling with mahogany. Also on the second floor was a Dickens Room, furnished in the style of the suite occupied by the writer in 1867 and 1868. Including facilities in the old annex, the new hotel embraced nearly eight hundred rooms. Because the annex remained open during construction of

The new Parker House, opened in 1927 (Boston Globe photo)

the new building, owners of the Parker House claimed—perhaps correctly—that theirs was the oldest continually operating hotel in the United States.

After its opening in 1927 the Parker House enjoyed a new burst of prosperity. But the financial crash of 1929 taught the Whipple Company a grim lesson in the realities of hotel economics. The Parker House was Boston's handsomest hotel, but Whipple had borrowed heavily to finance the new construction, and in the hard times that followed the crash there was little demand for plush hotels in Boston. In 1933 Whipple's mortgage was foreclosed, and the lender, First National Bank of Boston, transferred ownership to Glenwood J. Sherrard. Sherrard operated it until his death in 1958. In 1969 the hotel was acquired by the dynamic Dunfey family, owners of nearly a dozen hotels and restaurants in New England.

Under ownership of the Dunfeys—mother, Mrs. Catherine Dunfey, brothers, Bob, Jerry, Bill, Jack, Walt, and Roy—the Parker House became the nerve center of a rapidly expanding national and international hotel and restaurant chain. From New England the Dunfeys expanded their interests into New York, Pennsylvania, Maryland, Illinois, Georgia, Louisiana, Texas, and California. An agreement signed with Ireland's Aer Lingus in 1975 gave the Boston-based family management responsibilities for the London Tara Hotel and made them leaders of the world's fourth largest international airline and hotel group. By 1976 the number of Dunfey-owned or -managed guest rooms in the United States and England totaled more than seven thousand.

Beginning an extensive renewal program at the Parker House, the Dunfeys sought to make their historic ''flagship'' a showplace. The family name was prominently affixed to the hotel's marquises, signs, letterheads, and menus. If traditionalists complained that the name of Harvey Parker was nearly overwhelmed by the torrent of Dunfey family promotion and advertising, they admitted that the new owners showed a refreshing concern for the history of their Boston property.

Under the Dunfeys' management doormen, bellboys, hostesses, clerks, and other staff members, dressed in the costumes of the colonial era, greeted guests at the School Street entrance much as Harvey Parker did in the days of Longfellow and Dickens. In the mornings guests gathered for breakfast in the Revere Room just off the main lobby. In the afternoons and early evenings cocktails were served in the mezzanine-level Parker's Bar.

The main dining room—called simply Parker's—was redecorated in vintage Boston style, its menu expanded to include such nineteenth-century Parker House favorites as black bean soup, cream of oyster soup, Boston fish chowder, Haymarket haddock, Boston scrod, lobster, tripe, and Boston cream pie. Private banquet and conference rooms on the upper floors, bearing the illustrious names of Dickens, Holmes, Emerson, Longfellow, and Hawthorne, were the scene of private parties and convention gatherings.

Outside the hotel, visitors with an ear for poetry sometimes paused in the courtyard of Old City Hall, across School Street, or in the shadows of King's Chapel at the corner of Tremont to survey the walls of the hotel and remember the lines of Dr. Holmes:

> **Turn half-way round, and let your look survey**
> **The white façade that gleams across the way,—**
>
> · · ·
>
> **Such guests! What famous names its record boasts,**
> **Whose owners wander in the mob of ghosts!**

The ''white façade'' is darker now than it was in the days of Harvey Parker; the remembered voices of Longfellow, Dickens, and Holmes are nearly inaudible. But the ''mob of ghosts'' still stalks the halls and corridors of the palace inn—and will, if fate is kind, for a century yet to come.

3

Magnolia Days

THE GREENBRIER, WHITE SULPHUR SPRINGS

It is a warm afternoon on the veranda of a columned mansion. The singsong of mockingbirds echoes in the trees, and the scent of magnolias perfumes the air. Men in white linen suits relax in rocking chairs as a smiling black waiter sets a tray on the table before them. On it are a set of tumblers filled with ice, Bourbon whiskey, and sprigs of mint. At the foot of a nearby flight of steps, tethered horses paw a graveled road that leads from the veranda into a grove of trees. Standing at the veranda rail, women in colorful dresses admire the view of road, trees, valley, and mountains. A scene from the pages of Margaret Mitchell? A stage set from the back lot of Metro-Goldwyn-Mayer? A nostalgic flashback to plantation life in the antebellum South?

The scene described is none of these—but a vignette of twentieth-century hotel life on the portico of one of America's most historic resorts, the Greenbrier at West Virginia's White Sulphur Springs.

West Virginia's image as an industrial and mining state belies the long history it shares with its eastern neighbor, Virginia. Before 1863 the Mountain State was part of the Old Dominion, frequented by belles from Charleston and Savannah, whiskey-drinking politicians from Richmond and New Orleans, cotton and tobacco planters from the Carolinas and Mississippi. In the pro-Unionist movement that split West Virginia from Virginia, the voters of Greenbrier County favored secession, but the necessities of military defense brought all

counties west of the Allegheny Mountain crest into the new state—and White Sulphur Springs found itself four miles outside the Old Dominion. Separated by a line on the map from its traditional Southern neighbors, the resort remained psychologically and emotionally bound to its brothers and sisters in the old Confederate States.

Life in the Old South was not perfectly re-created in *Gone With the Wind*, nor is the flavor of resort life in the Old Dominion precisely preserved at the modern Greenbrier. But there is more than a close resemblance in each case. The proprietors of the Greenbrier have not turned back the clocks in an effort to re-create the style and tone of life at White Sulphur Springs in the nineteenth century, but enough of the bygone era has survived to convince all but historical purists that the tradition is alive and still very well.

Though the principal buildings at the Greenbrier were built in the early years of the twentieth century, they carry on a tradition which is much older. At least one structure still on the grounds dates from the days when Thomas Jefferson occupied the White House, and many were standing when Henry Clay and John C. Calhoun danced with crinolined belles in the White Sulphur ballroom. The President's Cottage, which today houses the Greenbrier Museum, was built about 1816 as the resort home of Stephen Henderson, a wealthy sugar planter from Louisiana. In later years it attained fame as the "Summer White House" of Presidents Martin Van Buren, John Tyler, Millard

Horses and riders beneath the soaring north portico of the Greenbrier, White Sulphur Springs (Courtesy of the Greenbrier)

The Presidents' Cottage, today the Greenbrier Museum (Courtesy of the Greenbrier)

Fillmore, Franklin Pierce, and James Buchanan. A plaque on the hotel grounds, erected by the Greenbrier's owners in 1940, marks the site of the great hotel that was the focus of resort life at White Sulphur Springs from 1857 until 1922—"The Old White," its affectionate admirers called it. Once acclaimed as "The Pride of the Old Dominion," The White was razed half a century ago, but its spirit survives in the great Georgian mansion that today carries on the springs tradition.

The mineral springs of Virginia are of ancient origin. They were frequently visited by the Shawnee Indians, who regarded them as "medicine waters" of great power and potency, and European settlers knew of them long before the American Revolution. In 1748 an eighteen-year-old surveyor named George Washington visited the earliest known of the Virginia springs—now Berkeley Springs—

that he knew as "Ye Famed Warm Springs." Warm Spring Baths was discovered in 1761, Sweet Springs three years later, Capon Springs, Howard's Lick, Hot, Healing, Salt Sulphur, Red Sulphur, Blue Sulphur, and Gray Sulphur Springs in the next two decades. But none was to be as celebrated or to make as lasting an imprint on the life of the Old South as White Sulphur Springs.

The first Europeans to explore the vicinity of White Sulphur Springs were probably French explorers from Canada, for the name *Ronceverte* appeared on Canadian maps before its English equivalent, Greenbrier. The name referred to a rough, prickly shrub that the explorers found in profusion in West Virginia. "Greenbrier, boldbrier, horsebrier, catbrier, squirrelbrier, devil's clothes line, whichever of its names you use," said naturalist Lyle Bryce, "it's a most troublesome bramble." The name of the shrub was applied to the river that flows southwestward through the Allegheny Mountains, to a low mountain in western Virginia and, later, to a county.

In a secluded valley of the Alleghenies, at an altitude of about two thousand feet, steady streams of water, heavily charged with sulphur and other minerals, flowed from openings in the ground— some from marshy pools, others from fissures in low formations of rock. The waters' smell, often described as that of an egg "half-boiled and half-rotten," was not pleasant to the uninitiated, but the earliest settlers seem not to have been bothered by it. Ignoring the sulphur water, they proceeded to clear oaks from the nearby fields, to plant corn and rye, and to put up rude cabins. Nicholas Carpenter, who settled in the valley around 1750, thought the spring water worthless, but he was much impressed by the rich bottomland that bordered nearby Howard's Creek and set seriously to work to farm it. Carpenter was killed by Indians in 1752, but behind him he left a wife along with a young daughter who, in 1766, married a storekeeper from Fincastle, Virginia named Michael Bowyer.

In addition to his storekeeping duties, Bowyer worked as a farmer, served as a church vestryman, and was a captain in the Revolutionary War. When the war was over, Bowyer asked his wife's mother to sell him her land at White Sulphur Springs. She did so and, in 1784, the former captain and storekeeper became master of a princely domain of 950 acres in the valley of White Sulphur Springs.

At the time he took title to the land, Bowyer was unaware of an incident that had occurred at the springs four years earlier and that was destined to alter the land and his own career drastically. In 1778 a woman named Amanda Anderson, badly crippled with rheumatism, heard from the Indians that the waters had miraculous restorative powers and prevailed on her family to drag her to the springs in a litter strung between two horses. At the springs she was laid in a hollow log, which was then filled with water and hot stones. As she bathed, Mrs. Anderson "drank freely of the fountain." Repeated daily, the treatment soon produced perceptible results. The invalid was able first to stand, then to walk slowly around her family's camp. At the end of several weeks she mounted a horse and rode happily away.

News of the crippled woman's recovery spread quickly. Soon other sufferers appeared at the springs to immerse their pain-wracked limbs in its medicinal waters and to drink deep drafts of the liquid. Access to the site was facilitated by a one-time buffalo path and Indian trail that snaked through the mountains and valleys of western Virginia, connecting the James River basin of the East with the Kanawha and Ohio River valleys of the West. The trail crossed Michael Bowyer's property and, after 1782, when some trees along the route were leveled and the trail renamed a "road," it brought flocks of visitors to the springs. There were a few log cabins on the property, but most of the travelers pitched tents near the water or, in summer, slept in the open air.

Not all visitors to Bowyer's property in the early years were health-seekers. Hunters found the mountain valley an ideal spot for their recreation, as did hikers and nature-lovers. From as far east as Alexandria, horsemen, roughly dressed in buckskins and broad hats and carrying long rifles at their sides, rode over the mountains and camped by the springs or on the nearby banks of Howard's Creek. They carried the wardrobes they would wear at the springs in their saddle bags, along with jugs of corn liquor, occasional bottles of French brandy, packs of cards, and pistols for shooting venison or highwaymen.

Sensing the profit that could be made from his property, Bowyer put up some guest cabins and in 1808 erected a large tavern building. Built of wood, the one-story structure had a large dining room, a bar, some lodging rooms, and a long porch that extended the length of the building.

After Bowyer's death in 1809 his son-in-law, James Calwell, took charge of the springs property. Calwell put up a row of cottages, enlarged the tavern, and built two spring houses.

The first spring house, erected sometime after 1810, was an open wooden structure of four pillars with a pyramid-like roof. The life-sized figure of an Indian queen, holding a bundle of arrows and a large bowl, stood at the peak of the roof. The second spring house was built a short distance from the first. It resembled a Roman temple, with a circle of twelve white columns that supported a low dome and a statue of Hygeia, the goddess of health, on top. Beneath the dome the spring opening was encased in an octagonal basin lined with marble. A circle of benches provided seating accommodations for about a hundred people. The year the second spring house was built has not been recorded, but it may have been 1815, the year General Andrew Jackson paid a visit to southwestern Virginia. When the old structure was being restored in 1964, a sealed box containing newspaper clippings was found embedded in one of the

The circular spring house at White Sulphur Springs (Courtesy of the Greenbrier)

columns. The clippings were of stories of the Battle of New Orleans, the bloody encounter in which Jackson won fame for a brilliant defeat of the British. The battle was fought in January of 1815; Jackson's visit to southwestern Virginia took place in October of the same year.

Two years after the heroic general's visit a famous politician stopped at White Sulphur. Henry Clay was serving his fourth term as Speaker of the House of Representatives when he arrived in July 1817 for a stay of three days. Returning from Washington to his plantation in Lexington, Kentucky, the "Great Compromiser" found the trail that passed through James Calwell's property a convenient route for his trip. The ledger entry of Clay's visit reveals that his room and board cost $1.50 a night ($4.50 for three days). Lodging his servant and stabling his three horses cost 75 cents a night for each (a total of $9). The horses consumed two gallons of grain (33 cents), and nine gallons were taken along for the rest of the journey ($1.50). Clay bought a dozen cigars (25 cents) and had his clothes laundered (68½ cents). His servant had three drinks, a dram of brandy upon arrival (12½ cents) and two grogs (6¼ cents each). The ledger does not record any liquid refreshment for the speaker, but the omission is not evidence that he abstained. Clay was as noted a drinker as he was an orator, and probably he took his spirits with his host—"sipping whiskey," perhaps, or "hailstorms," an early White Sulphur version of the mint julep. The total bill for Clay's three days at the springs was $16.51½.

Life at White Sulphur became more lively after Henry Clay's visit. The James River and Kanawha Turnpike, built along the route of the old Indian trail, opened to traffic in 1824. Wealthy planters were spending much of their time at the resort, many in cottages specially built for their use. Prominent among the early private cottages was the house built in 1816 for Stephen Henderson of Louisiana. Overlooking the domed spring house, Henderson's house was a two-story building of brick, with long white columns and a broad veranda. Another cottage, built nearby, was even more handsome. Erected around 1825 for Colonel Richard Singleton of South Carolina, it was an imposing white structure with a gleaming Greek colonnade.

More modest cottages were built in rows which were given imaginative names. Several were named for regions of the South—Virginia, Georgia, South Carolina, Alabama, Baltimore, Florida. One—Tansas—was named for a Louisiana Indian tribe. Another—Paradise—was named for the eventual destination of all good Southerners. Yet another—Wolf Row—was reserved for bachelors. "Unless you be young and foolish," warned an early visitor, "fond of noise and nonsense, frolic and fun, wine and wassail, sleepless nights and days of headache, avoid Wolf Row."

When cholera and yellow fever swept large portions of the South in the 1830s, word was spread that White Sulphur Springs was free of the pestilence. A desire to escape the disease, coupled with a yearning for social contact, brought increasingly larger crowds to the resort. Life on large plantations, where neighbors were often miles away, afforded little opportunity for mixing with members of "one's class." Gathered at White Sulphur, wealthy planters and their families could socialize while they looked for suitable marriage partners for their sons and daughters.

A ballroom with lodging apartments attached was built a short distance from the tavern. In the evenings plantation belles and beaux gathered in their finest dress clothes to dance to the music of a band. Henry Clay made frequent visits to the springs, where he divided his time about equally between the bar and the ballroom. On the dance floor the Kentuckian was a perennial favorite of the ladies. Colonel William Pope of Alabama—founder of the Springs' "Billing, Wooing and Cooing Society," a kind of introduction service for young men and women—directed the dances, setting up cotillion figures, supervising waltzes, directing the more familiar and consistently popular movements of the Virginia Reel. John C. Calhoun of South Carolina was a prominent visitor at the resort, where he joined ladies in the "Treadmill," a kind of ballroom promenade said to have been originated by Clay.

A young Philadelphian visited the springs in 1834 on the first leg of a journey "to see the world and pick up health." Writing under the pen name of Peregrine Prolix, he described the Virginia resort:

> The middle of the valley . . . is cleared of forest, care having been taken to leave a few noble trees for ornament and shade. The buildings consist of a frame dining room about one hundred and twenty feet long, with which is connected a large kitchen and bakery; a frame ball room with lodging rooms over it and at each end; two very large frame stables with eighty stalls in each, of which the exterior rows are open to the air; and many rows of cabins tastefully arranged around the larger edifices, and standing on rising ground. There are several straight and dusty walks laid out with rectangular art; and many artless paths more agreeable to the foot and eye. The cabins are, in general, clean; some suspicion of fleas I confess too, but I detected no bugs, which are perhaps kept away by the nature of the water, for Virgil says in the fifth book of his Georgics:
>
> Foetidum in aqua non gaudet sulphurea bedbug: which translated into the Virginia vernacular, means, "The stinking chinch does not like sulphur water."

Peregrine was impressed by the marvelous restorative powers of the springs which, he was told, cure "Yellow Jaundice, White Swelling, Blue Devils, and Black Plague; Scarlet Fever, Yellow Fever, Spotted Fever, and fever of every kind and colour; Hydrocephalus, Hydrothorax, Hydrocele, and Hydrophobia; Hyphochondria and Hypocrisy; Dispepsia, Diarrhea, Diabetes, and die-of-anything; Gout, Gourmandising, and Grogging; Liver Complaint, Colic, Stone, Gravel, and all other diseases and bad habits, except chewing, smoking, spitting and swearing." In addition to minerals, the waters contained what Peregrine noted was "a very strong infusion of fashion."

Since the latter was "an animal substance," he thought its "quantity cannot be precisely ascertained; it is supposed, however, to be gradually increasing, and no doubt contributes greatly to the efficiency of the water."

In the summer of 1837, amid a nationwide financial panic, President Martin Van Buren met a group of his advisers at White Sulphur to discuss rechartering the United States Bank. Visitors from Europe were occasionally seen at the springs, where they tasted the waters, inspected the grounds, and inevitably compared both to such celebrated Old World spas as Epsom, Vichy, Bad Nauheim, and Baden-Baden.

The Englishwoman Harriet Martineau was much impressed by the elegance of the springs' guests. Everybody was "gay and spruce," Miss Martineau wrote in her book, *Society in America.* "The gentlemen in the piazza in glossy coats and polished pumps, ladies in pink, blue and white; standing on green grass, shading their delicate faces and gay head-dresses under parasols. . . ." The American Mary Hagner—disguised for literary purposes as "Mark Pencil, Esq."—was even more enthusiastic. She described the resort in a chatty volume of travel memoirs titled *The White Sulphur Papers,* published at New York in 1839. "When we arrived at the springs," Miss Hagner wrote, "the company were going to dinner, and all the walks and avenues leading from the cabins were streaming with lively forms. A band of music was playing gaily in the portico of the dining hall; and the whole face of things had the look of enchantment. It seemed to us travelers, arriving at such a time, as if the inhabitants of some fairy isle were turning out to welcome the coming of expected strangers."

The English novelist and naval captain, Frederick Marryat, visited several Virginia watering places in 1837 but found White Sulphur "the only springs which are fashionable." He was taken by the beauty of the surrounding valley, the wooded hills, the tavern, the ballroom, and the rambling rows of cottages, but he was even more impressed by the guests. During his stay the cottage rows were always crowded and the dining room filled nearly to bursting by the company of no less than seven hundred persons who sat down to each meal. "It is astonishing," Marryat noted, "what inconvenience people will submit to, rather than not be accommodated somehow or another." The planters' fine dress and courtly manners struck him as "excessively aristocratical and exclusive" in a country which prided itself on its democratic in-

stitutions. Indeed, he thought White Sulphur the only place in the United States where society might truly be considered "select." He wrote:

Of course all the celebrated belles of the different States are to be met with here, as well as all the large fortunes, nor is there a scarcity of pretty and wealthy widows. The president, Mrs. Caton, the mother of Lady Wellesley, Lady Stafford, and Lady Caermarthen, the daughter of Carrol, of Carroltown, one of the real aristocracy of America, and a signer of the Declaration of Independence, and all the first old Virginian and Carolina families, many of them descendants of the old cavaliers, were at the springs when I arrived there; and certainly I must say that I never was at any watering-place in England where the company was so good and so select as at the Virginia springs in America.

James Calwell presided over White Sulphur Springs for more than forty years, watching it grow from an obscure mountain resort into one of the world's great spas, but he seemed unable to make it a financial success. He planned for years to build a great new hotel on the property but could not attract the capital essential to the project. When he died in 1851 at the ripe age of seventy-eight years, Calwell's springs were still crowded with the elite of Southern society, but he was hopelessly in debt. Poor management, his detractors said, caused his business failure.

Calwell's son William carried on after his father's death, but he found the debt he inherited a heavy burden. In 1853 he persuaded the state legislature in Richmond to charter a White Sulphur Springs Company and authorize the sale of five hundred thousand dollars worth of stock. When it appeared that the authorized sum would be insufficient to wipe the springs clear of debt and build a new hotel besides, the legislature authorized the sale of three times the original limit of stock. A group of businessmen in Baltimore considered taking the stock, as did a company of British investors, but the final sale was made in 1857 to eight Virginians headed by Commodore Matthew Maury. Shortly after the purchase the new owners broke ground for a new hotel.

It was advertised as the largest building in the South. It may in fact have been the largest in the United States. Four hundred feet long and one hundred twenty feet wide, it rose four stories above the gravel walks and spreading lawns of the old springs compound. Its main entrance was marked by a broad flight of steps, a sheltered porch edged with a row of Doric columns, and a gabled portico. At the summit of the roof a

*The Old White (*Harper's New Monthly Magazine, *August 1878)*

cupola-topped dome looked down on the cottages and springs.

The interior of the hotel was even more impressive than its exterior. Broad lobbies and corridors ran the length and width of the building. The ballroom was touted as "the largest and finest" in America, and the dining room, 300 feet long and 120 feet wide, was capable of seating no less than 1,200 guests. Sleeping accommodations were provided for seven hundred. With the surrounding cottages, the total lodging capactiy of the resort came to something over two thousand.

Opened in June 1858, the new building was grandiloquently named the Grand Central Hotel.

But the new name did not take. It was "Grand Central" in advertising leaflets and on the headings of hotel stationery, but to its guests it was always The White or The Old White. Even when new, the hotel seemed to epitomize the South, to symbolize its love of good manners, high style, and tradition, to typify the pride it took in its belles and beaux, sipping whiskey, Treadmill and magnolia blossoms. The hotel's handsome setting, classic architecture, and ample proportions all contributed to the illusion that it had always been at White Sulphur Springs, had always served the social, recreational, and cultural needs of the people south of Mason's and Dixon's Line. More important, The White was a focus of regional pride, proof to Virginians, Georgians, Alabamians, Missisipians, and Louisianians that the South was capable of doing things on a big scale, and doing them as well or even better than the North.

In the storm gathering over the nation the South's regional pride was by no means an inconsequential factor. As the 1850s drew to a close, the balls at The White seemed more brilliant than ever before, but there was a bitter, brittle quality to the brilliance. The season which opened at White Sulphur on June 1, 1860, saw the hotel and cottages crowded as usual. The nineteen-year-old Englishman, Baron Renfrew (better known to his subjects as Albert Edward, Prince of Wales, the future King Edward VII), was a visitor that year, as was John Letcher, the fifty-seven-year-old Governor of Virginia. The baron's visit was social—that of Letcher anything but. Baron Renfrew bedded down in a comfortable suite at The White. The governor camped out on Copeland Hill, an eminence above the domed spring house, with Company F of the Richmond Volunteers. The proprietors of the hotel installed a pistol gallery for the convenience "and necessity" of guests.

The fiery Virginia farmer and pamphleteer, Edmund Ruffin, was at the springs in 1860, as he had been the three previous summers. There he attempted to arouse support for his dream of a confederacy of Southern states free of the malign influence of the government at Washington. Ruffin organized the ladies of the resort into shooting clubs while Governor Letcher marched with his troops. Young Charley Bonaparte, grandnephew of Emperor Napoleon I and grandson of Jerome Bonaparte, often drilled with them. His family was spending the summer at White Sulphur, as was their custom, in the Baltimore Row cottage owned by Jerome.

Abraham Lincoln's election as president brought a pall of gloom to the South—a gloom that was coupled with an ominous spirit of defiance. Ruffin's proselytizing had little success before the Illinois rail-splitter took his oath of office as the nation's sixteenth president, but great success afterward. In April 1861 the North was shocked by news of the Confederate attack on Fort Sumter, South Carolina. But few who had visited White Sulphur Springs in the previous four years were surprised to learn that one of the first shots on Sumter was fired by Edmund Ruffin.

The war fiercely tested the loyalties of western Virginians. Many, including most who lived in the neighborhood of White Sulphur, were ardent supporters of the Southern cause and rallied enthusiastically behind General Robert E. Lee and his Army of Northern Virginia. Others were as firm in their support of the Union. Large numbers of settlers had come into western Virginia from Pennsylvania and other Northern states in the two decades before 1860. The loyalties of these transplanted Northerners were largely responsible for the pro-Union movement which culminated in 1863 in the decision to split Virginia into two states. But before the break came, there were troop movements at the springs and anxious moments for people who lived in the neighborhood.

The White opened in June 1861 for its usual summer season, with rates reduced "owing to the embarrassed state of the country," but the gaiety of previous years was notably absent. General Henry Wise, formerly Governor of Virginia, marched by the resort on the James River and Kanawha Turnpike in his advance on Charleston but fell back to White Sulphur when he was threatened by superior Northern forces. John Floyd, another Virginia governor-turned-general, brought to the springs a second force, threatening for a time to quarrel with the troops under Wise. General Lee hurried to the springs to mediate.

While Lee was in the area, he first saw the four-year-old gray horse that was later to become his favorite mount. Traveller, originally called Jeff Davis, had been raised at Blue Sulphur Springs, a few miles west of The White. He had been renamed Greenbrier before Lee purchased him in the fall of 1861 and, referring to the animal's reputation as a "fine traveller," gave him his final name.

All normal operations at White Sulphur had been suspended by August 1863, when Union General William W. Averell marched his troops over the turnpike toward Lewisburg, nine miles west of the springs, intent on seizing the law library at the Lewisburg courthouse. On August 26, near the eastern edge of White Sulphur Springs, Averell's force met a Confederate unit commanded by Colonel George S. Patton, grandfather of the celebrated Army commander of World War II. The encounter between Averell and Patton was bloody, resulting in 380 casualties and forcing the Union general's hasty retreat to the east.

Combat once again threatened the springs in June 1864, when Union General David Hunter marched over the turnpike and stopped at The White, then undefended by any Confederate soldiers. Though the general's force included two men who were later to achieve fame, Colonel

General Robert E. Lee with a group of his wartime associates. Taken at White Sulphur in the 1868 season. (Courtesy of the Greenbrier)

Rutherford B. Hayes and Captain William McKinley, Hunter's activities at White Sulphur were best remembered because of a memoir published by another captain in his unit, Henry Algernon Du Pont, a son of the Delaware munitions manufacturer who supplied much of the Union's powder during the war. Du Pont wrote:

> I reported to General Hunter about noon and made inquiry as to the hour for beginning the march. . . . I remarked, as I was about to depart, "General, I hear that you intend to burn the buildings here when we leave." He replied, "Yes, I intend to burn them all down." After a short pause, I said, "Don't you think, General, that the burning of these structures would be a military mistake?" This seemed to arouse him, and, raising his voice a little, he at once asked, "What do you mean, Captain, by that inquiry?" Looking him squarely in the eyes, my response was as follows: "I mean this, General—if we have later to occupy and hold this country, the White Sulphur Springs will be the natural point for our principal station, as so many roads converge here. Such being the case, the buildings as they stand would furnish excellent winter quarters for at least a brigade of troops." He said nothing but looked at me with some suspicion, I thought. In a few seconds, howev-

er, his expression changed and he quietly remarked, "Well, I had not thought of that," whereupon he instantly called his orderly and sent for the adjutant-general to report forthwith. Upon the arrival of this officer, Hunter said at once, "Colonel, I have changed my mind about burning the buildings here. Don't issue the order."

Spared by Du Pont's entreaty and Hunter's last-minute reprieve, the hotel and cottages at White Sulphur Springs survived the war and in the summer of 1865 made ready to throw open their doors to a new generation of guests.

There was a conscious attempt to re-create the ambience of life at the springs before the war. The hotel and cottages had been damaged in the fighting—the statue of Hygeia atop the spring house had been shot away, and furniture and draperies in the main building had been destroyed. A new stock company was formed by George L. Peyton to lease the springs and operate the hotel, and the buildings were repaired and repainted. A race track was opened, and an artificial lake was formed by damming Howard's Creek.

General Lee's arrival in June 1867 marked the

springs' return to the first rank of Southern resorts. The defeated Confederate hero had brought his wife Mary, badly crippled with arthritis, to the spa in the hope that the sulphur water would ease her pain. The Lees were accompanied by their son Custis, their daughter Agnes, Agnes' friend Mary Pendleton, and a maid. They set up in a cottage in Baltimore Row, where Mrs. Lee took all of her meals. The other members of the family dined in The White.

The hotel and grounds buzzed with quiet excitement the evening of the general's arrival. If, as expected, he appeared in the hotel parlor, how should the other guests receive him? He was universally beloved by Southerners but, as the commander of a defeated rebel army, he might be embarrassed by undue attention.

The discussion about how to receive him was still under way when the general appeared in the door of the parlor. A hush fell over the room as, one by one, every man and woman arose and stood in silence until the general took his seat. Assured that no demonstration would be made, Lee went regularly into the parlor on succeeding nights, where he enjoyed the quiet attention he received from all the guests. The general was a favorite companion in the parlor and dancing partner in the ballroom, but he preferred to spend much of his time alone, riding with Traveller in the hills above the springs, pausing here and there to admire the beauties of nature or to ponder the strange twists of his and Virginia's fate.

Lee and his family were back at the springs in 1868, when the general was joined by several of his wartime comrades-in-arms—Generals P. G. T. Beauregard, A. R. Lawton, Henry Wise, James Connor, Martin Gary, and John Bankhead Magruder. A Union general, W.S. Rosecrans, was also a guest that year. Meeting with Lee, Rosecrans suggested that the Virginian might want to sign a statement affirming his loyalty to the Union and promising the efforts of the South to treat the Negroes fairly. Lee agreed, asking only that the statement include mention of the South's desire to be treated fairly by the North and to be restored to self-government. Put in writing, the "White Sulphur Manifesto" was signed by Lee and thirty-one other ex-Confederates.

The Lees were at the springs again in 1869, the year of the famous "Peabody Ball." Given in honor of George Peabody, a Boston and London philanthropist who had given $3,500,000 to the Fund for Southern Education, the ball was the most lavish The White had ever seen. Two thousand people crowded the parlor, ballroom, and corridors the evening of the dance. The guests were "the most gifted, distinguished and gentle-blooded to be found in either section of our vast country," said a reporter for the *Richmond Whig,* adding: "Never has there been brought together a crowd of fair women and brave men which represented more largely the refined beauty, grace, worth and intellect of our country than that which did honor to Mr. Peabody." General Lee, as usual, enjoyed his 1869 visit to the springs though, commenting on it later, he admitted he "should prefer more quiet." Toward the end of August the sixty-two-year-old soldier left the springs for the last time, returning to his home in Virginia, from which he would make only three more trips—none of them to White Sulphur—before his death in October 1870.

Though White Sulphur was still a great Southern resort, changes were unmistakably in the wind. The year of Lee's last visit, 1869, was also the year the railroad came to the springs. Talk of building a rail line through western Virginia had been heard at least since the early 1850s, but the talk was not serious until 1867, when a conference of investors was held at The White to raise funds for construction. Wood burning locomotives of the Chesapeake & Ohio finally reached the springs in July 1869, when they were greeted by wildly cheering crowds. Four years later the last spike was driven in a road that joined the Chesapeake Bay to the Ohio River. Completion of the railroad was a triumph for the West Virginia resort, for White Sulphur Springs was the only major watering place on the entire C & O line.

If the Chesapeake & Ohio brought new crowds to White Sulphur, they were clearly of a different kind from those that thronged the resort in the days of Clay and Lee. Northerners were increasingly in evidence, as were families of moderate means. In the seventies and eighties The White—now universally The Old White—went through a succession of owners, each determined to restore the resort to its antebellum glory. But each was thwarted in his purpose by the hard realities of double-entry accounting. Expenses of running the hotel and springs were greater than they had been before the Civil War, and there were no more great Southern planters to contribute to the income. "We find the grass unmowed," wrote a disappointed visitor in the 1870s, "except by trampling feet; the gravel paths unweeded; steps leading into once favored summer-houses falling to decay; everything evincing taste in the original design, but unkempt as a beggar child's profuse and ringleted hair. The enigma is solved in a statement that the present proprietors have leased the property from a company who refuse to do anything toward repairs. . . .

"Yet nobody talks of the discomfort, nobody appears to feel it. Has not Fashion lifted each and all above the meanness of a comment on such petty details?"

There were still glittering balls in the summer, and belles and beaux who gathered in knots on the graveled walks or in the shade of the old spring house (the domed temple still stood proud and erect, though the pyramid-roofed building had long since been razed). There were distinguished visitors—Governor Wade Hampton of South Carolina, General P. G. T. Beauregard of Louisiana, Ben Hill of Georgia, Mayor Grace of New York, the Longworths of Ohio, the Prestons and Browns of Kentucky—who mingled pleasantly with the belles of old plantations. Grand dames still made dramatic entrances in the parlor and swirled in great circles across the ballroom floor. There was elegance yet at The Old White, but it was a decaying elegance. Visitors to the ballroom often found women with proud, historic names of the old south seated in arm chairs, watching the Treadmill, dressed in faded, nearly threadbare gowns decorated with treasures resurrected from old trunks—pieces of rare Brussels lace, perhaps, diamond solitaires, or strings of perfect pearls.

Finances at the springs were so bad that in 1882 the first mortgage on the property was foreclosed and a new Greenbrier White Sulphur Springs Company was organized to manage the property. The new proprietors drew up plans to expand the hotel by adding three wings to the 1857 structure so as to create a square measuring 450 feet along each side. One wing of the projected three was built before financial difficulties again beset the property and the expansion plans were scrapped. The nadir of White Sulphur's prosperity was probably 1894, the only post-Civil War year when the resort did not open for the summer season.

Business improved in 1895 and continued its upward trend through the final years of the century, spurred largely by increasing traffic on the Chesapeake & Ohio. When wealthy and important men arrived at the springs around 1900, they did not come in sleek carriages with liveried footmen and horses trailing behind, as in the days of Henry Clay, but in luxurious private railroad cars—the "wheeled palaces" of the new industrial age. One car might belong to J. Ogden Armour, another to

William K. Vanderbilt, others yet to Astors, Dukes, Drexels, and Biddles. The fortunes of White Sulphur Springs were increasingly linked with those of the railroad, and it was not surprising that the Chesapeake & Ohio should consider buying the property. An offer to buy the resort was made in the 1880s, but the railroad was not able to complete the transaction until 1910. The price—three annual installments of fifty thousand dollars each—was well within the means of the C & O, which had an annual income of nearly ten million dollars, and its executives reckoned it a promising investment. Proper development of the springs would attract large numbers of passengers to the C & O and add significantly to the already handsome profits of the railroad.

But first there was work to be done. The walls of The Old White had to be covered with a new coat of paint; splintered boards in the long veranda had to be replaced; the salons and parlors and grand ballrooms needed cleaning, repainting, and refurnishing. When these temporary improvements were completed, the railroad began a more ambitious program of expansion and development.

Architects from Philadelphia were summoned to design a large mineral bath to be fed by waters from the springs, and Junius Sterner, a New York architect, was commissioned to draw plans for a large new hotel. Construction of Sterner's seven-story, 250-room Georgian-style building began in 1910. By September 1913 the new building was ready to welcome its first guests.

The two hotels—The Old White and the new Greenbrier—were operated independently, though they were under common ownership. The Greenbrier was open year-round; The Old White only in summer. When both were open, there was much traffic between the two buildings—visits shared by guests, parties exchanged in the many parlors and ballrooms. A nine-hole golf course, the Lakeside, was opened in 1910; the eighteen-hole Old White course four years later. Tennis courts were built, a golf and tennis club erected, and new cottages put up at strategic points in the springs compound. By the end of June 1915 the C & O had supplemented its original investment of $150,000 with more than $2,000,000 worth of improvements.

In the years following World War I White Sulphur Springs was again acclaimed as one of America's most fashionable resorts. President Woodrow Wilson was a guest, as were General of the Armies John J. Pershing and the twenty-five-year-old grandson of White Sulphur's distin-

Front entrance of the Greenbrier (Courtesy of the Greenbrier)

guished 1860 visitor, Baron Renfrew. Like his grandfather, David Windsor carried the title of Baron Renfrew but, unlike his ancestor, he made no effort to conceal the fact that he was also the Prince of Wales. He arrived at White Sulphur in September 1919 in an elegant private railroad car but chose to walk from the train station to the Greenbrier, where a sumptuous suite was reserved for his use. After a few minutes in the hotel the prince was off to the spring house for a glass of sulphur water; then to the swimming pool and golf course for some exercise. In the evening he delighted the eligible socialites who gathered around him by dancing gracefully and playing the drums with the hotel orchestra.

Less noted than the prince's visit were the several vacations spent at White Sulphur by the Baltimore belle, Wallis Warfield, who visited the resort with her family and honeymooned there with her first husband, Navy Lieutenant Earl Winfield Spencer. Neither the prince nor Miss Warfield could have known that their paths would one day

meet at White Sulphur. When ex-King Edward VIII returned to the springs nearly three decades after his 1919 visit, he did so as the Duke of Windsor and Wallis Warfield as the Duchess, his wife.

By the beginning of the 1920s it was clear to many of White Sulphur's guests that The Old White was nearing the end of its useful life. More and more, guests preferred the modern comforts of the Greenbrier to the vintage charm of the sixty-five-year-old pre-Civil War inn. When in 1922 the old structure failed to pass a state fire inspection, the order was given to demolish it. Parts of the building were saved—mouldings, chandeliers, carved doors—for use in the growing Greenbrier complex.

A second eighteen-hole golf course was opened in 1925. In 1930 the hotel was expanded from 250 to 580 rooms. A residential wing was built, joining the Greenbrier with the bath building. The dining areas were doubled and an auditorium and a Virginia Wing containing lounges and an ''Old White

Club" added. The pre-Civil War cottages were refurbished and, where necessary, rebuilt. A colony of artists, teachers, and students was established in the cabins of Alabama Row. A private airport was built in 1929 and a polo field in 1932. The golf courses were redesigned in 1933 and 1934 and, in 1936, a twenty-four-year-old farmboy from Hot Springs, Virginia joined the Greenbrier staff as resident golf pro. In the years ahead Sam Snead was to win more than a hundred tournament prizes, including three Professional Golfers Association championships, three U. S. Masters titles, three Canadian Opens, two Western Opens, and a British Open title—bringing fame and honor to himself and the Greenbrier.

The resort survived the lean years of the Great Depression with little interruption, but the crisis of World War II was to affect it more directly. Two weeks after the Japanese attack on Pearl Harbor a contingent of 159 German and Hungarian diplomats arrived at White Sulphur. Because of its relative isolation and the ease with which it could be guarded, Secretary of State Cordell Hull had determined that the Greenbrier was a suitable place to house interred enemy diplomats. A contingent of Japanese diplomats, who arrived soon after the Germans and Hungarians, helped to swell the total number of the internees to nearly 1,400. In July 1942 an exchange of prisoners was accomplished, and the internees left the Greenbrier.

But the hotel's return to civilian use was brief. On September 1, 1942, the United States Army purchased the hotel for use as a hospital. Old murals, pictures, and engravings were hastily shipped off to storage, loaned to museums, and donated to Washington and Lee University, while a contingent of doctors, nurses, and technicians moved in with hospital beds and laboratory equipment. Operating as Ashford General Hospital, the hotel sheltered thousands of wounded veterans from the war front until it finally closed its doors on September 5, 1946.

Declared surplus property by the government, the springs complex with its 6,500 acres of surrounding land was offered for sale and repurchased by the Chesapeake & Ohio Railroad for a total price of $3,500,000. Led by its dynamic president, Robert R. Young, the railroad began a mammoth restoration project at the springs. Under the guidance of interior designer Dorothy Draper the lobbies and corridors were rearranged and repainted, the bedrooms refurnished, and the ballrooms and restaurants refurbished and redecorated. In April 1948 a grand opening party signaled the rebirth of the great hotel.

A fleet of airplanes converged on the Greenbrier airport, fourteen private railroad cars arrived at the train station, and a caravan of limousines crowded the driveway in front of the main entrance. The guest list included President and Mrs. Harry S. Truman, the Duke and Duchess of Windsor, Prince and Princess Alexander Hohenlohe, Lady Stanley, Lady Cochran, Lady Harry Oakes, and Lady Sheila Milbank; Mr. and Mrs. John Jacob Astor, Mr. and Mrs. Anthony Biddle Duke, Attorney General Tom Clark, Governors Clarence Meadows, William Tuck, and Charles Edison; Pearl Mesta, Elsa Maxwell, Bing Crosby, Fred Astaire, Louis B. Mayer, William Randolph Hearst, Jr., and J. Arthur Rank. Among the lesser-known guests were the Marchioness of Hartington—formerly Kathleen Kennedy of Boston—and her thirty-one-year-old brother, Congressman John Fitzgerald Kennedy. Awestruck, Igor Cassini (the Hearst newspapers' "Cholly Knickerbocker") reported: "We doubt that even the Sultan of Turkey, the Emperor of China, or the Czar of Russia, when those fabulous courts were at their peak, ever attempted anything on a more colossal scale." Cleveland Amory, less given to hyperbole, admitted the event was "the outstanding resort Society function in modern social history."

In the years that followed the 1948 opening a distinguished company of guests passed through the doors of the Greenbrier. The Duke and Duchess of Windsor made frequent stops. In 1956 President Eisenhower met the President of Mexico and the Prime Minister of Canada at the resort. Prince Ranier and Princess Grace of Monaco, Prime Minister Nehru of India, and Presidents Lyndon Johnson and Richard M. Nixon all made visits to the hotel.

In the postwar years White Sulphur also won recognition as one of the nation's leading medical clinics. The healing tradition, begun in 1778 when Amanda Anderson bathed in a hollow log at the springs, had continued to be a large part of the resort's attraction. Soon after the reopening of the hotel the medical and surgical staff of the C & O established a modern diagnostic clinic in the Greenbrier. Staffed by distinguished specialists, the clinic commenced a program of examining leading business executives from around the country.

As the twentieth century entered its final quarter, White Sulphur Springs remained one of America's most fashionable resorts. As a hotel it could and did compete favorably with newer inns

Aerial view of the Greenbrier (Courtesy of the Greenbrier)

in many parts of the country, but as a monument to history it had few rivals. The President's Cottage, occupied by a half dozen or so of the nation's chief executives, still sood on a hill above the principal compound guarding its museum of treasures—paintings, murals, photographs, furniture, and other memorabilia of the springs' two centuries of history. The domed spring house still hovered over the sulphur springs, as it had done every year since Andy Jackson beat the British at

New Orleans. The cottage occupied by Robert E. Lee in Baltimore Row faced the long walks and green lawns of the springs' grounds, as it did in the first years after Appomattox. The scent of magnolias perfumed the air, and the songs of mockingbirds echoed in the trees, as they had for centuries past and probably would for centuries to come. White Sulphur was old, but it was honored by time and, for loyal devotees, that fact alone was enough to commend it.

4

The Pride of State Street

THE PALMER HOUSE, CHICAGO

The summer of 1871 was unusually dry in Chicago. Only five inches of rain fell between July and October, less than an inch in the month preceding October 8. Twenty-seven fires struck the city in the first week of October, the largest devouring a four-block area, killing one person, and injuring four before it was brought under control. The city was a throbbing metropolis of 334,000 people that year, with thirteen major rail lines and heavy traffic along the Chicago River and the Illinois and Michigan Canal. It had always been susceptible to fire. More than six hundred blazes had erupted in the city in 1870, most of them beginning in barns, despite a local ordinance which forbade the use of open lamps or candles in places where straw or hay was stored.

Potter Palmer, traveling east to attend the funeral of a sister, was out of Chicago on the morning of October 8, but his presence was still very much felt in the prairie city. He was a vigorous forty-five years old, the "land man *par excellence*" of Chicago, in the words of a local newspaper, a dreamer of sorts, but also a doer. In the nineteen years since he arrived in the city from upstate New York, he had made a name for himself and a fortune of several million dollars, acquiring more land, leveling more lots, widening more streets, and building more buildings than any other half-dozen men in Illinois.

The story of Mrs. Patrick O'Leary and her clumsy cow has been dismissed by many as apocryphal, but there is no doubt that the fire which began in Chicago in the evening hours of October 8, 1871, originated in the cowshed behind the O'Leary home on De Koven Street. Mrs. O'Leary's son Jim, later a prominent gambler and politician, admitted that the fire began in his mother's shed but blamed it on the smoking of neighborhood boys and denied that the family cow had kicked over a coal-oil lamp. Mrs. O'Leary herself said the fire resulted from the carelessness of a neighbor who had been in the shed just before the flames broke out. Ignatius Donnelly, a Wisconsin reformer, had a more ingenious theory—saying that the entire Middle West had been made combustible by elements formed in the soil when a comet passed over the land several thousand years before. Whether or not the O'Leary bossy kindled the blaze, there is no doubt that it spread quickly and angrily from the shed on De Koven Street to nearby houses and stables.

An alarm soon went up from the fire-watch station atop the Cook County Courthouse, more than twenty blocks away, but the first engines were dispatched to the wrong location and, when firemen finally arrived at the O'Leary residence, they found the whole block in flames. Roaring menacingly, the fire gnawed at boardwalks, engulfed trees, and leapt narrow streets as it marched inexorably toward the river. Refugees fled wildly when the flames reached the opposite bank and began to invade the commercial and residential sections of the South Side. When, twenty-nine hours after the fire began, it was finally subdued, a

The Palmer House, Chicago, 1871 (Harper's Weekly, October 28, 1871)

scene of awful destruction spread out beneath the ruined towers of the courthouse. Seventy-three miles of streets had been swept by the flames, which had destroyed 17,500 buildings and made 100,000 people homeless. One hundred twenty dead bodies were recovered, but estimates of the total fatalities ran as high as three hundred. In all, $192,000,000 worth of property lay in smouldering ruins.

Potter Palmer rushed home to comfort his wife, who had remained behind, and to assess the destruction. His country house on the outskirts of the city had escaped the ravages of the blaze, and his wife had been unhurt, but the millionaire's house and stores on Lake and State streets had been devastated.

The Palmers had been married only fourteen months at the time of the fire. All of Chicago had regarded the middle-aged bachelor as a good catch when he took the twenty-one-year-old Bertha Honoré to the altar in July 1870. She was the daughter of a prosperous Chicago landowner, Henry Honoré, and one of the belles of the city, but her family's fortune was no match for Palmer's millions. The wedding had, according to the *Chicago Tribune,* excited "fashionable circles, commercial circles, and all other circles" for months before it took place. Bertha was radiantly beautiful in a Parisian gown of white satin, with veil of

Bertha Honoré Palmer as a young woman. Oil painting by Anders Leonard Zorn, 1893. (Courtesy of the Art Institute of Chicago)

Potter Palmer. Photograph taken by John Carbutt in 1868. (Courtesy of the Chicago Historical Society)

rose-point looped with orange blossoms. She and Palmer beamed broadly (though, no doubt, for different reasons) as they left the First Christian Church for a reception in the Honoré home and, a little later, left for a honeymoon in Europe.

Potter Palmer had begun his career in Chicago modestly enough by operating a dry goods and carpet store, but his business was so successful that by 1858 his store rose five stories above Lake Street and dominated all the businesses around it. During the Civil War he cornered the Northern market in cotton, making enormous profits when Southern supplies of the fiber dwindled to a trickle. He was the first large merchant in the country to offer credit and refund privileges to his customers. In 1865 he sold his store to Levi Leiter and an energetic young merchandiser from Massachusetts named Marshall Field. Palmer's brother Milton became a partner in the store, which operated under the new name of Field, Palmer & Leiter.

Palmer sold to Field in part because he was a wealthy man and did not need the income from his store, in part because he had grown weary of the everyday drudgery of merchandising. More important for the future of Chicago, he had decided there were better places to invest his money than in a dry goods emporium. Lake Street, crowded with three- and four-story buildings of brick and stone, was Chicago's principal business street in 1865. Palmer was convinced that the city would soon outgrow the narrow avenue and seek room for expansion along another thoroughfare. Dingy, narrow, and rutted, State Street was lined with a ramshackle collection of shanties, houses, and wooden stores. To develop State into a great thoroughfare would be easier and less expensive than attempting to rescue Lake, but the effort would require extensive investment. Palmer believed he was the man to lead the enterprise. Most of Chicago agreed. Soon after selling his store, he set about buying property on State Street and eventually acquired more than a hundred parcels that extended for a mile along either side of the avenue. He tore down houses and stores, widened the right-of-way, and began to put up new buildings.

One of the first merchants to consider moving to State Street was Marshall Field. Palmer offered to build a handsome new building for the merchant if he would leave Lake Street for the new avenue. The new building would rise six stories above the street, he said, be faced with limestone and Canaan marble, and be adorned with Corinthian columns. When Field and his partners agreed to lease the building for fifty thousand dollars a year, Palmer selected a site at the northwest corner of State and Washington and quickly began to erect the building. By October 1868 "Palmer's Marble Palace," as Chicagoans called the new home of Field and Leiter, was ready for business.

Now Palmer turned his eyes toward a site four blocks south, at the northwest corner of State and Quincy, where he announced he would build a hotel that would rival Chicago's finest hostelries, the Tremont, the Briggs, and the Sherman House. Construction of the new hotel, called the Palmer House, was begun in 1869. At the time of Palmer's marriage to Bertha Honoré the building was rapidly nearing completion—indeed, some Chica-

goans hinted that its lavish bridal suite was intended for the owner's own use. But Palmer's honeymoon was over by the time the hotel was finished, and the suite was made ready for other lovers.

The Palmer House rose eight stories above the street. It had been designed by the prominent Chicago architect, John Van Osdel, in Second Empire style, with columns along its first floor, tastefully corniced windows above and, at the top, a soaring mansard roof pierced with three tiers of dormers. More than five thousand visitors were on hand for the opening on September 26, 1870. "Had the occasion been a reception for the dignitaries of the nation," the *Tribune* reported, "it could not have been more fashionable. . . . The Palmer House is certainly the model caravanserai of Chicago, and more than equals the anticipations of our citizens, who expected something choice and elegant at the hands of its proprietor." The hotel had 225 bedrooms and dozens of salons, parlors, and lobbies. It was equipped with what the *Tribune* called "all the modern improvements"—gaslights, fire hoses on every floor, and a smoothly gliding elevator. For the entertainment of guests, the main salon was furnished with "two very fine pianos—one grand and one square—from the celebrated factory of W. Knabe & Co."

The Palmer House and "Palmer's Marble Palace" were the most notable of Palmer's Chicago properties in 1871, but they were not the only ones. Less than a year after he opened the hotel, the millionaire had begun construction of a second hotel at the corner of State and Monroe streets, about halfway between Field's store and the Palmer House. The decision to build a second great inn so soon after the opening of the first may have been prompted by concern over the projected Grand Pacific Hotel, a magnificent edifice with 100 private parlors and 450 single rooms, which John Drake began to build only a block from the Palmer House in 1871. Palmer's Quincy Street hotel compared favorably with the older Tremont, Briggs, and Sherman House, but the millionaire knew it would seem puny alongside Drake's Grand Pacific. To forestall his threatened rival, Palmer directed Van Osdel to design a new and even more luxurious hotel of 8 stories and 650 rooms. Construction of the new building was well under way when the hay in Mrs. O'Leary's cowshed flamed into history.

John Van Osdel had seen the fire approaching State Street on the fateful night and hurried from his West Side home to his downtown office, where he gathered books, papers, and records, then headed for the site of Palmer's new hotel. The wall of flames was approaching rapidly when the architect reached his construction office, hurriedly scooped up the plans for the building, and headed for the basement. There he dug a pit into which he carefully packed his accumulated books, papers, and plans, covering them with two feet of sand and a thick layer of wet clay. The blaze that passed over State Street a few minutes later leveled the walls of the rising hotel, cracked blocks of granite and marble, and twisted iron posts and beams, but it did not touch the plans the architect had buried in the basement pit.

Before the last embers of the fire had cooled, plans were announced on all sides to rebuild Chicago. Potter Palmer sold the site of Field's store at State and Washington, and the new owners announced that they would put up a massive new building for the merchant. John Drake had begun to reconstruct the Grand Pacific. With Van Osdel's

surviving plans as a guide and several million dollars in hastily arranged loans to back him, Palmer announced that he would begin to rebuild the hotel at State and Monroe.

Reconstruction work was under way by the end of 1871. The project was probably more extensive than any previously undertaken in Chicago, with masses of workers assembled at the site and wagons lined up for blocks in every direction waiting to unload their cargoes of brick and stone and cement. Anxious to speed the construction, Palmer ordered work to be carried on around the clock, with calcium lights suspended from cables and poles to illuminate the project at night. The Palmer House at State and Quincy was forgotten in the rising glory of the new building, to which its owner proudly transferred the name of "Palmer House."

If the former hotel had been Chicago's "model caravanserai," its successor was nothing less than a palace. Larger than the Grand Pacific, it was

The second Palmer House. Photograph taken in the late 1880's. (Courtesy of the Chicago Historical Society)

more elegant, more imaginative, more spacious than any hotel west of New York. The building stood eight stories tall and covered a full city block. Massive pillars and a graceful portico marked its main entrance on State Street, while a smaller but equally handsome portal on Monroe was reserved for ladies. Three ranks of Corinthian columns rose from the sidewalk to the base of the seventh floor, marked by a ledge which completely encircled the building. Above it, two floors of windows led to a chimney-covered roof of slate. At the corner of State and Monroe, a tower rose from the sidewalk to a soaring, flag-topped dome, nine stories above the street.

Inside, the building was a profusion of parlors and salons, reading, writing, and smoking rooms, elevators, and a maze of electric bells and lights which buzzed and flashed nervously. At every turn, features distinctive enough to excite gasps of awe presented themselves to visitors: The barber shop, called the Garden of Eden in honor of its proprietor, Mr. Eden, was paneled with mirrors and paved with slabs of marble in which hundreds of silver dollars were imbedded. Broad staircases of Carrara marble were reflected in long mirrors of Venetian glass. Throughout the building gas-burning chandeliers sparkled and glittered and dazzled like the jewels of an emperor's crown. The Grand Dining Room opened into a series of adjoining halls to afford more dining space than "any refectory west of the Alleghenies." The Roof Garden, a conservatory of marble and glass, was crowded with royal palms, trailing vines, and hanging baskets of flowers.

Despite Chicago's amazing rebirth, the fear of fire still hung over the city. By ordinance, wooden houses were forbidden in the central district, but buildings of brick and stone as well as those of wood had been consumed by the flames of 1871, and occupants of even the stoutest structures harbored a lingering uneasiness. When the owners of rival hotels advertised in the *Tribune* that their structures were completely fireproof (Palmer knew they were not), the millionaire angrily protested, challenging his rivals "to build a fire in the center of any chamber or room of the Palmer House . . . the furniture, carpets, mirrors, etc., to be undisturbed and the doors and windows to remain closed for one hour. If . . . the fire does not spread beyond the room, the party accepting the invitation is to pay for all damages done and for the use of the room. If the invitation is not accepted . . . I purpose, with the consent of the Underwriters of Chicago, to make the test myself." As expected,

the Underwriters did not consent, and none of Palmer's competitors dared to force the millionaire's hand. Whatever the outcome, the publicity such a preset fire would attract would have been priceless advertising for the Palmer House.

From its opening in 1873 the new hotel was warmly received by Chicagoans. Polished carriages lined up at the curb to discharge their cargoes of fashionable guests—men with flowing whiskers and silk hats, women with bustled dresses and sweeping ostrich plumes, gamblers and mining speculators, investors from Wall Street intent on surveying business opportunities in the new Chicago. Among the women who swept in and out of the Monroe Street lobby under the looming lanterns and canopy of the ladies entrance, none was more beautiful or more universally admired than the proprietor's wife, Bertha Honoré Palmer. The millionaire and his family had taken a lavish suite in the hotel, where they entertained in a style befitting his money and her social ambitions. She was admittedly a dazzling woman—a symphony of limpid eyes, sensuous lips, and long, silken tresses—dressed habitually in the latest Parisian gowns, with tiaras and brooches, necklaces and pendants to set them off. Before she was thirty, Bertha Palmer was acclaimed queen of Chicago society. The honor was due largely to her husband's wealth and her own beauty and charm, but it also owed much to her family's political connections. Bertha's sister Ida had married Frederick Dent Grant, son of President Grant, at the Honoré country home outside Chicago in 1874. The president was an occasional visitor at the Palmer House after the event, and Bertha was a frequent guest at the White House, where she made glittering appearances in Mrs. Grant's receiving line.

When in Chicago, visitors from abroad habitually found their way to the Palmer House, which they examined as if it were a mogul's palace in some oriental principality. The Englishwoman Lady Duffus Hardy put up at the hotel on the first night of her visit to Chicago in 1879. She found it "more like an elegantly appointed home than a mere resting place." She was impressed by the rich appointment of the bedroom suites, the abundance of bathrooms, the fine carpets and soft chairs. "Being cosily installed beneath this hospitable roof," Lady Hardy wrote, "one feels like 'poor *Joe*,' disinclined to 'move on.'" After two days on the road the traveler rejoiced in her warm bath, after which she descended to the Grand Dining Room. The menu was illustrated with drawings and mottos. On one side appeared a pigsty and a hovel labeled "Chicago forty years ago"; on the other was a gleaming metropolis captioned "The Chicago of to-day!" The table was piled high with food, so high that the lady for a time feared she would be unable to finish her meal. "If we had stayed for a month and eaten *pro rata* as at our first meal," she wrote, "we should have ruined our digestive organs and rejoiced in internal discords for ever afterward."

Rudyard Kipling put up at the hotel a few years after Lady Hardy's visit. A sterner critic and a keener wit than his countrywoman, Kipling professed to be alarmed by the vulgarity of the self-professed "boss" town of America. "I have struck a city,—" he wrote of his visit, "a real city,—and they call it Chicago. The other places do not count. San Francisco was a pleasure-resort as well as a city, and Salt Lake was a phenomenon. This place is the first American city I have encountered. . . . Having seen it, I urgently desire never to see it again."

Arriving at the railroad station, the doughty Britisher made his way through the city's swarming streets to the Palmer House, which he called "a gilded and mirrored rabbit-warren." "There I found a huge hall of tessellated marble," he wrote, "crammed with people talking about money and spitting about everywhere. Other barbarians charged in and out of this inferno with letters and telegrams in their hands, and yet others shouted at each other." A man who had drunk more than was good for him told the writer that the Palmer House was "the finest hotel in the finest city on God Almighty's earth." Kipling smiled condescendingly. "When an American wishes to indicate the next county or State," he noted, "he says 'God Almighty's earth.' "

Touring the city with a cabbie as his guide, the Englishman surveyed the tall buildings that crowded every block, looked down on the Chicago River, black with mud and oil, watched the endless flow of traffic across its bridges, and paid a visit to the stockyards. The cabbie thought Chicago a marvel, "a thing to be reverently admired." Kipling did not agree. Returning to his room in the Palmer House, he packed his bags, descended to the street, hailed another cab, and made his way to the railroad station. "I have seen the City of Chicago," he wrote as the puffing train headed east. "And I went away to get peace and rest."

Through the seventies and into the eighties the Palmers regarded the hotel as their home. Despite the coming and going of thousands of guests they managed to maintain a semblance of domesticity

The third Palmer House, completed in 1927 (Courtesy of the Palmer House)

in the sanctum of their private suite. By the early eighties their two sons were growing uncomfortable in the semi-public residence, and Potter Palmer was appraising a swamp-ridden stretch of the shore of Lake Michigan with a hungry investor's eye. The land, south of Lincoln Park and north of the city harbor, was a waste of sand dunes, stunted willows, and pools of stagnant water when Palmer sent a scow along the beach to scoop sand from the lake bottom and throw it on the shore. He bought large sections of the lake frontage, subdivided it, and sold off the parcels as home sites. The road which the city cut through his property was known first as North Shore, later as Lake Shore Drive. Palmer's decision to build his

The Empire Room of the new Palmer House. (Courtesy of the Palmer House)

home on a choice site in the new tract assured that it would become Chicago's choicest residential district.

The house that architects Henry Cobb and Charles Frost designed was unlike any Chicagoans had seen. It was a three-story mansion of Wisconsin sandstone and Ohio granite, with crenellated towers and turrets, looming pinnacles, and a grand *porte-cochère* to shelter arriving carriages. Its style was variously described as Rhine River *schloss*, Norman Gothic, or English battlement. Whatever its architectural pedigree, it was clear to observers that the building lacked nothing but a moat and drawbridge to pass as a baron's medieval close. Palmer had thought the house would cost close to ninety thousand dollars. Before it was finished, a million dollars had been spent, and the owner told his bookkeeper to stop entering

charges against it. He had no wish to know its final cost.

When they were not in the Palmer House or in their castle on Lake Shore Drive, the Palmers were traveling in England, in France, in Germany. Bertha had developed a taste for fine art nearly as lusty as her appetite for glittering jewels, and she was helping her husband assemble a collection. Her favorite artists were the French Impressionists—Degas, Manet, and Monet. At home she was an occasional dabbler in civic affairs and an early, if tentative, champion of women's rights. She was chairman (not chairwoman) of the international committee which put up the government-supported Woman's Building at the Columbian Exposition in Chicago in 1893. The speech she gave at the building's opening was pretty: "Even more important than the discovery of Columbus, which we are gathered together to celebrate, is the fact that the General Government has just discovered woman." But reporters were more concerned with the *grand dame's* appearance than with what she said—recording that she was gowned in yellow satin and velvet, wore a tiara in her hair, and had ropes of magnificent pearls at her neck.

Potter Palmer was occasionally active in civic affairs. He was an early manager of the YMCA and organized the Chicago Baseball Club. With such Chicago notables as Cyrus H. McCormick, Marshall Field, and George M. Pullman he organized a Citizens League to help check crime and discourage drinking among juveniles (being careful not to interfere with the imbibers in the Palmer House bar). But his civic ambitions were not overweening. He declined an offered post in President Grant's cabinet, preferring to spend his working hours in the little cage behind the reception desk in the Palmer House—counting money, studying faces, giving orders. In his last years he grew reclusive, refusing to leave his dressing room on the sunny side of the castle on Lake Shore Drive for any but the direst of physical necessities.

Potter Palmer was seventy-six when he died in May 1902. Bertha was only fifty-three, still vigorous, still radiantly beautiful. Her rosy outlook on life had not been noticeably changed by the terms of Palmer's will, in which he left all his considerable estate to her. Marshall Field shook his head disapprovingly. "A million dollars is enough for any woman," the merchant muttered. But it would clearly have not been enough for Bertha Palmer.

She spent money lavishly—taking houses in London and Paris, buying art and jewels and antiques, vacationing in New York and Newport and Florida, entertaining on a grand scale in her Lake Shore castle. But she was far from profligate. She kept a wary eye on affairs at the Palmer House, bought and sold property wisely, and invested in more than sixty thousand acres of land near Sarasota, Florida. When she died in 1918, Bertha Palmer's estate was worth about twice what her husband had left her sixteen years before.

The old Palmer House still stood proud and erect on State Street. Though in the 1920s its long pillars and soaring corner tower, darkened by decades of smoke and soot, were murky and its roof was covered with a film of grime, its Venetian mirrors still sparkled, its elevators still hummed, its electric call bells and lights still flashed and buzzed nervously, as in the days of Potter Palmer. The old hotel was a monument to Chicago's past, but a costly one for Palmer's two sons to maintain. All around it stood buildings of fifteen, twenty, and twenty-five stories, nascent skyscrapers that hid their heads in the clouds and cast long shadows across the entrance to the Palmer House. Where carriages had once lined up to discharge ladies and gentlemen of fashion, smoke-belching automobiles now rumbled and coughed and growled. The broad expanse of State Street was now a confusion of trucks and buses and electric trolleys, with horns and clanging bells and crowds of shoppers wandering about in profusion.

To make better use of the Palmer House site, trustees of the Palmer estate began to tear down the old building and put up a gleaming new Palmer House. Finished in sections, the new building was in its way as distinctive as its predecessor. It rose 24 stories above State Street, had 2,250 rooms, and cost more than $20,000,000 to finish. The first half was opened in 1926, the second in 1927.

The Empire Room of the new Palmer House became a showplace in Chicago. During the World's Fair of 1933 an unknown ballroom team, Veloz and Yolanda, entertained in the room, won the hearts

Conrad Hilton. Photograph by Fabian Bachrach. (Courtesy of Hilton Hotels Corporation)

of the city, and stayed for thirteen months. They were followed by a long line of performers that included Guy Lombardo, Ted Lewis, Maurice Chevalier, Sophie Tucker, Eddie Duchin, Jimmy Durante, and Hildegarde.

Business at the hotel slowed perceptibly during the years of the Great Depression, but not enough to seriously imperil Palmer House profits. Even in 1933, the gravest year of the economic crisis, its gross operating profit exceeded one million dollars.

The earning power of the Palmer House and its continuing reputation as queen of Chicago hotels were the principal reasons for Conrad Hilton's interest in it in 1945. In a career of a little more than thirty years Hilton had astounded the world of hôteliers by building a modest savings of five thousand dollars into a nationwide chain of hotels. His purchase of New York's Plaza in 1943 marked his entrance into the world of luxury hotels. In 1945 he bought Chicago's Stevens, a gargantuan convention hotel of nearly three thousand rooms, widely and perhaps accurately advertised as the world's largest.

But the hotel magnate hankered for something better. He visited the Palmer House, ate in its dining room, walked in its long corridors. He thought it was "as regal and dignified and sound as the Queen Mother herself." When he confided to a friend that he was thinking of asking the Palmer trustees if the hotel was for sale, the friend laughed. "Might as well ask the Windsors if Buckingham Palace is on the market," the friend said.

But Hilton did ask, and was surprised to learn that the trustees would consider a proposal. The offer he made—a total purchase price of just under twenty million dollars—was accepted, and on January 1, 1946, Hilton took over the Palmer House.

In September 1971 the Palmer House celebrated the completion of its first century of business. Conrad Hilton, a hearty octogenarian, was on hand for the ceremonies, as was William Edwards, Executive Vice President of the Hilton Corporation, and Chicago's perennial Mayor Richard J. Daly. Bands played, toasts were offered, and speeches recited, as the hotel began its second century. Mayor Daly, himself something of a Chicago institution, reflected the thoughts of many when he said: "Throughout the country and the world, there is no better known nor more highly esteemed hotel institution than the Palmer House. . . . People who have been in and out of our city think of the Palmer House when they think of Chicago."

Potter Palmer would have beamed, and Rudyard Kipling sneered, had they been on hand to hear the mayor's words. But their differences of opinion would not have altered the fact. For better or worse, the city and the great hotel were wedded. At least for the foreseeable future, there was little prospect that they would part.

5

A Dream of Gold and Silver

Excerpted from "The Splendid Caravansary," *American History Illustrated,* October 1974.
Copyright © 1974 The National Historical Society.

THE PALACE, SAN FRANCISCO

From the beginning, the Palace Hotel was recognized as a symbol of its age—the proud fulfillment of the West's most confident dreams, the embodiment of the best and worst of its opulent frontier grandeur. No building in all of California better symbolized the self-assured swagger, the brimming self-confidence of that boisterous epoch of gold and silver. It was only fitting that it was called the Palace, and that it was built in San Francisco, the quintessential metropolis of the Gilded Age.

The city itself was a monument of sorts. Only twenty-five years before the opening of the Palace, San Francisco had been a huddle of huts at the edge of a cove crowded with abandoned ships. In less than three decades the sandy streets of the town had spread from the wind-swept wastes of Portsmouth Plaza to the steep slopes of Russian and Telegraph hills. San Francisco was born in the first flush of the gold fever and drank eagerly from the river of yellow wealth that poured from the Mother Lode of the Sierra Nevada, but by the second decade of its existence its wealth derived as much from silver as from gold. In 1859 the Comstock Lode was discovered beneath the floor of a flinty Nevada desert. The richness of its deposits soon exceeded even its discoverer's fondest dreams, as Comstock silver poured into San Francisco even more plentifully than Sierra gold, and speculation in Nevada mining claims became an unquenchable fever. From all over the world men and women flocked to the Golden Gate to drink from the glittering cup that was San Francisco.

San Franciscans knew that the city had no need for another hotel, but they also knew that need was not the measure of the dream—at least in matters that concerned William C. Ralston. More than any other man, Ralston symbolized the strutting self-confidence of the frontier city. Brash, energetic, resourceful, he had been in San Francisco scarcely twenty years when he broke ground for the Palace Hotel, but in that twenty years he had moved mountains. Formerly a ship's carpenter and clerk, he had come to California in 1853 as agent for a New York steamship line. He arrived too late to be classed as a Forty-Niner, but soon enough to reap the benefits of the state's first frenzied decade of gold-seeking. When his employers opened a bank, he learned their business and soon became a resident partner. He eventually formed his own partnership and by 1864 was able to organize the Bank of California, the largest depository in the West. Agencies at Virginia City and other Nevada boom towns gave Ralston and his partners control of some of the richest of the Comstock mines, and their personal wealth and influence grew with those of the bank.

With almost unlimited financial resources and a seemingly inexhaustible store of energy, Ralston took the lead among the city's growing coterie of promoters. He built woolen mills and dry docks, opened carriage and watch factories, financed irri-

The Palace Hotel, Market Street, San Francisco. Only Lotta's Fountain, at the intersection of Market, Geary, and Kearny Streets, remains today. (Courtesy of the University of California)

gation projects, and planned iron works to provide rolling stock for California's projected network of railroads. His house on Pine Street near Leavenworth was one of San Francisco's showplaces, and his country home, called Belmont, twenty miles south, was the state's most palatial private dwelling. A visitor to Ralston's country villa in 1875 compared it to a sprawling summer hotel. No one bothered to guess how much the mansion, with its rambling wings and galleries, stables and grounds, had cost the banker. It was only money, and San Franciscans knew that money meant nothing to Ralston.

If anyone doubted that the Squire of Belmont was San Francisco's first citizen, his announcement in 1872 of plans to build a great new hotel effectively silenced them. It would be the largest building of its kind in the United States, he said, a massive edifice of marble and brick and iron that would mark San Francisco's coming of age, signifying the closing of one era and the beginning of another. Not the least, the hotel would also brilliantly cap the career of William Ralston.

There were already a half-dozen hotels of taste and elegance in the city. The Lick House and the Occidental, on opposite sides of Montgomery Street, were San Francisco's finest hotels in the 1860s, and they maintained their prestige even after they found competitors in the Russ House, the Baldwin, and the Grand. Handsome though they were, these hotels were all to be eclipsed by Ralston's new edifice.

As a site for his hotel the banker chose sandy flatlands south of Market Street, where Montgomery Street came to an end. A new thoroughfare, called New Montgomery, was cut through the block between Market and Howard. At a cost of four hundred thousand dollars, enough land was purchased to complete a square block. As his architect Ralston hired John Gaynor and sent him east to study the construction of America's leading hotels—the Palmer House and Grand Pacific in Chicago, the New Windsor and Sturtevant House in New York. When Gaynor returned, plans for the new hostelry, to be called the Palace, were drawn.

It would be built in the form of a giant rectangle, with its long sides extending 350 feet along New Montgomery and its shorter sides 275 feet along Market. In all it would cover an area nearly twice that of Chicago's Grand Pacific. Like the caravansaries of ancient Araby—large, enclosed inns that sheltered desert caravans—the hotel would be built around a spacious central court that would supply light and air to the interior rooms. To connect it with the street, the court would have a circular driveway, permitting guests to alight from their carriages on a floor of polished marble in the inn's very heart.

The building was to rise seven stories above the street and contain nearly eight hundred rooms—more than Paris' huge Grand Hotel. Vertical bands of bay windows, a characteristic feature of San Francisco architecture, would cover the outside walls, and the central court would be capped with a vaulted dome of glass.

Early in 1873 a high board fence was thrown up around Ralston's Market Street property as excavation for the hotel began. The digging was itself a considerable task, for there was to be a basement and, below it, a sub-basement covering the entire block of two and a half acres.

When the site was excavated, work on the foundations began. They were of arched masonry, twelve feet deep, more than two feet thick, and heavily laced with iron. Stout brick walls rose above the foundations. Three hundred masons, laying as many as three hundred thousand bricks in a single day, worked at the site. Before it was done, the hotel would consume more than twenty-four million bricks. To satisfy this gargantuan appetite, brickyards along the length of the Pacific Coast strained to their utmost capacities.

Fires had repeatedly struck San Francisco and, to minimize the danger of holocaust at the new hotel, Ralston adopted novel means. Automatic fire detection devices were installed in every room. A series of artesian wells was drilled on the site and a huge reservoir sunk in the basement. Seven tanks were installed on the roof to insure adequate water even if the city's supply should fail. The tanks and reservoir were connected with a net-

William C. Ralston (Courtesy of the Bancroft Library, Berkeley)

work of 5 miles of pipes, 350 outlets, and 20,000 feet of hose.

By the spring of 1875 construction of the hotel was nearing completion and visitors were admitted to the premises. Standing on the floor of the inner court, they gazed with amazement at the soaring tiers of balconies, the long columns and arches, the expanses of sun-splashed marble. From the central court, visitors passed into the hotel office, a marble-flagged chamber 65 by 55 feet; the men's and ladies' reception rooms, each 40 feet square; and the grand dining room, 150 feet in length, the largest in the West.

Modern inventions were displayed throughout the building. One hundred twenty-five miles of wire permitted the operation of electric call buttons in each room. Telegraphic instruments in the service pantries on each floor connected with the dining room and main office. Because telephones and electric lamps were still too primitive for practical use, gaslights illuminated the vast building, but there were sixteen clocks, marvelously powered by electricity, which ran in perfect unison. "Tubular conductors" were installed on each floor to carry mail and small parcels throughout the building. An air-conditioning system with more than two thousand vents provided fresh air for each bedroom, bathroom, and closet. Five hydraulic elevators, called "rising rooms" by the visitors, provided access to the Palace's loftiest heights. They were spacious chambers with long mirrors and comfortable seats on which passengers could repose during transit.

The Palace Hotel's spacious central court (Courtesy of the Sheraton-Palace Hotel)

"The furnishing of the hotel," wrote a visiting reporter, "has been attended to in a style corresponding with the magnificence of the building. The greatest care has been given to selecting furniture, upholstery, table-ware, bedclothing and everything necessary to throw the charm of a luxurious and refined home around the spacious rooms and stately halls." Marble, rosewood, and ebony, elaborately carved and polished, gleamed throughout the building, and the walls of the public rooms, painted a delicate shade of pink, blushed like the cheek of a peach.

When the hotel's exterior walls emerged from their mantle of ladders and scaffolds, they revealed a dazzling array of bay windows, white walls, and gold trim. A reporter for *Leslie's Illustrated Newspaper*, published in New York, visited the building and described it for his readers: "Striking as is the vastness of the building when viewed from a point near at hand, to get a true idea of its comparative size one must see it from the Bay, east of the city. Viewed from this standpoint it is the most conspicuous object in the view, and looming up above the sea of houses, presents a grand and imposing appearance."

The hotel opened for business on October 2, 1875, but its formal inauguration was on October 14 at a gala banquet in honor of the Civil War hero, General Philip Sheridan. Crowds gathered in the Grand Court as Sheridan and Governor Romualdo Pacheco entered to the accompaniment of Suppé's *Poet and Peasant Overture* and William Sharon, one of Ralston's partners and newly elected United States Senator from Nevada, stepped to the edge of a second-floor balcony to address the assembled visitors.

"In the crowning hour of victory," Sharon said, "in the presence of this grand witness of your skill in the mechanic arts, in this glorious temple of hospitality amid all this flood of light and music, I experience an almost overwhelming sadness. I miss, as you do, the proud and manly spirit of him who devised this magnificent structure, and under whose direction and tireless energy it has been mainly reared. I mourn, as you do, that he is not with us to enjoy this scene of beauty."

Sharon's audience did not miss the import of his remarks. Even as the Palace had been readied for its opening, Ralston's Bank of California had been shaken by rumors of a failure in the Comstock Lode. San Francisco had been the victim of a score of financial panics, but the scare of 1875 had a particularly bitter bite. Depositors stormed Ralston's headquarters, demanding the money that was not

William Sharon, U.S. Senator from Nevada (Courtesy of the Bancroft Library, Berkeley)

there, and on August 26 the citadel of Western commerce was forced to close its doors. The following day the body of William Ralston was found floating in San Francisco Bay. Was the tycoon's death a suicide, as many speculated, or a sardonically coincidental accident? San Franciscans were still arguing the cruel twist of Ralston's fate when his magnificent hotel opened its doors and Senator Sharon extended his arms in a gesture of bittersweet welcome.

The visit of General Sheridan established a pattern of social events at the Palace. Thenceforth, heroes and conquerors were frequently welcomed in its balconied court. Generals Grant and Sherman, surrounded by decanters of brandy and swirling clouds of cigar smoke, reminiscing about their days in arms, spent many evenings in the hotel's elegant salons. There were hosts of other distinguished visitors—financiers and tycoons, artists and actors, musicians and reigning princes.

In time the list of Palace notables read like a roster of the great and near-great of the age: Rockefeller, Morgan, Carnegie, and Pullman; Henry

Ward Beecher and Carrie Nation; James J. Jeffries and the Prince of Siam. Rudyard Kipling and Oscar Wilde were guests, as were Judge Oliver Wendell Holmes, Jr. and Presidents Hayes, Harrison, and McKinley. One of California's ex-governors, the railroad tycoon Leland Stanford, occupied a suite at the northeast corner of the hotel while his forty-room mansion on Nob Hill was being built. The "Divine" Sarah Bernhardt moved mountains of baggage into an eight-room suite at the Palace in 1887, and in 1894 Eugene Sandow, the world's "most perfect physical specimen," appeared in pink tights in the Palace's Maple Room, where he flexed his biceps, expanded his chest, and invited reporters to punch him in the stomach.

From the beginning the Palace was renowned for the sophistication of its haute cuisine. When the hotel opened in 1875, its staff of 150 waiters was the largest in the world, and its chefs and cooks boasted that they could serve any guest with delicacies indigenous to his own country. The boast was frequently made good, to the delight of visitors from such diverse countries as Russia and India, Greece and the South Sea Islands. In addition to its menu of continental cuisine, the Palace popularized a variety of distinctly Californian fare—mountain and valley quail, grizzly streaks, rainbow trout, sole, bass, and abalone. The small California oyster, with its faintly coppery taste, became a favorite of epicures after it appeared in the Palace's cocktails and omelets, and Pudding a la Sultan, a creation of Palace chef Ernest Arbogast, was a perennially favorite dessert. The wine cellars were always full, stocked with the best of Burgundy and Bordeaux and an ample supply of the robust, if not distinguished, vintages of California's own Napa and Sonoma Valleys.

After Ralston's death the Palace, as well as the villa at Belmont, fell into the hands of Senator Sharon. The diminutive banker, a mild-mannered man with a drooping mustache and piercing gray eyes, had once served as agent in the Bank of California's powerful Virginia City, Nevada office. Though he lacked the magnetism of his deceased partner, Sharon was shrewd and ambitious. From 1875 until 1881, while he served Nevada in the Senate, the unobtrusive millionaire divided his time between Washington and a suite in the Palace. He entertained lavishly in the hotel, as he did at Belmont, though his activities attracted little attention in either place. He was a juiceless little man, San Franciscans thought, worthy of notice only because of his millions.

Opinions of the senator changed rapidly when he was arrested in his suite at the Palace and charged with the crime of adultery. It was shocking enough that Sharon should have dallied with a comely young woman, as the complaint against him alleged; it was even more startling to learn that his misconduct should constitute the crime of adultery. Sharon's wife of twenty-three years had died in 1875, and it was generally supposed that he had remained unmarried. The adultery complaint was dismissed for technical insufficiency, but the mystery of the Senator's marital status was not so easily put to rest.

In 1883 a civil complaint was filed against him by a woman calling herself Mrs. Sarah Althea Sharon. It asked for a divorce, claimed alimony, and asked for a division of the community property. The plaintiff, a handsome, thirtyish woman, produced a handwritten contract which purported to be an agreement of marriage. She claimed that she had lived as the wife of the sixty-four-year-old senator for three years in reliance on the purported contract. Sharon denounced the instrument as a forgery and vowed to give legal battle. Sarah won the first skirmish when a judge ordered Sharon to pay her alimony, but her claim to be recognized as the senator's wife and to share in his estimated fifteen-million-dollar fortune ultimately failed in the appellate courts. The "juiceless" senator died in 1885, still denouncing the purported contract. Sarah, disillusioned and embittered, ended her days in a mental hospital.

From its earliest days the Palace was a favorite rendezvous of touring musicians and singers. The Polish pianist, Ignace Paderewski, sojourned in the hotel on more than one of his spectacular American tours, and the Italian diva, Adelina Patti, made the Palace her headquarters for a succession of celebrated "farewell" tours. The Neapolitan basso, Antonio Scotti, first visited the hotel in 1901, when he sang at the Grand Opera House nearby and entertained hotel guests by parading through the corridors in a wardrobe of dazzling clothes. Scotti returned in 1905, this time in the company of a golden-voiced tenor named Enrico Caruso who, after his opera performances, entertained guests in the hotel by drawing deft caricatures of local personages and bantering in a confusion of English, Italian, and French. "I like temperance," cooed Caruso, shaking his massive head, "but I like too the little thing to drink, and the macaroni, and—oh, yes!—the roast beef. I love the roast beef. I love it too much."

Scotti and Caruso were back in the Palace in April 1906 as part of the Metropolitan Opera Company's spring tour of the West. *The Queen of Sheba,* which opened the Metropolitan's run at the Grand on April 16, was a disappointment to the audience, but Caruso's portrayal of Don José the following night more than made up for the opening slight. " 'Carmen' rechristened itself for San Francisco last night," critic Blanche Partington wrote in the San Francisco *Call.* "For the season, at least, it is 'Don José.' Caruso is the magician." His bows completed, the tenor returned to his hotel. Not long after midnight, he slipped into the Palace bar to join other members of the company for a round of cognac.

The Metropolitan's conductor, Alfred Hertz, had returned to his hotel room at a respectable hour in preparation for his conducting chores the following night. At a quarter past five in the morning Hertz was awakened by a jarring movement and the sound of creaking timbers. He leaped from his bed and made his way to the door just in time to hear basso Robert Blass shouting in an adjoining room: "Earthquake!"

Dressing hurriedly, Hertz raced to Caruso's room, where he found the tenor sitting upright in his bed and weeping. The men embraced, while Caruso babbled hysterically that they were doomed, all doomed, and that he had lost his voice. When Hertz urged him to try to sing, the tenor went to the window, opened it, and startled pedestrians on the street below by intoning majestically:

La fanta mi salva,
L'immondo ritrova . . . .

Satisifed that his vocal chords were still intact, Caruso dressed and, with Hertz, rushed to the lobby.

The conductor did not share the tenor's belief that they were all doomed. Though the Palace had not been unscathed by the earthquake, its massive walls and foundations had withstood the vibrations remarkably well; the structure had not been impaired. Hertz noted with surprise that an old Chinese servant was already at work, calmly and quietly cleaning the easy chairs and carpets of the lobby.

What damage the hotel had sustained could have been easily repaired. Within a week, perhaps two, the building could have been restored to normal. Could have been restored, that is, had it not been for the fire.

Neither Caruso nor Hertz could know that columns of smoke were already curling from the wooden tenements south of Market Street, racing across the sandflats, licking at the edges of the business district. Fire crews could only watch the progress of the flames with hopeless resignation. The city's water mains had been broken by the earthquake, and the fire hoses that alone could save San Francisco from disaster were dry.

Soon the small fires joined in a giant blaze that marched inexorably toward the heart of the city. To save the Palace and other large buildings near it, fire fighters decided to dynamite the Monadnock Buliding, a new structure immediately behind the hotel. But the charges were badly placed

and the building was hardly moved. Flames swept through it and lunged at the walls of the Palace.

A crowd that had gathered on a hill above the city let out a cheer as jets of water spouted from the hotel's roof and Ralston's reservoirs were put to a do-or-die test. But the cheer proved only to be the last hurrah for the hotel. The building was deserted when the wall of flame engulfed it, chewing at its timbers, devouring its carpets and floors, reducing its brick and marble and iron to a twisted, blackened rubble.

Like its builder, the Palace Hotel was dead.

But the dream it represented was not forgotten. Even before the ashes of destruction cooled, a

The last portal of the Palace Hotel to fall to the wreckers' balls after the 1906 earthquake and fire (Courtesy of the Bancroft Library, Berkeley)

The glass-canopied Garden Court of the rebuilt Palace Hotel. (Courtesy of the Sheraton-Palace Hotel)

spirit of determination gripped San Francisco. Because more than two-thirds of the city had been leveled, many Easterners expected that the site would be abandoned. San Franciscans knew the city would be rebuilt.

Streets were cleared of rubble. Water mains were reconnected, gas mains repaired, trolley lines straightened, electric lights rewired. Fire-blackened walls were razed and the foundations for new buildings laid. Throughout the city the sound of hammers and saws signaled the rise of the new San Francisco.

To keep the tradition of the Palace alive, a small, wooden "Baby Palace" was hurriedly constructed a few blocks from the site of the ruined hotel. It had only twenty-three rooms, but it was fitted with some style, and its grill was presided over by Ernest Arbogast, the same chef who had made the

Palace an epicurean delight. When the charred walls of the hotel were leveled and the rubble hauled away, workmen descended on the site in force.

The new hotel followed the plan of the old, though there were differences. The original Palace had been a marvel of white and gold, with tiers of bay windows on every side; the new inn was more sedate, with walls of gray brick and granite and a single row of iron balconies beneath its cornice. The circular driveway and Grand Court, where the carriages of nabobs and generals had once assembled in queues, were gone, replaced by a glass-canopied dining room called the Garden Court. Framed by double rows of marble pillars, ornamented with mahogany paneling and crystal chandeliers, it was a handsome room and a worthy successor to the old Grand Court. Adjoining the

Garden Court on one side was the Rose Room, a ballroom with ivory woodwork and rose-colored draperies and, on the other, a large restaurant. Beyond a set of glass doors was the men's grill, with a heavy-timbered Gothic ceiling and red tile walls. Adjoining the grill was the bar, warmly wrapped in oaken panels and ornamented with a Maxfield Parrish mural of the Pied Piper of Hamelin. The upper floors housed reception rooms, private dining salons, and nearly six hundred guest rooms. Total cost of the new hotel was set at eight million dollars.

A reporter who attended the hotel's grand opening on December 15, 1909, wrote glowingly: "Three years ago there was a tent restaurant on the old Palace lot serving coffee and sinkers to dusty laborers. . . . Where in the stories of enchantment has imagination equalled this transformation?" William Ralston's son was on hand to open the hotel with a golden key, after which the key was floated from the roof at the end of a cluster of balloons. Glistening in the sun, it boldly headed out through the Golden Gate.

Unlike its predecessor, the new Palace was not the undisputed queen of San Francisco's hotels. The new Fairmont, which crowned the summit of Nob Hill, was a splendid structure, as was the towered St. Francis, which faced the grassy expanse of Union Square. Both hotels were frequented by increasing numbers of fashionable guests. But the Palace offered something more than either of its competitors. It offered tradition, a sense of the continuing past, a link with a city, now largely vanished, that had flourished before the earthquake and fire. However popular the new hotels might become, the Palace would continue to occupy a special place in the affection of old San Franciscans. The Garden Court was as impressive a room as any in San Francisco, and it was widely regarded as the social and cultural center of the city. There, potted palms nodded gracefully beside banquet tables. There, orchestras played for debutante cotillions and fashionable balls, and young men and women, misty-eyed and ruddy-cheeked, plotted dreams of the future.

When notables visited San Francisco, they usually found their way to the Palace. In 1919 President Woodrow Wilson, on a tour of the West to seek support for the League of Nations, addressed 1,500 members of the Chamber of Commerce in the Garden Court. In July 1923 Wilson's successor, Warren G. Harding, suffering from a bad case of "indigestion," rushed from a speaking engagement in Seattle to a suite in the Palace, where

Mayor James Rolph, Jr. and American Medical Association President Ray Lyman Wilbur greeted him apprehensively. The day after his arrival the President's condition worsened. Then he gradually began to improve. On Thursday, August 2, while he was lying in his bed, Harding suffered a sudden and unexpected seizure. Doctors were summoned, and Secret Service agents battled to keep back reporters who crowded the Palace lobby. A few minutes later lights were dimmed and a solemn voice announced, "Your President is dead."

Herbert Hoover and Franklin D. Roosevelt were guests at the hotel, as were Hollywood celebrities Don Ameche, Cesar Romero, Douglas Fairbanks, Loretta Young, Tyrone Power, and Darryl F. Zanuck. During World War II Bob Hope rehearsed for one of his Armed Forces radio shows in the Palace, and in 1959 Soviet Premier Nikita Khrushchev addressed a combined gathering of the World Affairs Council and the California Commonwealth Club in the Garden Court.

Five years before Khrushchev's appearance the Palace had undergone the greatest change of its post-1906 history. In the fall of 1954 it was announced that Mrs. William Johnstone, granddaughter of Senator Sharon, had sold the great hotel. *Life* magazine published the picture of a broad-faced man with piercing eyes and thinning hair resting his hands on a balcony above the Garden Court. The man in the picture was Ernest Henderson, president and chief mover of the rapidly expanding Sheraton Corporation. He had come to San Francisco to survey the latest of his many hotel acquisitions.

San Franciscans, who cherished tradition more than most other American city-dwellers, were outraged by the sale. "It's the trend of the times, isn't it?" Mrs. Johnstone told a reporter for *Time* magazine. Trend or no, veterans of the Palace lobby refused to recognize the hyphenated name, Sheraton-Palace. An editor for the San Francisco *Chronicle*, noting a menu item advertised as being served "at Sheraton Hotels everywhere," protested that San Franciscans would never take to "syndicated ragout of beef." The item was dropped from the menu, but the hyphenated name remained—even after 1968, when the Sheraton chain was acquired by the trans-national conglomerate, International Telephone and Telegraph. In 1973 a Japanese corporation called Kyo-Ya, a subsidiary of the Kokusai Kogyo conglomerate of Tokyo, acquired the hotel. Management remained in the hands of the Sheraton Corporation, and the name remained Sheraton-Palace.

But old San Franciscans still regarded it as the Palace. The city's continuing affection for the hotel was demonstrated on October 18, 1975, when 450 diners paid $100 each for the honor of attending a centennial banquet in the Ralston Room of the hotel. Proceeds of the banquet were earmarked for the San Francisco-based California Historical Society, which sponsored the dinner and the ball which followed. Men and women in period costumes filled the Garden Court to overflowing as they danced to the nostalgic music of Ernie Heckscher's society orchestra.

The centennial outpouring of affection for the Palace was evidence, if any was needed, that the hotel still held a fascination for San Franciscans. The reason for their feeling is not difficult to discern. A city destroyed and rebuilt in the figurative winking of an eye—as San Francisco was in the first decade of the twentieth century—needs something that suggests permanence, a tie with its roots, a link between generations pulled further and further apart by the tensions of modern life. A century after its opening the Palace was such a tie, such a link—a dream of gold and silver endlessly renewed in the memory of a grateful city.

6

A Retreat for the Nabobs

DEL MONTE LODGE, PEBBLE BEACH

Sebastian Vizcaino, a Spanish merchant-turned-navigator and explorer, was the first European to set foot on California's Monterey Peninsula. It was a crisp day in mid-December 1602 when the doughty captain, commander of an exploring fleet of three small vessels, entered a spacious bay on the coast of Central California and set his flagship to anchor. Wooded mountains rose up on three sides of the sheet of water, a handsome plate of blue fringed by a lip of glistening sand. It was the finest port the explorer had seen on his voyage north from Mexico, and in his report to his patron and superior, the Viceroy of New Spain, he described it exultantly. Mindful of the importance of his discovery, Vizcaino named the bay for the viceroy, the estimable Count of Monterey.

Two hundred seventy-seven years later an ambitious railroad baron laid his eyes on the same peninsula, the same wooded hills, and the same bay that had excited Vizcaino's enthusiasm. Without hesitation, Charles Crocker decided to make Monterey the site of the grandest resort hotel on the Pacific Coast.

Between Vizcaino's discovery and Crocker's decision the bay and peninsula had been witnesses to grand events of history. The sandaled missionary, Junipero Serra, had put ashore at Monterey Bay in 1770, the year the town of Monterey was founded. The friar's headquarters were at Carmel, across the pine-clad hills to the south, where a tile-roofed adobe mission rose up from broad fields of mus-

tard and mallow. Until 1850, when California became the thirty-first state of the American Union, Monterey was the seat of the Spanish and Mexican governors, whose word was law in all the territory from the ocean shore to the far-off peaks of the Rocky Mountains. But when the government left Monterey and the center of business and population shifted north to the roistering city of San Francisco, Monterey settled into a somnolent dream.

It was a picturesque town of adobe and tile and shadowed balconies, with rutted streets of sand below and flocks of wheeling gulls above. Tourists, seeking relief from the noise and excitement of San Francisco and the Sierra gold fields, made occasional excursions to the old town, but their visits were few, and they excited little notice even among the *señoritas* who peered discreetly from behind barred windows or the mustachioed *vaqueros* who loitered in the murky recesses of the town's *cantinas*. If Sebastian Vizcaino had sailed into Monterey Bay in 1879, he would have seen a few white-washed walls and tiled roofs on the greensward that rose up from the bay shore, but little else would have changed. Piney forests still spread from the rocky prow of Point Pinos to the summit of Mount Toro. A ribbon of snowy sand still met the lapping waves of the bay. And a broad vista of blue still swept from the rocky southern arm of the bay to the redwood forests of Santa Cruz, twenty miles to the north.

Charles Crocker's decision to build a grand hotel beside Monterey Bay was typically bold and im-

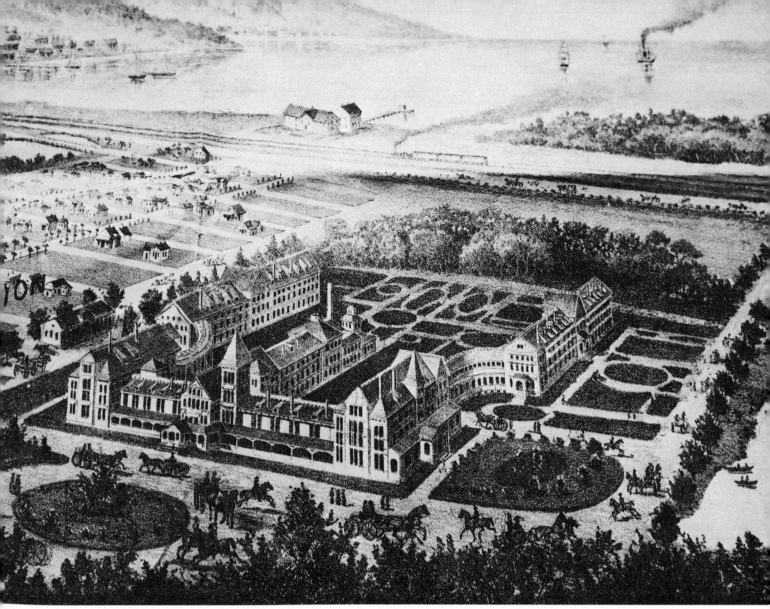

Artist's view of Hotel del Monte (foreground). The town of Monterey and Monterey Bay are in the background. (Courtesy of the Monterey Public Library)

petuous. All his life he prided himself on being "a doer, not a talker," and even his enemies admitted that the description was apt. He was a big man who normally weighed more than 250 pounds and, though his periods of intense activity alternated with other periods of equally intense inactivity, he had accomplished miracles in his fifty-seven years.

He was one of the celebrated quartet of railroad barons (Leland Stanford, Collis P. Huntington, and Mark Hopkins were the others) who had built the great Central Pacific Railroad from San Francisco to Ogden, Utah and, thereafter, planned and executed the even more extensive Southern Pacific Railroad. Stanford was a politician, a Civil War governor of California who was twice elected to the United States Senate; Huntington was a hard-driving, cool-thinking business executive whose flair for making money was equaled only by his talent for making enemies; Hopkins, tall, spare,

and stooped, was a non-smoker and non-drinker who seldom ate meat, rarely spent money on himself, and never completely got over the embarrassment of being a multi-millionaire. Huntington was the brains of the "Big Four," as the quartet of barons were invariably known. Stanford was the politician and contact-man and Hopkins the voice of caution and restraint. But Crocker was preeminently the doer—the engineer, the builder, the driver. He often complained that Stanford had done nothing for the railroad between 1863, when he turned the first shovelful of earth, and 1869, when he drove the last spike. Crocker had spent much of that time in the saddle, riding among the hordes of coolies who worked on the road, giving orders, shouting commands, wiping streaks of sweat and splotches of alkali dust from his ruddy face.

When the Central Pacific was completed,

Crocker contemplated his future gloomily. He could retire to a comfortable office somewhere in San Francisco or New York, shuffle papers and ponder figures, but he knew he would be unhappy if he did. He thought seriously of selling his shares in the Pacific Improvement Company—the corporate shell that embraced the railroad and the Big Four's other investments—but eventually thought better of the idea. He resumed his title as corporate vice president, put on weight, and spent the next fifteen years trying not to become a slave to his job. Much of his time was spent on long trips along the coast, inspecting properties—coal and gold mines, cattle ranches, irrigation projects—that he always talked of buying, and often did.

On one of his trips he happened on the old Spanish town of Monterey. Development of the former capital had been seriously hampered by its remoteness from the mines of the gold country, but even more by the fact that all the land in its vicinity was controlled by a single man. David Jacks, a Scottish-born former storekeeper, was as roundly hated in Monterey as Huntington was in San Francisco. He had bought up the town's "pueblo lands"—thirty thousand acres of choice seashore and hillside—for three cents an acre at a sheriff's sale in 1859. In Spanish and Mexican days the land had been guarded as the town's patrimony, and it rankled old residents to see the dour Scot, his red beard flowing in the Pacific breeze, marching across the hills and valleys of the Monterey Peninsula as if he were a baron and the peninsula his barony. Shrewdness in making loans, coupled with complete lack of compunction in foreclosing on mortgages, had enabled Jacks to acquire additional thousands of acres. By 1870 he was Monterey County's richest man, but also one of its most uneasy. Whenever he drove his carriage to the county seat, he prudently returned by a different road than he had set out on, to confound the ambushers who perpetually lay in wait for him.

Jacks' domain was prosperous, but there were chinks in the baron's armor. In 1874 he had built a narrow-gauge railroad between Monterey and the county seat and had borrowed heavily to complete it. But the depression of the seventies kept traffic on the railroad disappointingly low, and payments on the narrow-gauge's mortgages soon fell into default. In the fall of 1879 the Big Four, always ready to take advantage of an opportunity, purchased the mortgages and started foreclosure proceedings. For once in his life, David Jacks sensed failure.

But the future was not to be all black. As they

proceeded with the foreclosure, Charles Crocker and his partners Stanford and Huntington (Hopkins had died in 1878) opened negotiations for the purchase of large sections of Jacks' other peninsula property—the old *Pescadero* and *Pinos* ranches on the coast south of Monterey and a choice plot of wooded land on the bay shore north of the town. Reeling from the effects of the depression, Jacks was happy to exchange a little part of his barony for a pile of ready cash. At the agreed price of five dollars an acre, he reckoned he had made a handsome profit on the thirty-five thousand acres he sold to Crocker and the Pacific Improvement Company.

Without delay the Southern Pacific made plans to tear up the narrow-gauge road and lay a standard-gauge line in its place. In December 1879 Crocker was quoted by a reporter for the San Francisco *Chronicle:*

"Everything is ready. We shall lay the road with new steel rails, which are already on the ground. As to the rolling stock and material of the narrow-gauge road, we have already sold rails, engines, cars, turntables, water-tanks and everything else to the Nevada Central Railroad Company. . . . Our inten-

Charles Crocker (Courtesy of the Bancroft Library, Berkeley)

tions regarding Monterey are to make it a first-class watering-place in every respect, for which it is well-adapted. . . . We shall build a handsome depot and a splendid hotel in a locality not yet determined. . . . The hotel will be completed and ready for occupancy by next season. We shall run trains through in three hours, and plenty of them. By this means we shall make Monterey almost a suburb of San Francisco.''

Crocker's plans were ambitious, but it soon became evident that he intended to fulfill them. By January 1880, when the standard-gauge railroad was completed, Crocker had chosen the site for his hotel. It was a plot of several hundred acres of choice land that bordered the bay shore just north of Monterey. Early explorers had often camped on the site, where cypresses clutched at pyramids of sand and lofty pines crowded the shores of a looking-glass lake. It was reputed to be the sunniest spot on the shore of Monterey Bay, a vale of perpetual sunshine, immune to all but the most piercing of sea fogs. The plot, moreover, was studded with magnificent trees—pines and cypresses and spectacularly gnarled oaks with long, twisted limbs hung over with gossamer veils of Spanish moss. And the sound of the surf, beating quietly on the beach, was never far away.

In February a vast construction crew assembled at the hotel site. Materials arrived in crowded boxcars as construction began. The plan was impressive. The inn was to be three stories high and more than three hundred feet long. There were to be pinnacled towers and balconies, long latticed verandas, sweeping flights of steps, and tiers of dormer windows. Crocker watched intently from his seat in a carriage nearby as work proceeded on the structure. At first the hotel was called the ''Stanford.'' Later, it was more mellifluously christened the ''Hotel Del Monte.'' By the beginning of June 1880 the great resort was ready for guests.

The hotel stood in a sumptuous park of nearly a hundred acres, all enclosed with a white picket fence. Broad carriage-ways led from the building's main steps to the gingerbread depot, nestled at the base of towering dunes by the bay shore. There was a grand bathhouse on the beach, enclosed with glass, large enough to accommodate five hundred bathers, and the lake on the grounds—

Hotel del Monte in 1882 (Harper's New Monthly Magazine, October 1882)

fancifully dubbed the "Como"—was fitted with a landing and floated with a fleet of graceful gondolas. Viewed from the outside, the building was a maze of gables, towers, verandas, loggias, and balconies, all painted a tasteful pearl gray. Inside it was a wonderland of white—white walls, white ceilings, white stairways, white floors. At night, inside and out, Del Monte blazed with the blue-white flames of nearly a thousand flickering gaslights.

Even before ground was broken for the hotel, an expectant air hung over Monterey. In December 1879 the San Francisco *Chronicle* announced: "The little Spanish-Mexican town of Monterey, after a Sleepy Hollow repose of half a century, is once more to be awakened to a life of fashion and commercial activity." By May 1880, when the hotel was nearly finished, the Monterey *Californian* was able to report a large increase in the town's population. "Stores are going up on all sides," the *Californian* said, "and although rent has increased one hundred per cent., not even an old adobe building, capable of sheltering a family, is to be found empty."

The new depot at Del Monte bustled with horses, sleek carriages, and a glittering array of guests. The railroad moguls, Crocker, Stanford, and Huntington, made grand entrances, with retinues of family, friends, and servants trailing behind them. Company officials made frequent visits. Society editors, coming down from San Francisco for a day or a week, wrote glowing accounts of the resort for their readers and hinted broadly that a weekend—or a summer—at Del Monte would be useful to anyone who sought favors from the influential railroad. Soon ambitious businessmen and obsequious dowagers alike crowded the railroad cars that regularly arrived at Del Monte station.

A parade of illustrious guests affixed their names to the hotel's register: governors and senators, bankers and industrialists, speculators and investors. All were welcomed with open arms by the hospitable Del Monte staff.

In September 1880 Civil War hero General William T. Sherman arrived at Del Monte accompanied by none other than the President of the United States, Rutherford B. Hayes. There was a grand ball to welcome the guests. Hayes abstained from the dancing, though his traveling companion did not. "General Sherman joined in the festivities with a relish," the *Californian* reported. "He is a good dancer and a great favorite among the ladies."

Another general arrived at Del Monte in July 1886. No Yankee warrior was Mariano Guadalupe Vallejo, but a Spanish-Californian, native of Monterey, and once semi-feudal commander of the vast northern frontier of California. The seventy-nine-year-old don had returned to the city of his birth to participate in the fortieth anniversary celebration of the American conquest of California. It was a day of fervent Yankee exultation. Vallejo raised the Spanish and Mexican flags at the Monterey Custom House in a nostalgic tribute to the vanquished sovereigns of the old capital, then retired to his room at Del Monte. In the evening he wandered alone in the gardens and on to the veranda, where he sat smoking cigars and thinking long thoughts of old Monterey.

Not all observers of the grand hotel welcomed its arrival in the old town. Robert Louis Stevenson, the gaunt Scottish writer who had sojourned in Monterey in the fall of 1879, looked on the resort with undisguised distaste. "The Monterey of last year exists no longer," he wrote in *Fraser's Magazine* in 1880:

A huge hotel has sprung up in the desert by the railway. Three sets of diners sit down successively to table. Invaluable toilettes figure along the beach and between the live oaks; and Monterey is advertised in the newspapers, and posted in the waiting-rooms at railway stations, as a resort for wealth and fashion. Alas for the little town! it is not strong enough to resist the influence of the flaunting caravanserai, and the poor, quaint, penniless native gentlemen of Monterey must perish, like a lower race, before the millionaire vulgarians of the Big Bonanza.

Others, less emotional than Stevenson, wondered if the prosperity Del Monte brought to the little town was real or illusory. The great bathhouse was often half empty, and the long, crescent beach nearly deserted. A reporter for the San Francisco *Stock Report* visited the bay shore and expressed surprise that "not a bather was to be seen, except some Chinese fishermen hauling in their nets." The same reporter, needling Crocker, complained to him of the chilling bay waters fed by the icy flow of the California current. "My suggestion to Crocker to supply his guests with sealskin bathing suits with India-rubber outsides," the reporter wrote, "made him give a sort of sickly smile and shrug his shoulders, which extend well down to his knees." The hotel was usually crowded, but its fashionable guests were content in their picketed park, and when they went for drives in the old town or along the rugged outer coast of the Monterey Peninsula, they were antiseptically detached. They brought shiny dollars to Monterey, but the dollars were spent in the grand hotel, and few strayed to the adobe town. In 1890 the Census Bureau certified Monterey's population as 1,662, 266 more than in 1880, but a scant nine souls more than the population of thirty years before. The "flaunting caravanserai" was not, perhaps, as great a threat to old Monterey as Stevenson had imagined.

Whether or not Montereyans welcomed the hotel, it was clear that Crocker was pleased with it. Del Monte was the mogul's pet, a semi-private reserve in which his word held more weight than that of any of his railroad partners. He set the management policies for the hotel, insisting that it be run on the vague but chivalrously hospitable principle that "what ladies and gentlemen do is their own business and that ladies and gentlemen never annoy ladies and gentlemen." Crocker was in the hotel one evening when one of the guests, feeling the effects of too many after-dinner brandies, wandered through the empty lobby making speeches and smashing glass and furniture. Reminding his manager that "what ladies and gentlemen do is their own business," Crocker forbade him to interfere with the boisterous guest. "Let him break anything he wants," Crocker said, "so long as he does not do it in an objectionable manner. But be sure to charge him generously for what he destroys—and on top of that add a generous operating profit."

Crocker had homes scattered throughout the country—a handsome mansion in Sacramento, a splendid palace on Fifty-eighth Street in Manhattan, a Taj Mahal on the summit of San Francisco's Nob Hill—but these monuments to his magnificent wealth did not please him half as much as Del Monte, and he spent much of his time in the hotel.

One of Crocker's proudest boasts was that Del Monte was a wholly fire-proof building. There was water in abundance, pumped from artesian wells on the property, and a ready crew of firemen, prepared at a moment's notice to man the hoses. But fire has a way of overcoming man-made obstacles, as Crocker was to learn in the spring of 1887. A few minutes before midnight on April 1 of that year, a fire kindled somewhere in the sprawling hotel raced along a corridor, descended a stairway, gathered force and speed in a dimly lit salon, then erupted in a hungry, all-consuming wall of flame. In an hour the Hotel del Monte lay in a smoldering heap of ashes. No one was injured in the conflagration, but the loss to property was considerable. A special train rushed the hotel's three hundred guests

to San Francisco, where they arrived in what a reporter for *Harper's Weekly* called "a pitiable state of temporary poverty." In Monterey an army of stiff-collared valets and uniformed footmen remained behind to sift through the ruins in a laborious search for lost jewelry and gold pieces.

Crocker was discouraged, but not daunted, by the holocaust. In a few days he announced plans to rebuild the hotel. Workmen returned to the site, and railroad boxcars filled with lumber and bricks and glass once again crowded Del Monte Station as the hulking figure of Charles Crocker took up its accustomed point of vantage in an oak-shaded carriage. The new hotel rose proudly on the site of the old, duplicating its gables and towers and verandas. By the end of summer, fashionable carriages again crowded the graveled concourse in front of Del Monte's main steps as maidens lolled in gondolas on Lake Como and young men and women crowded the great bathhouse on the beach.

Crocker was sixty-six years old when the hotel was rebuilt. Despite frequent efforts to diet, he still weighed more than 225 pounds, and his health was wavering. In New York he had been thrown from his carriage and injured so badly that he was confined for several weeks to his bed. Back in California, he returned once again to Del Monte, confident that a rest would restore him to health. When on August 14, 1888, word reached San Francisco that the builder of Del Monte was in a diabetic coma, his eldest son and a group of doctors boarded a special train. The train moved swiftly and surely over the 125 miles that separated the city from the resort, but it arrived too late by minutes to see the patient alive.

The hotel's operation continued after Crocker's death much as it had before. New features were added gradually: a sprawling, oak-shaded golf course, claimed to be California's first; a polo field; a column-edged Roman plunge; and a spectacular carriage road that hugged the rocky seacoast west and south of Monterey. The road—first called the "18-Mile Drive," later shortened to the "17-Mile Drive"—became the best-known section of seacoast in California. It was a chain of breathtaking natural wonders—twisted rocks, gnarled cypresses, curving bays, and angry surf—that was often and not unfavorably compared to the French Riviera.

There were outposts of Del Monte at selected spots on the Monterey Peninsula. In the little town of Pacific Grove, west of Monterey, was the wooden El Carmelo Hotel, priced more moderately than Del Monte. In Carmel Valley, just south of the Peninsula, were hunting lodges maintained for Del Monte guests. In 1909 a rambling lodge of logs was built in the forest at Pebble Beach, a spectacular cove on the 17-Mile Drive. The lodge was a convenient resting place for those who took excursions on the drive, equipped as it was with a dining room, lounges, and a great hall warmed by a fireplace so large it took two men and a truck to fill it with logs for an evening's blaze. In 1915 a row of cottages, connected with the lodge by a covered bridge, was built at Pebble Beach. Many travelers preferred the informal atmosphere of the lodge to the most fastidious surroundings of Hotel Del Monte, and it soon became a popular weekend resort.

Leland Stanford had died in 1893; Collis P. Huntington, the last of the Big Four, in 1900. Following Huntington's death the Eastern stockbroker and railroad speculator, Edward H. Harriman, bought a controlling interest in the Southern Pacific. But control of Del Monte did not pass with the railroad. After their sale of the Southern Pacific, heirs

of the Big Four retained the Pacific Improvement Company and its not-inconsiderable stable of remaining assets: seventy-four townsites scattered across the country; valuable land in Buffalo, New York and in Louisiana; the Carbon Hill coal mines near Washington's Mount Ranier; the Guatemala Central Railroad; and Hotel Del Monte with its surrounding properties.

In 1915 an exuberant young Yale graduate-turned-California water engineer was put in charge of the Pacific Improvement Company and its Monterey Peninsula assets. Samuel F. B. Morse was a grandnephew and namesake of the famous nineteenth-century painter and inventor of the telegraph. At Yale the husky Morse had been captain of the football team and a friend of a young Californian named Templeton Crocker, a grandson of the builder of Del Monte. After graduation, Morse came West to make his fortune. Introduced to the Crocker family in San Francisco, he quickly captivated them with his charm and energy.

For a while Morse was put to work on an irriga-

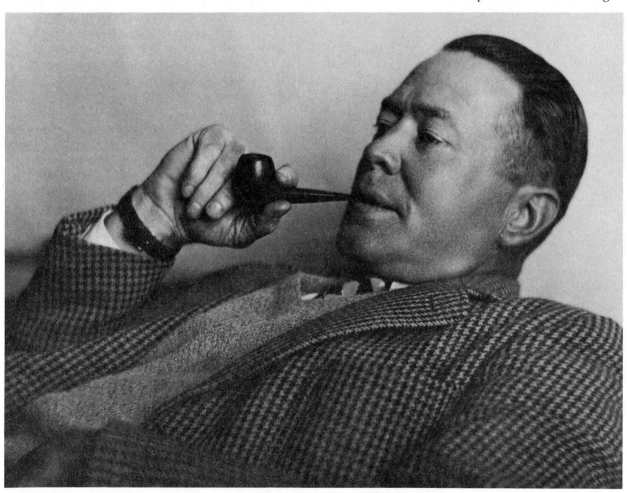

Samuel F.B. Morse (Courtesy of the Bancroft Library)

The spectacular golf links at Pebble Beach in front of Del Monte Lodge (Courtesy of the Pebble Beach Corporation)

tion project in California's great Central Valley. Then he was sent to Monterey and charged with the duty of liquidating the old Pacific Improvement Company. Morse was able to sell most of the company's assets, but he could not bring himself to part with Del Monte and its properties. In 1919 he secured financial backing in San Francisco and, with investor Herbert Fleishacker as his principal partner, formed the Del Monte Properties Company, which promptly took possession of the hotel at Monterey, the lodge at Pebble Beach, and the related properties in Carmel Valley and on the 17-Mile Drive.

Behind his desk as much as on the college gridiron, Morse was an impressive figure—a strapping six-footer, handsome, with a polished Ivy League manner and an infectious enthusiasm for anything and everything that pertained to Del Monte. He was as much at home in the saddle at Del Monte's Carmel Valley dude ranch as in the elegant salons of the old hotel. His dark hair blowing in the breeze, his white teeth clamped on a smoldering briar pipe as he strode across his broad domain, he seemed every bit as regal as Charles Crocker had seemed in the old days at Del Monte station, every bit as baronial as David Jacks had seemed on the wind-swept coast of the *Pinos* and *Pescadero* ranches. Morse's growing circles of admirers, noting his easy air of assurance and authority, dubbed him "Duke of Del Monte." The name was as descriptive as it was catchy, and it stuck.

During the early years of Morse's stewardship Del Monte was plagued by a succession of fires, but in each case the "Duke" was able to turn the flames to his own advantage. In 1917 a blaze of mysterious origin attacked the log walls of the lodge at Pebble Beach, leveling the building. Morse promptly rebuilt the structure. The new lodge was a handsome structure with gleaming white walls, looming windows, and broad terraces that commanded sweeping views of the forest surf. Between the lodge and the ocean the "Duke" laid out spectacular golf links that quickly became the most celebrated in California.

In 1924 flames attacked the old Hotel Del Monte for a second time. Fire trucks responded to the alarms, and well-placed charges of dynamite saved two wings of the building, but the towered central portion was totally consumed. Again rising to the challenge, Morse began to rebuild the hotel. The new Del Monte was a massive Mediterranean villa with soaring arches, tiled arcades, broad loggias, carved and painted ceilings, and a lofty central tower that loomed boldly above the surrounding forest of oak and pine. The hotel's reopening was celebrated on May 8, 1926, with a gala banquet in the main dining room, a spectacular hall more

than two hundred feet in length. Mayor James Rolph, Jr. of San Francisco was on hand to make a speech. Two orchestras played as guests dined happily on Mousse de Saumon and Breast of Spring Chicken Del Monte. Mindful of the Prohibition strictures of the Volstead Act, no wine list was in evidence. But guests were determined to enjoy themselves, and alcoholic beverages flowed freely.

With the lodge at Pebble Beach and the hotel at Del Monte, Del Monte Properties Company had acquired title to most of the land acquired by the Big Four from David Jacks. Portions of the property that were still virginal were divided into commodious homesites which sold at a brisk pace in the 1920s. A home with a Pebble Beach address—or, better yet, frontage on the spectacular 17-Mile Drive—became a mark of distinction among the rich and nearly rich of California society. On summer days, when wisps of cooling fog blew in from the Pacific and shrouded the eighteenth hole of the golf links at Pebble Beach, refugees from the sweltering heat of San Jose and Los Angeles headed toward Del Monte. Many bought home-

The new Del Monte Hotel, today the administration building of the United States Naval Postgraduate School (U.S. Naval Postgraduate School)

sites, some for retirement, others for weekend retreats.

By 1929 selling real estate at Del Monte had become an even more lucrative business than operating the lodge and hotel. Despite its profitability, Morse never permitted the business to be "high pressure." Land was shown to lodge or hotel guests only if they first showed an interest in it, and plots were sold only to buyers who shared Morse's belief that development of Del Monte land should always enhance and never detract from its natural beauty. Whether or not it was good for business, Morse adhered to a strict policy of natural conservation, boasting that under his stewardship Del Monte would remain as beautiful as it had been in the days of the explorer Vizcaino.

It was not easy to adhere to the policy, particularly in the depths of the Depression that followed on the heels of the boom of the twenties. Del Monte was no less vulnerable to the financial crisis than other luxury industries, and real estate sales in Pebble Beach and on the 17-Mile Drive declined as precipitously as did hotel and lodge patronage. Fogs rolled gloomily over the now-deserted golf links at Pebble Beach as real estate contracts gathered dust in pigeon holes. And the great Hotel Del Monte stood nearly empty in its picketed park by the shore of Monterey Bay.

With the outbreak of World War II the hotel was leased by the U.S. Navy for use as a pre-flight training school. Del Monte Properties Company remained on the scene, maintaining the grounds, serving more than six million meals to the tens of thousands of hungry trainees who passed through the place during the war. The company resumed control of the hotel after the war, but in 1948 it was sold to the government for use as a Naval Postgraduate School.

Sadly, Del Monte employees moved from their familiar quarters in Monterey to the lodge at Pebble Beach, now universally known as Del Monte Lodge. The lodge soon took up where the hotel left off, becoming the headquarters of the vast Del Monte Properties complex—the humming nexus

The new Del Monte Lodge. A green of the celebrated Pebble Beach golf links is in the foreground. Photo by William C. Brooks. (Courtesy of the Pebble Beach Corporation)

of the 17-Mile Drive, the Del Monte Forest, the complex of golf courses, polo fields, and dude ranches.

Now Hollywood stars, handsome in their stylish tweeds, golf togs, and bathing suits, were regular visitors at Del Monte. Del Monte became the site of the annual California State Amateur Golf Tournament and the even more-celebrated Bing Crosby Pro-Amateur Tourney. From the single row of cottages built at Pebble Beach in 1915, Del Monte Lodge had expanded its bedroom accommodations to more than 150 by 1975. It was not the largest hostelry on the Central California coast, but it was surely the most fashionable.

Samuel F. B. Morse died in 1969. But his memory lived on at Del Monte, as did that of his predecessor, Charles Crocker, the railroad baron who started it all in 1880. The hotel and the lodge had changed much in the years since Crocker sat in his oak-shaded carriage watching workmen raise the walls and towers of the old hotel. But the peninsula and bay, still starkly beautiful, had changed hardly at all. If the doughty Sebastian Vizcaino were to sail past the peninsula and drop anchor in Monterey Bay in the midst of the twentieth century, he would have no trouble recognizing his wondrous discovery. That fact, as much as any other, was a tribute to the wisdom and restraint of the builders of old Del Monte.

7

$$\mathcal{Where\ Trade\ Winds\ Blow}$$

THE MOANA AND THE ROYAL HAWAIIAN, HONOLULU

For the better part of a century past, the Hawaiian Islands have been acclaimed as a vacationer's paradise, a mecca for travelers from North America, the South Pacific, and exotic capitals of the Orient. Modern travelers, contemplating for the first time the profusion of resort hotels that push their lofty heads above the clouds at Honolulu, would find it difficult to imagine a time when the islands' only accommodations were huts of bamboo and grass or open-air taverns with sleeping rooms attached. Yet such was the condition of the "Paradise of the Pacific" only a little more than a century ago.

When Mark Twain arrived in Honolulu in March 1866, he tarried at the dock for an hour of conversation, during which time his more energetic fellow-passengers took all the available rooms in town. The writer resigned himself to a night in his steamer cabin, a night which he thought would be uneventful, but which proved to be anything but. The tropical air was so stiflingly hot that Twain at length resolved to dress "in a manner unnecessary to describe." He found the clouds of mosquitoes that drifted around him "rather troublesome," but rejoiced when he realized "that the two million I sat down on a minute ago will never sing again." There were no nets on the ship to help him in his combat with the insects. Later, when he settled into a guest room in Honolulu and got hold of a gauzy tent, he mastered a plan of defense. Holding up the tent on one side, he waited until all the mosquitoes got in, then himself got out, lowered the net, and slept soundly on the floor.

If a local tradition may be believed, the mosquitoes, like Twain, were visitors to Hawaii. According to an often repeated story, they had arrived in Honolulu in 1826 in a cask of water from Mexico. Surveying the town and the surrounding country, they found the scenery, the balmy climate, and the local population much to their liking and decided to settle down. Missionaries blamed the insects' advent on the natives' sinful ways, claiming the winged marauders were sent as punishment from Heaven. Since the mosquitoes' arrival in Honolulu corresponded roughly to the arrival of the missionaries, the natives—unsophisticated in the complex theology of sin—blamed the foreigners for the bugs. Travelers began to come in numbers a few years later. In time the four groups—natives, missionaries, tourists, and mosquitoes—arrived at an uneasy but tolerable peace.

There was a sprinkling of lodging houses and inns in Honolulu in the 1850s and '60s—an American Hotel, really a collection of cottages; a Hotel de France; and a dingy National Hotel and Billiard Saloon, which faced the waterfront. When His Royal Highness, the Duke of Edinburgh, second son of Britain's Queen Victoria, visited the islands in 1869, he was put up in style in the house of Hawaii's King Kamehameha V. But other visitors found accommodations scarce, uncomfortable

84

Diamond Head and Waikiki, Hawaii before the advent of the palace inns (Courtesy of the Bancroft Library)

and, above all, lacking in style. Steamships and square-riggers were appearing with increasing frequency in the harbor at Honolulu, their decks crowded with troops of wide-eyed tourists—men in frock coats and boiled shirts, women in silks and ostrich plumes, all eager to bask in the tropical sun, to feel the trade winds on their faces, to enjoy a week or a month in the "Paradise of the Pacific."

For years the need for a large hotel was the subject of general conversation in Honolulu. A public meeting to consider the subject was held in 1865, and the king's ministers took up the issue soon after. Kamehameha V was the last of a distinguished line of Hawaiian monarchs who claimed direct descent from the legendary "Napoleon of the Pacific," Kamehameha the Great. Though he was an intelligent man with a mind and will of his own, Kamehameha V depended heavily on the advice and counsel of his cabinet, which consisted mostly of Americans.

Two of the king's advisors, Finance Minister John Mott Smith and Judge Charles C. Harris, believed that the kingdom should erect a grand hotel. The tourist trade was growing rapidly, and a hotel worthy of Honolulu and the islands could not be built solely with private capital. The king owed it to his subjects, argued Smith and Harris, to put up a worthy building. Six months passed before Kamehameha expressed an opinion. "I think favorably of the Government building a hotel," he said finally. The decision made, Smith and Harris set to work to implement it.

A block of land in downtown Honolulu was selected as the site of the new building. "Hotel bonds," issued on the credit of the kingdom, were floated to raise the construction costs, with proceeds payable not in interest, but in shares of the projected rent. Concrete blocks, fabricated on the site, were used to build the walls. Work began in May 1871 and continued through the end of the year. When finished, the hotel was an imposing structure of three stories with broad *lanais* or porches across its façade and a turret-like observatory on top. Its inner chambers glistened with polished woods and crystal, China, ivory, and silver. Overstuffed couches and settees crouched in the shade of potted palms. The bedrooms, paneled in varnished pine and crowded with lounging chairs, opened on the *lanais*. A commodious dining room ran the width of the second

The Royal Hawaiian Hotel, opened in February 1872 (Courtesy of The Bancroft Library, Berkeley)

floor. Next to it was a large parlor and lobby connected with the ground by two semicircular stairways. Outside, the observatory and *lanais* looked down on sweeping lawns studded with tamarinds, algarobas, and breadfruit trees and a long horseshoe drive that led from a nearby street to the entrance stairways.

The new hotel was leased to Allen Herbert, a former San Francisco hotêlier, who opened it on February 29, 1872, with a grand banquet and ball. The ball was attended by Kamehameha V, his retinue of advisers and attendants, and a swirling throng of missionaries, tourists, and mosquitoes. Though officially named the Hawaiian Hotel, the new inn was soon known throughout the kingdom as the "Royal Hawaiian."

The total cost of the hotel, pegged at $116,528 by dollar-wary bookkeepers, was considerable even by royal standards, and it troubled many islanders. The amount in excess of $42,500 had been borrowed on the personal responsibility of Smith

and Harris and, when they petitioned the legislature to have the kingdom assume the obligation, a heated debate erupted. Opposition leaders complained that the hotel had been built without legislative authority and that it had more than doubled the national debt. But the king supported the ministers, a majority of the legislature supported the king and, in the end, Smith and Mott were relieved of their debt.

From the day of its opening the Royal Hawaiian was the center of social life in Honolulu. To show the favor in which he held the new inn, Kamehameha ordered the renovation of an old grass hut on the hotel grounds for use as a council chamber. The *lanais* and corridors were perpetually crowded with representatives of the islands' varied population—women in *holokus* and *muumuus* and wide-brimmed hats under curling ostrich plumes; men in white ducks and flannels and straw hats circled with bands of peacock feathers; sea captains in braid and brass, visored caps and polished boots. No less cosmopolitan than the guests were the varied members of the hotel's staff. Bellboys from the Canary Islands and the Azores carried luggage. A Portuguese day clerk and a Chinese night clerk registered guests. A Greek chef presided in the kitchen, and a German barber cut the hair of male guests. The head steward was an Alsatian, his wife a Parisian. Beaming at the throngs that crowded the Royal, the American proprietor, Allen Herbert, bragged that travelers were turned away with "monotonous regularity." He was not surprised by the fact. "Here is artistry in its highest sense," Herbert exulted. "And all six minutes to the steamer wharf!"

One of the liveliest attractions of the hotel was the Royal Hawaiian Band, which gave regular concerts in a pavilion on the grounds and delighted natives and visitors alike with its unique combination of European melodies and native tunes. Organized as a royal institution in 1870, the band achieved distinction after 1872 when Captain Heinrich Berger, late of Kaiser Wilhelm's Prussian Musik Corps, was named Kapellmeister to Kamehameha V. As Kapellmeister, Berger took charge of the Royal Band, instilled it with military discipline, and quickly transformed it from a ragtag aggregation into a first-rate marching band and orchestra. Its members were all Hawaiians, but Berger trained them so thoroughly in European techniques that they could toss off polkas and schottisches as readily as native *hulas*. When steamships arrived at the wharf in Honolulu, the mustachioed captain and his troop of musicians, handsomely attired in military uniforms, were on hand to serenade the passengers with Hawaiian ballads and airs. When the elite of Honolulu society gathered in the Royal Hawaiian Hotel for banquets and balls, Berger and his musicians played rousing Offenbach overtures and Strauss waltzes. On Sundays, when sunlight dappled the lawns around the hotel and families gathered to picnic beneath the great tamarinds and algarobas, the Royal Hawaiian Band played concerts from its pavilion bandstand.

Berger worked closely with musical members of the royal family. David Kalakaua, who became King of Hawaii in 1874, wrote the words and Berger the music for "Hawaii Ponoi," the islands' national anthem. King Kalakaua's sister, Princess (later Queen) Liliuokalani, wrote the words and hummed the melody of the even more celebrated "Aloha Oe," which Berger arranged for orchestra. Effective as they were with Strauss and Offenbach,

the musicians of the Royal Band did not bring audiences to their feet until they laid down their European instruments and began to sing native love songs and rhythmic chants in the ancient traditions of their island ancestors.

The handsome, bewhiskered King Kalakaua—"Merry Monarch" of his island realm—was a frequent visitor at the Royal Hawaiian Hotel. His royal residence, Iolani Palace, occupied a square opposite the hotel, but he spent so much time in the inn's Suite 17 that it became known as the "King's Room." Kalakaua was also a frequent and enthusiastic patron of the hotel bar where, in good democratic style, he stood to the brass rail with his friends and subjects, ordering when it came his turn, "liquidating the check" by digging into his royal pockets for clinking gold and silver coins when it came time to pay.

Foreign visitors were impressed by the hotel's commodious rooms and tasteful appointments. The Englishwoman Isabella Bird came to Hawaii in 1873 after visiting Australia and New Zealand. The long harbor and palm-fringed beach of Honolulu inspired her with a sense of awe, but the hotel convinced her that "in this fairy land anything might be expected." Miss Bird thought the Royal "the perfection of an hotel." "Hospitality," she wrote, "seems to take possession of and appropri-

King Kalakaua (Courtesy of the Bancroft Library, Berkeley)

ate one as soon as one enters its never-closed door. . . ."

> Everywhere, only pleasant objects meet the eye. One can sit all day on the back verandah, watching the play of light and colour on the mountains and the deep blue green of the Nuuanu Valley, where showers, sunshine, and rainbows make perpetual variety. The great dining-room is delicious. It has no curtains, and its decorations are cool and pale. Its windows look upon tropical trees in one direction, and up to the cool mountains in the other. . . . The hotel seems the great public resort of Honolulu, the center of stir—club-house, exchange and drawing-room in one. Its wide corridors and verandahs are lively with English and American naval uniforms; several planters' families are here for the season; and with health seekers from California, resident boarders, whaling captains, tourists from the British Pacific Colonies, and a stream of townspeople always percolating through the corridors and verandahs, it seems as lively and free-and-easy as a place can be, pervaded by the kindliness and bonhommie which form an important item in my first impression of the islands.

The American traveler Charles Nordhoff found the bill of fare at the Royal a never-ending source of surprise. Delicacies rarely encountered in the United States were abundant in the islands and common on the Royal Hawaiian's tables: plump strawberries, golden oranges, bananas and coconuts, guavas, mangos, taro, breadfruit. Nordhoff, enjoying the flying fish that he tasted at the hotel, called it "the most tender and succulent of the fish kind," but he had reservations about the Hawaiian national dish, *poi,* a paste of pounded taro roots. "Fresh or unfermented," Nordhoff wrote, "poi has a pleasant taste; when fermented it tastes to me like a book-binder's paste, and a liking for it must be acquired. . . ."

The San Francisco poet and essayist Charles Warren Stoddard was a frequent visitor in Honolulu both before and after the Royal Hawaiian was built. He was comfortable enough in the grass huts that crowded the capital before the advent of the hotel, but he took quickly and easily to the caravansary and on all his later visits rushed from the steamer wharf to the inn. His favorite spot in the hotel was the glass observatory that perched atop its roof, a vantage point from which he could inspect all of the city and much of the surrounding

Semi-circular lanais of the old Royal Hawaiian Hotel (Photo Hawaii)

ısland. On one of his visits Stoddard described the kaleidoscopic panorama that presented itself from the observatory:

> **It was the war-whoop of a Mynah bird on the window-sill that called our attention to old Diamond Head, which at that moment was glowing like a live coal, the picture of a red-hot volcano with the smoke rubbed out; there was a strip of beryl sea behind it, and at its base a great plain fretted with the light green shade of the Algeroba—this was framed in the sashes on one side of the cupola.**
>
> **On another side, mountain peaks buried their brows in cloud and wept copiously, so sentimental was the hour of our communion; forests of the juiciest green drank these showers of tears.**
>
> **Turning again, we saw the sun-burnt hills beyond Palama, and the crisp cones of the small volcanoes, and more sea, and then the exquisite outline of the Waianae Mountains, of a warm, dusty purple, and with a film of diffused rainbows floating in the middle distance. . . .**
>
> **There was but one window left; it opened upon a sea stretching to the horizon, and mingling with the sky, a shore fringed with tapering masts, and crested, sentinel palms; and beneath us the city submerged in billowy foliage through which the wind stirred in gusts and eddies.**

Stoddard's friend, Robert Louis Stevenson, visited the hotel in 1889. Belle Strong, Stevenson's daughter-in-law, who had been living in Honolulu for several years before the writer's visit, introduced him and his party to the city's principal attractions. The night of Stevenson's arrival Belle entertained him at a grand banquet in the Royal Hawaiian Hotel, a feast which was attended by members of Stevenson's family and a delegation of prominent Hawaiians. The dinner of roast beef and wine was, to Belle's mind, undistinguished, but Stevenson had survived on meager rations during his last week at sea and took great pleasure in the meal.

Before coming to Hawaii, the Scot had explored the Marquesas, Tuamotu, and Tahiti and had already amassed a great store of South Sea tales with which to regale his dinner companions. Two days after the hotel banquet, Stevenson was formally presented to King Kalakaua. The gaunt story-teller and the strapping king soon became good friends, exchanging visits aboard Stevenson's yacht and at the king's seaside villa at Waikiki. The two shared a laugh when, during a breakfast at Iolani Palace, the king asked the writer's mother, Mrs. Margaret Stevenson, how she liked the music of the Royal Hawaiian Band, and she replied politely that it was very nice and did not bother her in the least. After a few days in Honolulu Stevenson and his family

put up in a bungalow at Waikiki, where the beach and the surf afforded him the solitude he needed for his writing.

Waikiki was southeast of Honolulu, a seaside suburb of the city, five miles by carriage or horse-drawn trolley from the Royal Hawaiian Hotel. It was a breathtaking stretch of sea and shore—white sands studded with coconut palms and a foam-flecked surf guarded by a great reef of coral—all overshadowed by the crater mountain, Diamond Head. In the 1870s and '80s Waikiki was a popular bathing beach for residents of Honolulu. C. F. Gordon-Cummings, an Englishman who visited the islands in 1879, remarked that "Waikiki is to Honolulu as Brighton is to London." Local writers referred to it as the Long Branch, Newport, or Trouville of Hawaii.

As early as 1875 Allen Herbert set up a cottage at Waikiki where guests of the Royal Hawaiian could spend a day or enjoy a morning or evening bath in the ocean. In 1881 the *Hawaiian Gazette* wondered why some enterprising person did not put up a hotel at the beach. "A properly conducted place, nicely fitted," said the *Gazette*, "would pay." In the late eighties Herbert opened his private home at Waikiki as a branch of the downtown hotel, but the place was a makeshift affair and not the resort the *Gazette* envisioned. After 1891, when Hamilton Johnson joined Herbert in the management of the Royal Hawaiian, the Johnson residence on the beach, called "Waikiki Villa," was denominated the "seaside annex" of the hotel. A single Chinese servant was posted on the premises to attend to the needs of guests. After a few years canvas-covered cottages were built around the villa, a larger building was put up next to it, and Waikiki's first full-fledged hostelry was opened as the Seaside Hotel.

But the Seaside was too small to satisfy the rapidly growing demand for hotel accommodations at Waikiki. While visiting California, King Kalakaua had died unexpectedly in San Francisco's Palace Hotel in 1891, and his sister and successor, Queen Liliuokalani, had been deposed two years after she assumed the throne. A short-lived Hawaiian Republic established in 1893 was followed by American annexation of the islands in 1898.

As the nineteenth century drew to an end, tourists by the tens of thousands were flocking from the mainland to the new American territory, all eventually finding their way to Waikiki. Businessmen in Honolulu, appraising the flood of tourists with satisfaction, made plans to put up a new hotel to accommodate them. A plot of land just east of the Seaside Hotel, where a spreading banyan hugged low dunes of sand, was selected as the site of the new inn. Led by John George Rothwell, English-born and formerly secretary to the Hawaiian Minister of the Interior, a company was formed which raised upwards of one hundred thousand dollars to finance the project. Architect O. G. Traphagen was commissioned to design a building, and in September 1899 construction began.

The new hotel was christened the Moana, Hawaiian for "ocean." As designed by Traphagen, it was a rectangular building of four stories, with commodious parlors and saloons, a billiard room, a library, and a large dining room that extended on stilts over the edge of the surf. From the day of its opening in March 1901 the Moana was the pride of the budding Hawaiian tourist industry. As the only major resort in the islands and the first large hotel at Waikiki, it was crowded from dawn to midnight by throngs of wide-eyed tourists. A newspaper reporter said it rivaled "the finest hotels on the mainland or Continent" and praised its carefree atmosphere, attributable, he said, to "the swash of the surf, the strains of music and the

clinking of glasses of bubbling wine." Troops of sun-bronzed beach boys crowded the long surf in front of the Moana. Some were Americans, others native islanders, many a mixture of Oriental, European, and Hawaiian ancestries. All were splendid athletes, dazzling visitors with the strength and speed with which they swam through the crashing surf or piloted their skimming surf boards over the lips of curling waves.

A continuing program of improvement and enlargement added to the facilities of the Moana. A three-hundred-foot pier was built into the ocean, with a covered pergola at the end fitted with seats for spectators and a bandstand where Hawaiian musicians could play. In 1918 two concrete wings were added to the hotel building, enclosing the Moana banyan and creating a shaded *lanai* which became known as the Banyan Court. After World War I a new generation of tourists flocked to Waikiki and the Moana. Actors and actresses from far-off Hollywood frolicked in the surf and soaked up sun on the beach in front of the hotel. Aviatrix Amelia Earhart was a guest at the Moana, as was Edward, Prince of Wales, who put up in a lavish suite in April 1920.

The Moana Hotel. (Photo Hawaii)

In the first decade of the twentieth century the Royal Hawaiian in downtown Honolulu continued to attract tourists. In 1907 a group of United States congressmen with wives and children in tow arrived at the Royal on an "investigative tour" of the islands. The Territorial Legislature, which had appropriated fifteen thousand dollars for the visitors' expenses, hoped the pioneer "junket" would result in favorable consideration of Hawaiian interests in Washington. But not all of the congressmen stayed in the Royal. Some registered at the Moana; others at the Alexander Young, a large and modern hotel erected in downtown Honolulu in 1900. A doctor's and a dentist's office had been added to the Royal complex; comfortable cottages nestled beneath trees on the park-like grounds; semicircular *lanais* had been added to the principal building, extending the old second-floor veranda; and the eaves and roof had been decorated with colored electric lights and a circular sign, outlined with lights, that proclaimed "Aloha" to arriving and departing guests.

But the old hotel was feeling the competition of the newer Moana and Alexander Young. With greater and greater frequency the lobby stood nearly empty, and the broad *lanais* were deserted. In 1917 the hotel was sold to the Honolulu YMCA, which operated it as an Army and Navy YMCA until 1926, when it was demolished to make way for a new YMCA building.

The Royal Hawaiian was gone, but not forgotten, by the islanders who remembered its glory. The dream of building a new hotel to carry on the tradition of the old was nurtured by a group of businessmen in the islands and on the mainland. Edward Tenney, president of Honolulu's powerful Castle and Cook Company—one of the "Big Five" of island commerce—joined William P. Roth, manager of the San Francisco-based Matson Navigation Company, to make plans for a new hotel in Waikiki. A one-time island stock broker who had married Lurline Matson, heir to the navigation company, Roth loved luxury and believed there were enough well-heeled people who shared his tastes to make a grand hotel at Waikiki a reality.

In 1925 he and Tenney laid the keel for a great new steamship, the *Malolo* (Hawaiian for "flying fish"), which was designed to dominate passenger traffic between San Francisco and Honolulu. They also made plans to build a lavish hotel at Waikiki to house the *Malolo's* passengers when they arrived in the islands. Tenney and Roth negotiated with the Territorial Hotel Company, which controlled both the Moana and the Seaside Hotel, and

worked out a partnership agreement under which the site of the Seaside would be made available for the new inn. Plans were completed by October 1925. A landscape architect was commissioned to fill twelve acres around the building site with lush tropical foliage, and six hundred acres of land four miles distant were leased for development as a golf course.

Though the hotel site, fed by natural springs, was marshy, architects Warren and Wetmore, used to building on the bedrock of Manhattan Island, were confident they could securely anchor the new building's foundations. When the half-finished structure began to sink in the mud, Matson sent a frantic call to a retired Navy engineer who managed to save the building with additional (and expensive) bulwarks. The structure was larger and grander than any Waikiki had ever seen. Thirty-five thousand barrels of cement were consumed in its construction, as were 75 miles of wire cable, 50 tons of stucco, and more than 9,000 gallons of paint, stain, and lacquer. When finished, the hotel building stood six stories tall and included four hundred rooms. Remembering the historic hostelry in downtown Honolulu whose "seaside annex" had once occupied the site of the new inn, the hotel was named the Royal Hawaiian.

It was a handsome structure of stone and brick covered with pink stucco. Long rows of Moorish arches lined the seaside façade, with terraces and balconies above. Its roof was surmounted with tiled towers and cupolas that completed the Moorish design. From the day of its opening in February 1927 the new Royal Hawaiian was universally and affectionately known as the "Pink Palace of the Pacific."

Twelve hundred guests crowded the hotel on the night of its grand opening. The celebration began with a concert by the Royal Hawaiian Band (Captain Berger no longer wielded the baton, but his influence still pervaded the orchestra). A black tie dinner began at 7:30 and lasted two hours—barely enough time for the dazzled diners to essay the menu of Coupe Czarine, Jordan Almonds, Celery Hearts, Mixed Olives, Green Turtle Soup Kamehameha, Supreme of Mullet Albert, Medallions of Sweet Breads Wilhelmina, Mousse of Foie Gras Princesse, Squab-Chicken Casserole Mascotte, Salad Lurline, Royal Givree, Gourmandise, and Moka.

Diners staggered from the banquet hall to the beach *lanai* on the ocean front of the hotel, where they watched an historical pageant. Led by Princess Kawananakoa (who could have been Hawaii's

Seaside view of the new Royal Hawaiian Hotel (Courtesy of Sheraton Hotels in the Pacific)

queen if the monarchy had survived) and supported by a band of warriors and *Kahili* bearers, the eighteenth-century beach landing of Kamehameha the Great was reenacted. When the king was safely seated on his ceremonial throne, the whole party repaired to the hotel ballroom, where they danced into the night.

The *Malolo* was late for the Royal's opening. Launched at a Philadelphia shipyard in 1926, she had smashed into another ship on her maiden voyage, necessitating a return to the yard for half a million dollars in repairs. When she arrived in Hawaii in November 1927, she was greeted enthusiastically despite disturbing rumors that she had a tendency, like her namesake the flying fish, to roll in heavy waters. Whether or not the rumors were true, the *Malolo* and her younger sister the *Lurline* transported hundreds of thousands of pas-

sengers from the mainland to Honolulu and back. Under her new name of *Matsonia* the ship served the Pacific trade for more than two decades, earning a warm spot in the hearts of regular visitors to the islands.

The new Royal Hawaiian Hotel, opened only two years before the crash of 1929, got off to a shaky financial start, but it was a rousing social success from the first. Fourteen thousand guests were registered in the first five years it was open. Mary Pickford and Douglas Fairbanks, idols of the silent screen, were among the hotel's earliest and most celebrated visitors. They stopped off on a trip around the world, during which they wrote a series of syndicated columns about the sites they saw. "Of all the places Douglas and I visited on our trip around the world," cooed "America's Sweetheart" in one of her columns, "Honolulu is the most beautiful and alluring.'' The Great Depression did not prevent Mrs. Lamont Du Pont of Wilmington, Delaware from spending the entire summer of 1931 at the Royal Hawaiian and enjoying every lazy minute of it. Nor were honeymooners Mr. and Mrs. Nelson Rockefeller and Mr. and Mrs. Henry Ford II dissuaded from enjoying the luxury of the Waikiki palace. Others who refused to be intimidated by rumors of starvation on the mainland were Annie, Viscountess Cowdray; her granddaughters, Hon. Nancy and Hon. Joan Pearson of London; and entertainer Al Jolson and his bride, Ruby Keeler.

The Royal Hawaiian was taken over by the Navy during World War II as a rest and recreation center for personnel of the beleaguered Pacific Fleet. But by 1946 it was back in the hands of the Matson Navigation Company, which operated it and its neighbor, the Moana, much as they had in the balmy twenties and thirties. The two hotels—the lordly "Pink Palace" and the homey "Queen of the Banyan Court"—still dominated the sands, the palms, and the coral-ringed surf of Waikiki.

But the profile of the beach changed dramatically in the 1950s. Industrialist Henry J. Kaiser led the forces of change when he bought a twenty-acre plot of land and developed it into the sprawling resort-hotel complex known as the Hawaiian Village. The Village was followed by looming resort towers—the Halekulani, Princess Kaiulani, Ilikai, Imperial Hawaiian, and Káimana Beach. The Sheraton Hotel Corporation, chief rival of Conrad Hilton's chain of nationwide hotels, acquired the Moana and the Royal Hawaiian in the late fifties. The Moana was sold to the Japanese-based Kokusai Kogyo, Ltd. in 1959, but Sheraton retained control through a long-term management agreement.

The Sheraton chain brought vast changes to the old hotels. A curving, sixteen-story tower wing was built on the Diamond Head side of the Royal Hawaiian; a twenty-nine story Sheraton-Waikiki

February 1, 1927. One thousand two hundred people crowded into the Royal Hawaiian for its opening ceremonies. (Courtesy of Sheraton Hotels in the Pacific)

(one of the ten largest hotel buildings in the world) on the other. A row of shops on Kalakaua Avenue crowded the grove of palms that guarded the Royal entrance. A modern, 150-room Surfrider addition was built adjoining the Moana, its name changed to Moana Ocean Lanai after a Japanese investor erected the 431-room Surfrider Hotel on the opposite side of the old building.

From the deck of an ocean liner the tourist of today must survey the skyline of Waikiki carefully to identify the Moana and the Royal Hawaiian. Ashore, the old buildings are more easily discovered. Much has changed at the hotels, but much remains as it was in the early days of the century when beach boys crowded the ocean *lanais* and sleek Packards and Pierce-Arrows pulled up to the palm-shaded entrances. In 1972 the Moana was added to the National Register of Historic Places. Its seventy-fifth anniversary was celebrated in March 1976; the fiftieth anniversary of the Royal Hawaiian in February 1977.

The flavor of old Hawaii survives in many places in modern Honolulu—in the stately halls of Iolani Palace, in the heart of the city, on the wind-swept summit of Diamond Head, and in Kapiolani Park, the palm-studded expanse of green that flanks Waikiki on its landward side. But the old spirit is captured as well, perhaps better, in the Moana and the Royal Hawaiian. In the evenings, when trade winds blowing in from the ocean gently rustle the palms of the great banyan trees, when the rhythmic tunes of a Hawaiian band float through the lobbies and halls, you may forget for a moment that you are in the center of a modern American city and dream of a secluded isle in a tropical sea, untroubled by the dilemmas of life in the atomic age. The dream, of course, is an illusion, but the illusion seems preciously real in the Moana and the Royal Hawaiian.

8

Queen of the Glory Years

HOTEL DEL CORONADO, CORONADO

San Diego was a bubbly young city, small, but glowingly confident of its future when a railroad executive from Evansville, Indiana arrived in the town in the fall of 1885. Elisha Babcock was only thirty-six years old, but poor health had persuaded him to abandon his home and job in Indiana and seek his fortune in the glowing warmth of southern California. Babcock's decision to come west in 1885 reflected the similar decisions of tens of thousands of his fellow Americans. Tired of the freezing winters and sweltering summers of the Eastern and Midwestern states, these latter-day Forty-Niners hoped to find rest and repose—and at least a chance for good fortune—in the idyllic climate of the far southwestern corner of the country.

Southern California had been sorely neglected in the three decades since California achieved statehood—decades in which the western foothills of the Sierra Nevada had poured forth a dazzling river of gold and San Francisco had grown from a sleepy waterfront village to a throbbing metropolis, the only real "city" west of the Rockies.

The population of the northern half of the state had grown dramatically in those years, but that of the south had changed hardly at all. Pigs still dug for roots in the plaza of old Los Angeles, as they had in Spanish and Mexican days, and clucking chickens still paraded in the dusty streets of San Diego.

All that changed in the middle of the 1880s as southern California felt the rumbling vibrations of

its first great real estate boom. The arrival of the transcontinental railroad in Los Angeles was a major impetus to the boom, but its effects were felt far beyond, extending from the long sands of Santa Monica beach northwest of Los Angeles to the languid bay of San Diego nestled on the coast just north of the Mexican border.

Trainloads of Easterners and Midwesterners arrived in southern California eager to buy plots of land, to sink wells, to build houses and plant small farms. Land prices doubled, tripled, and quadrupled in the short space of a few months. County courthouses were flooded with subdivision maps as scores of newly christened towns and "cities"—some little more than gleams in the eyes of their promoters—dotted the sprawling landscape. There had been booms in southern California in the sixties and seventies, but those flurries seemed tame compared to the feverish excitement of the eighties. When a branch line of the Santa Fe railroad reached San Diego in November 1885, giving the port a valuable rail connection with the East, the little town was confident that it would share generously in the bounty of the boom.

The San Diego Peninsula—what later generations were to know as Coronado—was hardly an impressive sight in 1885. A low arm of sand and grass, washed on the south and west by the Pacific surf and on the north and east by the lapping blue waters of San Diego Bay, it divided the inland water from the open sea. At its southern end it was joined to the mainland by a tenuous thread of

Aerial view of Hotel del Coronado. The hotel and Coronado Peninsula are in the foreground; San Diego in the background. (Courtesy of Hotel del Coronado)

sand—the "Silver Strand," San Diegans called it. At its northwestern extremity the peninsula broadened to form two low knobs of land: one a mesa, carpeted with grass and chaparral and fringed with a glistening beach; the other a broad, island-like plateau that extended northward and westward like the spur of a fisherman's hook to form the low, southern shore of the entrance to San Diego Bay.

Babcock had come to San Diego for his health, but he was aware that money was to be made in the real estate boom, and he surveyed the empty peninsula longingly. When the Spanish-Californian Don Pedro Carrillo held title to the tract in the 1840s, the whole of its approximately four thousand acres was not valued at more than a thousand dollars. San Francisco lawyers Archibald

Peachy and Frederick Billings had joined with New York investor William Aspinwall to buy the property in the fifties, paying a little more than ten thousand dollars for their title.

With H. L. Story, a Chicago piano manufacturer, at his side, Babcock rowed from San Diego across the bay to the peninsula in the fall of 1885 and marched in high boots through the grass and chaparral to hunt jack rabbits and coyotes. The fresh sea air envigorated his lungs, and the southern sun, warm even in November, kindled fire in his blood. A group of San Diegans had talked of building a resort on the peninsula, but they had been unable to raise sufficient capital for the project. Babcock was intrigued by their idea, sure it would succeed if money enough to complete it could be found. Working with Story, he organized a syndicate of investors and in December 1885 completed purchase of the entire tract of 4,185 acres for the grand sum of $110,000.

At once Babcock and Story made plans to develop the peninsula. Chaparral was cleared and surveyors set out to plot the boundaries of homesites and streets. Fresh water was pumped to the site through a pipe laid on the floor of the bay, and tracks were laid for a local railroad that would meet a ferry terminal at the shore. The whole development was christened Coronado.

In Chicago the publishing firm of Rand, McNally issued a handsome, twenty-four-page prospectus for Babcock's Coronado Beach Company. The company was capitalized at one million dollars, the prospectus announced, and included three subsidiaries—the Coronado Beach and Water Company, the San Diego and Coronado Ferry Company, and the Coronado Railroad Company. "We have left nothing undone," the promoters proclaimed in their prospectus, "—preparatory to offering of Coronado beach to the esthetic [*sic*] as an Elysium, the more practical and less critical as a home, to the invalid as a sanitarium, or to the fashionable as a seaside resort of unrivalled beauty."

To spur development of the projected real estate subdivision, Babcock planned to erect a grand hotel on the ocean shore. "To a vast number of people," the prospectus continued, "the word HOTEL has a double meaning. It signifies their home as well as a place of temporary meals and lodging. . . ." Seemingly oblivious to the fact that Coronado was still a wasteland, the prospectus proceeded to describe the lavish inn that Babcock proposed to raise:

> **Inside the Hotel del Coronado, the guest is at once gratified and delighted with the perfection of all the appointments. You wonder if you are in a fairy palace or a hotel of the 19th Century. The soft Persian rugs, the Oriental tapestries, the antique design of the furniture, the luxurious baths, the odor of orange and pomegranate blossoms, all appeal to you and you join in the throng of devotees to Coronado the Lovely. . . . Close by the hotel is the lawn tennis court, and when the guests, costumed like the knights of old time appear, you might imagine yourself transplanted to the court of Louis the 14th.**

Though his hotel had been boldly announced, Babcock did not yet have the money to build it. Hoping to replenish the rapidly shrinking treasury of his Coronado Beach Company, he announced that parcels of subdivided land would be sold at auction. The first sale, held on November 13, 1886,

was a rousing success. More than six thousand people—some in skiffs, others in motor launches, most on the windy deck of Babcock's newly commissioned ferry, the *Coronado*—crossed the bay to hear the bids and watch the hammers fall. Hot air balloons hovered over the peninsula as a crew of eager salesmen spread over the sand. Prospective buyers were promised free tickets on the ferry, free water service for a year, and free passage on the projected Coronado street railway if they would sign their names to land contracts. The first parcel was sold to a San Diego attorney for $1,600. Before the day was over, the happy attorney was offered two thousand dollars for the same plot. Sales were nearly as brisk on the following days, in time aggregating between $100,000 and $400,000 a month.

In Indiana Babcock had been acquainted with James W. Reid, an architect for the railway of which he had been an officer. Writing from San Diego, the ebullient promoter informed the architect of his purchase of the San Diego Peninsula and of his plan to build a grand hotel on its western shore. At Babcock's urging, Reid and his brother Merritt, also an architect, agreed to visit San Diego and inspect the property. Boarding the Santa Fe in Evansville, they arrived in San Diego in December 1886 and were quickly whisked to the sandy peninsula. Reid noted a few newly built

Elisha Babcock (Courtesy of Hotel del Coronado)

houses at the ferry terminal and rows of tents beside the road to the hotel site, but little else that relieved the barrenness of the land.

When they arrived at a rise of ground near the ocean's edge, where the southern mesa met the northern end of the Silver Strand, Babcock planted his feet in the sand. "Right here," he said firmly. "We must build a place that people will like to come to long after we are gone. I have no time. It's all up to you."

The Reids were not eager to abandon their Midwestern homes to join a speculative venture on the coast of southern California, but their reluctance dissolved when they contemplated the grand view from the proposed hotel site. "Looking to the west was the vast and placid Pacific," James Reid recalled, "with the Coronado Islands in hazy view; on the north, the entrance to the Bay, guarded by towering Point Loma. On the east stretched the level area soon to be covered with homes; beyond that was the bay and city, and still beyond was the mesa and mountains. . . . The scenic beauty of the island and the excitement in the air put one at once in sympathy with this impatient enthusiasm. Anything seemed possible. . . ." Babcock impulsively called a stenographer to the spot and began to dictate a description of the hotel:

> It would be built around a court . . . a garden of tropical trees, shrubs, and flowers, with pleasant paths . . . balconies should look down on this court from every story. From the south end, the foyer should open to Glorietta Bay [a cove in San Diego Bay] with verandas for rest and promenade. On the ocean corner there should be a pavilion tower, and northward along the ocean, a colonnade, terraced in grass to the beach. The dining wing should project at an angle from the southeast corner of the court and be almost detached, to give full value to the view of the ocean, bay, and city.

The Reids hastened to prepare rough sketches for the building and to draw up lists of the lumber, brick, and other materials needed to build it. Work was started on a brick kiln, a planing mill, and a small iron works at the site, as James Reid hurried to San Francisco to procure the necessary timber and workmen. Square-rigged ships were loaded with mountains of redwood, fir, and pine, as well as with armies of pig-tailed Chinese workmen provided through the offices of San Francisco's Chinese Six Companies.

Back at Coronado, earth samples were taken along the ocean shore to determine the safest spot to lay the hotel foundations. Ground was broken in March 1887. Following Reid's preliminary

sketches, laborers worked feverishly around the clock, raising walls, balancing timbers, securing and leveling rafters and girders and buttresses. Though Reid's designs were only a step ahead of the workmen, his developing plan was a marvel to behold.

The main building of the hotel centered on a court or patio that stretched for 150 feet on one side and 250 on the other. Around the court was a maze of gables, balconies, galleries, stairways, verandas, loggias, arcades, and bulging bays. Most of the building stood four stories in height, but a profusion of towers and turrets, cupolas, spires, and gaping dormers, piercing the sky like the minarets of a sultan's mosque, raised the building's height in some places to five stories, in others to six or seven.

Descriptions of the structure varied as much as the wide-eyed gawkers who came out from San Diego to inspect it. Its gracefully curving towers and occasional clipped gables prompted some to describe it as a Queen Anne palace. Others, impressed by its looming turrets and tiered dormers, thought it a neo-Norman castle. Its walls and towers and stairways were built entirely of wood— seasoned Illinois oak, rough-sawn California redwood, green Oregon pine. The coal-burning fireplaces that adorned most of the bedrooms raised a forest of chimneys that blended with the maze of towers and spires to cast feathery profiles against the sky. In his puffing pre-hotel prospectus Babcock had described his inn as "Coronado the Lovely," suggesting that its elegance was suffused with an oriental splendor. Had the hotel been set down in an Arabian desert, with date palms nodding at its doors and hump-backed camels tied up to its steps, it might have passed for the pleasure dome of a wild-eyed sheikh or Aladdin's fairy palace. But it did not sit in an Arabian desert, and it was not a chieftain's manse. It was an American palace, a nineteenth-century resort, a monument, extravagant yet tangibly real to the daring of real estate promoters in southern California's "Glory Years."

The statistics of the place were impressive. There were 399 private bedrooms, most with windows that opened on the inner court as well as the outside galleries. On the ocean side the verandas were screened from the wind with long walls of glass. The combined length of the galleries, verandas, and balconies was more than two miles. Two thousand tons of rock and thirteen thousand barrels of Portland cement went into the building's foundations. The vast dining hall, the Crown

Room, was sixty-one feet wide and more than 150 feet long. Uncluttered by pillars or posts, it rose from damask-covered walls to a vaulted ceiling of golden sugar pine. At dinner more than a thousand people could be comfortably seated at its tables. The circular Grand Ballroom, ensconced at the base of a soaring tower that overlooked the ocean, was 160 feet in diameter and approximately fifty-five feet from floor to ceiling. From the hotel's main lobby guests could ascend to the upper floors in a handsome cast-iron elevator caged with gilded bars and doors.

The hotel's most dazzling attraction was its lighting system. Electricity had been used to illuminate hotels in New York and Chicago before the Coronado was built, and Henry M. Flagler had installed a vast electrical system in his Ponce de Leon Hotel in St. Augustine, Florida in 1887. But on the Pacific Coast no hotel had a system as vast as Babcock's. More than 3,500 incandescent fixtures burned in the building—square-paned lanterns, long, drooping lampions, glittering chandeliers, all tied through miles of electric wires to the hotel's own power generating plant.

Outside the building was a host of attractions. The central court and the sloping land that led down to the sea were planted with lawns and a profusion of trees and shrubs—umbrageous palms, scented oranges, flaming hibiscus. Imported ostriches paraded in a nearby compound. There was a race track and a boathouse for yachts. At the bay shore shiny rail cars met the ferry to transport visitors to the hotel entrance.

Workmen were still on the site in February 1888 when the Coronado's doors opened to the public. The first guest to sign the register was Nelson Morris, a millionaire cattleman, who settled down with his family and servants in a sumptuous suite of nine rooms. Morris was followed by Don A. Sweet, assistant to the vice president of the Santa Fe Railroad, who put up in a handsome suite nearby.

Within weeks the hotel was crowded with celebrated guests from all over the country. Eagerly, reporters for San Diego newspapers reported the arrival of merchant princes Marshall Field and Montgomery Ward, industrialists Harvey Firestone and John Studebaker, meat packer Philip Armour, the "floury" Pillsburys and the "yeasty" Fleischmanns.

Mark Twain's sometime literary collaborator, the novelist and essayist Charles Dudley Warner, visited Coronado while the walls of the hotel were rising and later when the concourse in front of the

Artist's rendering of Hotel del Coronado, 1890 (Harper's New Monthly Magazine, *December 1890*)

main entrance was crowded with the carriages of arriving millionaires. Writing in *Harper's New Monthly Magazine*, Warner praised the caravansary and its long beach as a "marvellous scene of natural and created beauty." "Taking it and its situation together," he continued, "I know of nothing else in the world with which to compare it. . . . If this great house were filled with guests, so spacious are its lounging places I should think it would never appear to be crowded; and if it were nearly empty, so admirably are the rooms contrived for family life it will not seem lonesome."

Estimates of the Coronado's cost varied widely. An 1887 issue of *San Diego Illustrated* set the cost of the building at $600,000, that of the furnishings at

Luxuriously furnished private suite at Hotel del Coronado (Courtesy of Hotel del Coronado)

another $400,000. The out-buildings and landscaping, yacht club and race track, ferry line and railroad undoubtedly pushed the final bill well above the published figures.

The boom which gave birth to the hotel had been expected to pay for it, but even before the palace was finished there were signs of trouble. The Santa Fe trains which pulled up to the station in San Diego were no longer crowded with hordes of Easterners and Midwesterners. Prices of local real estate plummeted, and a deathly quiet fell over the land sales office at Coronado. The bubble had risen grandly, and it burst as dramatically. By the middle of 1888, even as workmen were putting the final touches on the hotel, the "Glory Years" of the boom passed quietly into history.

Desperate, Babcock sought financial assistance. H. L. Story contributed to the hotel's coffers, as did Jacob Gruendike and the Hoosier businessmen Josephus Collett, Heber Ingle, and John Inglehart. Though substantial, their contributions were not enough to keep the huge hotel afloat. Seeking more capital, Babcock approached a young San Franciscan named John D. Spreckels. Son of the millionaire sugar manufacturer and shipper Claus Spreckels, John had visited San Diego on his sleek yacht *Venetia* in 1887. Sensing opportunity in the

town, he began to invest in local businesses—water works, banks, a wharf, street railways.

Spreckels was impressed by the grandeur of the hotel on the beach. In 1887 he bought Story's one-third interest in the property and, as need arose, made loans to Babcock to help keep it open. When payments on his loans fell into arrears, Spreckels began foreclosure proceedings. By 1894 title to Coronado—the hotel, the railroad, the ferry, and all the surrounding land—had passed into the San Franciscan's hands. Babcock remained in the hotel as manager.

Under its new ownership the Coronado commenced a program of improvements. A polo field was laid out, tennis courts leveled and paved, a Japanese Tea Garden plotted and planted, and a curving breakwater built along the ocean shore. Lured by advertising, celebrities in increasing numbers visited the hotel. Notable among the early visitors were the "Divine" Sarah Bernhardt who, resplendent in flowing robes and long, silken tresses, gasped with arms aflutter at the lofty ceilings and soaring stairways as she swept through the lobby; the bearded President Benjamin Harrison who, stern and proper in silk hat and morning coat, paused on the high veranda to fill his lungs with the bracing sea air and admire the crashing surf; President William McKinley who, bundled in a great-coat and surrounded by guards and secretaries, threaded the Silver Strand in a bumping coach and four; Thomas Edison, who inspected the power plant and network of incandescent lamps that illuminated the hotel; daredevil Glenn Curtiss, the pioneer airplane pilot who in 1911 flew the first seaplane from a grassy field on North Island, the upper half of Spreckels' Coronado domain.

Hollywood film stars were frequent guests after 1918: John Barrymore, hair tousled, eyes gleaming wildly as he soliloquized grandly from a patio balcony; Mary Pickford, smiling demurely from beneath cascades of golden curls; Charlie Chaplin, swimming happily in the surf; cowboy star Tom Mix, lounging on a sun-splashed veranda. Ramon Novarro and Anita Page were at Coronado in the twenties to film their silent melodrama, *The Flying Fleet*, the first of dozens of Hollywood epics to be

shot in and around the fairy palace.

In 1904 Elisha Babcock left Coronado, to be succeeded as manager by John J. Herman. In 1918 Spreckels sold the North Island half of his Coronado holdings to the federal government for the tidy sum of five million dollars. Without delay the Navy dispatched Lieutenant Earl Winfield Spencer, Jr. to North Island to organize a new Naval Air Station on the land. While awaiting construction of the commander's quarters on the base, Spencer and his wife, formerly Wallis Warfield, occupied a two-room suite at the Coronado.

In 1920 the hotel was visited by the shy but romantic Prince of Wales. David Windsor, as the prince was sometimes known, was twenty-six years old and the first member of Britain's royal family to visit California when he attended a grand banquet and ball at the Coronado in April 1920. More than a thousand guests were on hand to

The Crown Room, Hotel del Coronado's vast dining hall (Courtesy of Hotel del Coronado)

The Coronado's spacious central court (Courtesy of Hotel del Coronado)

greet the prince, handsome in black tie and striped trousers. Among the assembled guests were Lieutenant Spencer and his dark-haired wife. Mrs. Spencer admired the prince from afar, but she did not meet him at Coronado. Her fateful encounter with the heir to the British throne did not take place until 1930, when she was Mrs. Ernest Simpson and he thirty-six years old and still unmarried. The prince's equally fateful decision to renounce his glittering titles—King of Great Britain and Ireland, Emperor of India and the British Dominions Beyond the Seas—for the love of Wallis Simpson was not made until 1936. By then he and the Mrs. Winfield Spencer of Coronado had won a secure place in the roster of the world's great lovers, enshrined in legend as memorably as Heloise and Abelard, Romeo and Juliet, Rudolph of Hapsburg and the Baroness Marie Vetsera.

Though it was noted as a rendezvous of the chic

and fashionable, Coronado was also a popular resort for young families of modest means. On weekends and during summers, mothers and fathers, troops of children following behind them, came from throughout southern California to assemble before the cottages of Tent City, south of the hotel building. Opened in 1902, Tent City embraced long rows of canvas-covered tents, thatched huts, restaurants, a library, and a dance pavilion. From a stage in front of a music shell a military band, resplendent in visored caps and gold-trimmed coats, regaled visitors with Sousa marches, Viennese waltzes, and the latest strains of Victor Herbert's operettas.

John Spreckels died in 1926, but the great Coronado lived on after him. In 1948 the Spreckels heirs parted with the inn, which passed through the hands of Barney Goodman and John Alessio before M. Larry Lawrence and his Hotel del

Coronado Corporation acquired it in 1963.

In the decades since Elisha Babcock and H. L. Story first marched through the grass and chaparral of the Coronado Peninsula in search of rabbits and coyotes, San Diego had changed mightily. Gone was the seaside village of the 1880s. In its place stood a throbbing metropolis, a skyscraper-studded, freeway-veined industrial and commercial center of three-quarters of a million people. The transformation from village to metropolis had been more spectacular than any metamorphosis the real estate boomers of the "Glory Years" could have hoped for. As San Diego grew, the long Coronado Peninsula also changed dramatically. The grass and chaparral were gone, replaced by rows of homes and stores and the sprawling complex of the Naval Air Station organized by Lieutenant Spencer in 1918. Ferries no longer transported passengers from the city to the bayside depot of the Coronado Street Railway. A sleek bridge of concrete and steel now soared over the bay and onto the sandy peninsula within easy sight of the hotel towers and spires.

There had been changes, too, at Hotel del Coronado. A new convention facility, Grande Hall, and a two-hundred-room hotel addition, Ocean Towers, opened in 1973. A Prince of Wales Grill adorned the main building, as did five new conference rooms—the Hanover, Tudor, Stuart, York, and Kent. But the changes did little to mar the Victorian splendor of the place. Under Lawrence's leadership, the building was redecorated in period style. Painters were employed full time to keep its maze of towers and verandas sparkling and fresh. A museum of hotel history was maintained in the building, and tours regularly conducted. In recognition of its historical significance, the Coronado was in 1970 named a California State Historical Landmark. A year later, it was listed in the National Register of Historic Places. In October 1977 the National Park Service elevated the hotel to the status of a National Historical Landmark. In dedication ceremonies held in the hotel's Garden Patio, a plaque was unveiled commemorating the designation and proclaiming that the building

John D. Spreckels (Courtesy of Hotel del Coronado)

"possesses national significance in commemorating the history of the United States of America."

Tour guides at Coronado boast that the old hotel is the largest wooden Victorian building in the United States. If it is not the largest, it is surely the most spectacular—an Aladdin's palace set down on a strand of Pacific sand, an improbable fairy tale castle of wood and glass, a building that should never have been, but was, and is, and—in a drab and uncertain future—will continue to be a monument to the splendor and extravagance of the "Glory Years."

9

A Mile High Legend

THE BROWN PALACE, DENVER

The Brown Palace in Denver is not America's oldest historic hotel, nor is it the largest. It is not the most opulent of the country's great caravansaries, nor its most storied. The history of the Brown is less spectacular than that of San Francisco's Palace, less glamorous than that of Pebble Beach's Del Monte Lodge, less venerable than that of Boston's Parker House. But there is a quality to the Brown and its history that exists in no other American hotel—a character that marks it apart and sets it above all the others.

It is a Western House in the tradition of the mountain men and buffalo hunters who swarmed over the plains and climbed the forbidding peaks of the Rockies in the second half of the nineteenth century. In its heyday it was as ready for adventure as the long rifles of George Armstrong Custer's Seventh Cavalry, as nobly stoic as the Cheyenne Indians who sometimes camped on its doorstep, as boldly theatrical as Colonel William F. Cody, who liked to plan tours of his Wild West Show from a suite in the hotel. The Brown is more than a great Western inn, more than a lingering reminder of the Rocky Mountains' hell-bent-for-leather mining days. It is a stage on which a chapter in American history has been played and perpetually replayed in fact and fanciful legend, a chapter in the national epic that will continue to fascinate the country and the world as long as "good guys" and "bad guys" shoot 'em up in Western movies and little boys play cowboys and Indians on crowded streets—which is to say that it will probably last forever.

The Brown Palace opened its doors in 1892, two years after the American frontier—that indefinable line that separated the settled from the unsettled portions of the country—had, according to records of the United States Census Bureau, ceased to exist. The hotel was not witness to the opening of the West, but it was witness to its closing, an event in many ways more dramatic, more flamboyant and spectacular than any other part of the epic. Denver was a thriving city of more than one hundred thousand people in 1892, no mere mountain boom town. A maze of rail lines and interchanges clogged its western and eastern approaches: the writhing tentacles of the Fort Worth & Denver City, the Rock Island, the Colorado & Southern, the Denver & Rio Grande, and the Union Pacific. Substantial buildings of brick and stone thrust their roofs above the huddled mass of wooden houses and stores, remnants of the city's salad days as a gold camp and mountain trading center. There was a Grand Opera House and a sumptuous hotel, one of the most elegant in the country, to proclaim Denver's emergence as a social and cultural center of aspiration if not yet solid achievement.

The history of Denver's hotels was as long and nearly as colorful as that of the city itself. The first house of hospitality was, appropriately, a saloon, inaccurately named the Hotel de Dunk, which opened its doors in 1858, a year and a half before Denver City was incorporated. Early the following year the log-and-mud Eldorado Hotel opened

Denver's Brown Palace Hotel (Courtesy of the State Historical Society of Colorado Library)

under the aegis of the self-styled "Count" Murat, a barkeep and occasional barber, and his partner, a certain Smoke. When Horace Greeley arrived in the town in the summer of 1859, the Denver House, more generally known as the Elephant Corral, was in full operation, its guests clinking glasses around the clock to the accompaniment of a screechy orchestra.

Greeley was impressed by Denver, but not favorably. He had come to deliver a lecture on intemperance and must have despaired of his purpose when he sauntered through the barroom of the Elephant House and out onto the noisy streets. In a letter to his newspaper readers the Eastern visitor said that he found "more brawls, more pistol shots with criminal intent in this log city of 150 dwellings, not three-fourths of them completed, nor two-thirds of them inhabited, nor one-third fit to be, than in any community of equal numbers on earth."

When the mining magnate H. A. W. Tabor opened the Tabor Grand Opera House in 1881 (he had earlier built a similar theater in Leadville), all of Denver turned out for the event. Noted for its lavish decorations, its large stage, and its great curtain emblazoned with a scene of an ancient Roman city falling to ruin, the Tabor was host to all the grand theatrical personages of the day—Lily Langtry, Richard Mansfield, Helena Modjeska, Sarah Bernhardt, and young Minnie Maddern, later the celebrated Mrs. Fiske.

The Windsor Hotel, which opened about the same time as the opera house, was built by British capitalists, but it was leased by Tabor and managed by him and his energetic partner, William H. Bush. Bill Bush was a minor but indispensable player in the Colorado epic. In 1871 he had been hired by Henry Teller, later United States Senator, to manage his Teller House hotel in booming Central City, some fifty miles west of Denver. At the Teller House Bush had extended lavish hospitality to visiting dignitaries, twice hosting banquets for Ulysses S. Grant, and had earned for himself a reputation as a man of ability and substance. In 1879 he moved to Colorado's newest boom town, Leadville, south of Central City, where he operated the Clarendon Hotel. Next door stood the house of H.A.W. Tabor. Bush and Tabor became friends and close business associates and, when Tabor moved to Denver and opened his Grand Opera House and Windsor Hotel, Bush was installed as manager of both properties.

The Windsor was a palace of sorts, with a sixty-foot mahogany bar, a grand banquet room, and a

ladies' "ordinary" where respectable women were encouraged to eat in public. It also boasted a complement of Russian and Turkish baths. "These oriental ablutionary parlors," the hotel advertised, "are elegantly fitted up and handsomely furnished with white marble." To Bush belongs the credit (or blame) for introducing Tabor to a divorcée from Central City, Elizabeth "Baby" Doe, who became the magnate's mistress and in 1883 his wife. "Baby" Doe's first postnuptial act was to precipitate a quarrel and lawsuit between Tabor and Bush that resulted in a bitter estrangement between the men. By then Bush had acquired a controlling interest in the Windsor and could not be forced out. He employed the millionaire's son Maxcy as his assistant and began to look about for his own opportunities in Denver.

Henry C. Brown, the Ohio-born carpenter whose name was to be applied to Denver's greatest inn, was an unlikely candidate for hotel immortality. Seventy-two years old in 1892, he had arrived in Denver three decades before and set

Henry C. Brown (Courtesy of the State Historical Society of Colorado Library)

up a carpenter's shop on the banks of Cherry Creek. In the sixties he had homesteaded 160 acres east of the center of town, paid the nominal sum of $2.50 an acre for his land, and built a little frame house with his own hands to perfect his claim. Normally mild-mannered, the carpenter rose to heroic stature when he met a marauder intent on ousting him from the property at the doorstep of his house. Standing at the door with a finely honed hatchet in his hand, Brown threatened to cut off the intruder's legs if he did not get off his land.

As Denver grew out from its infant center, Brown's domain became more and more valuable. To assure that the city would remain the political as well as the economic center of Colorado, the carpenter gave the territorial government ten acres of land as the site for a capitol building. He had prospered enough by 1867 that he was able to build a stylish brick building to house his own bank and the offices of his *Denver Tribune*. By 1890 most of Brown's homestead land had been crossed by streets and a sprinkling of new buildings, and he was reckoned as one of Denver's wealthiest men. He had retained at least one piece of his pioneer homestead, a triangular slice of sand and grass at the corner of Seventeenth and Broadway. The lot was known to Denverites as the "cow pasture," from Brown's practice of milking a brindle cow on the property, a habit he continued years after his 160 acres had made him a millionaire.

The idea of building a hotel on Brown's cow pasture was originally Bill Bush's. Denver's center of fashion and commerce was moving south and east of Larimer Street in the late eighties, and the Windsor was already suffering from a perceptible decline in patronage. Bush took a lease from Brown on the pasture property and, with the English investor James Duff as his partner, made plans for a great new hotel. A massive basement was excavated, and foundations of granite and Portland cement were laid. Then the flow of English capital halted, and work on the hotel ground to a stop. In the spring, water flowed down from the nearby hills and filled the foundations to overflowing. In winter, the pond froze over, affording school children a handy skating rink. Bush called on Henry Brown for financial assistance, and the carpenter advanced a large sum to revive construction. Work progressed on the first three floors, then again ground to a halt. Exasperated, Brown took personal charge of the project, determined to see it to completion.

Frank E. Edbrooke, the hotel's architect, was as determined as Brown to erect a worthy palace, and his plans for the new building were nothing short of spectacular. Reams of paper weighing, in the aggregate, nearly two tons, were covered with masses of diagrams and drawings. With Edbrooke supervising the workmen, the hotel began to rise above its unfinished lower walls, a massive pile of columns, arches, and looming windows.

From its cavernous basement to its roof nine stories above the surface of Broadway, the hotel was supported by a skeleton of steel beams. Outside, the first story was faced with pink Platte Canyon granite; those above it with Arizona brownstone. A series of arches on the seventh floor measured twelve feet between piers, and a carved cornice three feet high completely enclosed the triangular structure. Bays, supported by cantilever beams, shaded the main entrance, which was spanned with elliptical arches. Inside, tile-covered columns rose from a spacious lobby through tier upon tier of wrought-iron balconies. At the top was a soaring canopy of stained glass. The court was dominated by two columns of Mexican onyx. Quarried in Coahuila especially for the new hotel, the columns weighed a ton and a half each and, between them, supported a fourteen-foot-high mantel. A forest of potted palms crowded the lobby. Water was supplied to the building by two artesian wells, sunk on the site to a depth of seven hundred feet.

Statistically, the hotel was impressive. It had six hydraulic elevators, four boilers, 90,000 feet of electrical wire, 4,200 incandescent lamps, seven ventilating fans, a large steam laundry, an ice manufacturing plant, 318 guest rooms, 160 tile mantels, 75,000 tons of ornamental iron, and 142 bath and toilet rooms that contained thirteen carloads of plumbing fixtures. The building would have distinguished New York's Fifth Avenue. In Denver, it was nothing less than a wonder.

Published figures estimated the cost of the hotel at $1,500,000. Bill Bush and Maxcy Tabor, who managed it, were reported to have invested another half million in its furnishings. But the cost of piles like this one has a way of eluding precise computation, and the total investment may well have exceeded two million dollars. If the thrifty Brown doubted the wisdom of his decision to bankroll the building, he could not have been displeased by the fruits of his lavish expenditure. The H.C. Brown Palace, as the hotel was officially named, seemed eminently capable of fulfilling its owner's proud boast that it would "last a thousand years." From its roof a vast panorama spread out

The lobby, Brown Palace Hotel (Courtesy of the Denver Public Library, Western History Department)

before the millionaire carpenter's eyes—south across undulant hills to the new resort city of Colorado Springs, westward to the ramparts of the Rockies, eastward across broad plains nearly to the edge of Kansas.

Workmen were still in evidence when the hotel opened for business in August 1892 with a banquet for three hundred members of the Grand Order of Knights Templar. Visitors streaming into Denver for the event clogged Union Station with a profusion of polished carriages and lurching, horse-drawn cabs. A second, more elaborate opening took place on January 28, 1893, with a grand banquet and ball. The ladies' parlor and grand salon were embowered for the occasion with flowers and ferns. Mrs. Maxcy Tabor received in a gown of white satin trimmed in Point Duchesse lace and decorated with knots of violets. At midnight, according to a reporter for the *Denver Republican*, guests sat down to a "bountiful collation" of Prague ham, Strasbourg foie gras, and Volga sturgeon eggs, served with more domestic but equally palatable products from Bush's 480-acre Windsor Farm. Mumm's Extra Dry was the wine of the evening, but claret in abundance was available for those whose appetites favored moderation.

Brown took a handsome suite in the new hotel, where he spent much of his time lolling on one of the balconies above the central court. When he contemplated the enormity of his financial undertaking, he was a little uneasy, but he did not begin to worry seriously until the latter part of 1893, when economic conditions took a sudden turn for the worse and a silver panic severely depressed Colorado's mining economy. To make ends meet, Brown took a $650,000 mortgage on the hotel, confident he would be able to pay the principle and interest when the price of silver rose and his investments improved. But the recovery did not come as hoped, and the millionaire fell more deeply into debt. Soon his mortgages totaled an alarming eight hundred thousand dollars. When Bill Bush died in 1898, Maxcy Tabor took stern measures to balance the hotel's shaky accounts. He ejected Bill's brother James and joined with the U.S. Mortgage Company in an effort to foreclose on Brown's mortagages. The old carpenter appealed to Winfield Scott Stratton of Colorado Springs, who had made millions on Pike's Peak. Stratton assumed the two mortgages, paid up the delinquent principal and interest, and permitted Brown to stay on in the hotel until his death in 1906.

Despite its financial difficulties, the hotel was a

Maxcy Tabor as a youth. Photographed in Augusta, Maine. (Courtesy of the State Historical Society of Colorado Library)

resounding social success. Leaders of business and finance made it a regular stop on their frequent continental crossings, pausing in the hotel bar long enough to reflect on the fact that their polished boots, when perched on the long brass rail, rested

Colonel William F. Cody, better known as "Buffalo Bill," circa 1897 (Courtesy of the State Historical Society of Colorado Library)

nearly half-way between the Atlantic and Pacific coasts. The realization invariably prompted them to raise an extra glass or two in celebration of the geographical nicety.

Titans of the dramatic and musical stage were welcome visitors at the Brown: Lillian Russell, the Barrymores—John, Lionel, and Ethel—Amelita

Galli-Curci, Ernestine Schumann-Heink. Colonel William F. Cody, silver-bearded captain of "Buffalo Bill's Wild West Show and Congress of Rough Riders," planned transcontinental tours of his road show from a suite at the Brown. Diva Mary Garden, after singing in Denver one night, returned to her room at the Brown to discover that a fourteen-thousand-dollar diamond brooch was missing. The police were summoned, and an all-night search for the missing bauble ensued, but it could not be found. Late the following night John Barry, the Brown's head porter, was putting a departing traveler into a cab when he glanced down at the curb and spotted the missing brooch. Mary Garden was delighted to recover her missing jewels, and John Barry was pleased to pocket his hundred-dollar reward.

Politicians found the Brown as much to their liking as the actors and musicians. William Jennings Bryan, whom John Barry remembered as a "friendly cowboy," was campaigning for the presidency (as usual) when he bedded down at the Brown. Theodore Roosevelt held the office Bryan hankered after when the Rough Riding Colonel arrived at Denver's Union Station in 1905 and paraded up Seventeenth Street to the doors of the Brown Palace. Setting up in the Presidential Suite on the eighth floor, Roosevelt set a precedent for succeeding chief executives, who found the Denver hostelry as much to their liking as did T.R. Woodrow Wilson spent the night of September 25, 1919, in the Brown in the midst of a speaking tour to advocate American membership in the League of Nations. Warren G. Harding arrived in June 1923, but canceled a banquet in his honor when a reporter covering his tour was killed in an automobile accident in nearby Bear Creek Canyon.

Among socialites the Brown was a perennial favorite. The pleasure-loving Evalyn Walsh McLean maintained an apartment in the hotel in the years 1906 to 1908. Born in Denver, the daughter of an Irish-born woodmaker and sometime miner named Tom Walsh, Evalyn had been raised in the gold town of Ouray in the southwest corner of Colorado. One day when she was ten years old, her father returned from his Gertrude mining claim with fire in his eyes. "Daughter," he announced excitedly, "we've struck it rich." Evalyn Walsh was one of the United States' richest women when she married Edward McLean, heir to the *Washington Post* and *Cincinnati Enquirer* newspaper publishing empire—and one of the world's richest women when she bought the legendary Hope Diamond from Pierre Cartier. Weighing forty-four and a half carats, the Hope had a reputation for giving its owners bad luck, but Evalyn was not daunted by the fact. "Bad-luck objects are lucky for me," she told Cartier. The lovely blue stone was surrounded by a host of lesser diamonds. The jeweler's asking price, $154,000, was well within Mrs. McLean's budget, and in 1911 she became the diamond's mistress.

A more frequent and less elegant guest of the Brown was the delightfully preposterous Margaret Tobin Brown. Like Evalyn Walsh, Maggie Brown was the daughter of an Irish laborer, a ditch digger in Hannibal, Missouri. She was seventeen years old when she went to Leadville, Colorado in 1884 and nineteen when she married James J. Brown, manager of one of the local mines. Brown made about two million dollars after gold was discovered in Leadville's Little Jonny (*sic*) mine in 1896, but Maggie Brown behaved as if her husband's fortune were at least two hundred times that amount. She set herself up in an ornate house in Denver, a cottage in Newport, Rhode Island, and apartments in New York and Paris. Out of earshot of the Denverites who knew better, she claimed she was the wife of "Leadville Johnny," owner of the mine in which her husband had been employed. When she tired of this charade, she dropped hints that she was the wife of the owner of Denver's Brown Palace. Mrs. Brown's penchant for wrapping her shoulders in expensive furs, even in warm weather, prompted Denverites to call her "Colorado's unique fur-bearing animal."

After 1912, when she heroically helped several dozen fellow passengers scramble to safety from the sinking ocean liner *Titanic*, she was referred to in the press as "The Unsinkable Mrs. Brown." When her Denver town house was rented out, Mrs. Brown liked to put up in the Brown Palace, where she paraded through the corridors singing off tune and brandishing a swagger stick. An irrepressible social climber, she longed to be accepted by polite society and made several unsuccessful attempts to change her first name from the plebeian Maggie to the more aristocratic (she thought) Molly. A generation after her death in 1932, the change was finally effected, when Broadway audiences and later movie fans around the world sat down to enjoy the hit musical, "The Unsinkable Molly Brown."

All was not comfort and elegance even in boom-time Colorado, as a few of the state's millionaires sometimes paused to reflect. For every rags-to-riches story, there were a dozen tales of poignant disappointment. For every "Unsinkable"

Maggie Brown, there were scores of women who toiled over washboards in chinked mountain cabins while their husbands searched indefatigably and unsuccessfully for the elusive "big strike." For every Evalyn Walsh McLean there were hundreds of urchins prowling the slanting streets of Central City, Leadville, Ouray, and Cripple Creek, hungering for scraps of bread, begging for discarded shoes with which to warm their freezing feet.

Bon vivants and big spenders were aghast in 1901 when Simon Guggenheim, whose father

Margaret Tobin Brown, "The Unsinkable Molly Brown" of Broadway (Courtesy of the State Historical Society of Colorado Library)

Meyer had made millions in Leadville copper, financed a Thanksgiving dinner for a group of indigent children. Parson Tom Uzzel hosted the feast, which drew the astonishing number of 1,500 waifs from Denver's streets into the Brown. They assembled in the dining room like wide-eyed gnomes, staring in disbelief at the slabs of marble and polished onyx that towered above them. There was wealth in abundance in the mountains of Colorado, but it was clear that not all Coloradans shared in the wealth.

Though it was conceived at the lingering end of the era of cowboys and Indians, territorial marshals and frontier desperados, the aura of six-guns and shoot-outs hung over the Brown long after it had disappeared from other less elegant surroundings. As late as May 1911 the hotel bar was the scene of one of the most celebrated exchanges of hot lead in Denver's history. The participants in the melodrama were wine agent and bedroom adventurer Louis Von Phul and Harold Frank Henwood, Von Phul's rival for the affections of Isabelle Patterson Springer, the wife of a banker and rancher. For some time before the crisis Mrs. Springer had maintained a home in Denver, a country estate, and a suite on the sixth floor of the Brown that she used for amatory adventures.

On the evening of May 24 the Springers were guests of Henwood in his box at Denver's Orpheum Theatre, where they watched a vaudeville show. Von Phul went to the Broadway Theatre to see Fanny Brice, Bert Williams, and "75 Anna Held Girls" in a performance of the "Follies." After the show Henwood saw the Springers to their Brown suite, then joined a group of twenty or so other men for a nightcap in the hotel bar. When Von Phul entered the bar, he strode over to his rival, stuck his finger in his glass, and knocked him down. Lying on the floor, blood streaming from his mouth, Henwood fumbled inside his coat. Withdrawing a revolver, he proceeded to empty it in Von Phul's direction. Three shots struck the wine merchant. A fourth hit an attorney from Colorado Springs and a fifth a sampling works owner from Victor. Von Phul and the man from Victor died in the hospital. Henwood's trial was predictably sensational, producing scandalous bits of gossip that were liberally sprinkled across the front pages of newspapers. The defendant was convicted and sentenced to life in prison. The Springers were divorced, and the old bar was eventually converted into a dining room.

Despite the closing of the bar, old-time adventure continued to stalk the Brown. The journalist and bon vivant Lucius Beebe was in the hotel's Ship Bar in September 1946 when Ronald Smith, a veteran of World War II, interrupted the cocktail hour with an unseemly display of gun-shooting skill (or lack of it). Firing wildly, Smith shot a medical student and wounded a college president and an advertising man who had, until the interruption, been nursing a brace of dry martinis. In the ensuing scramble glasses and furniture were smashed with abandon. Beebe "doubted that the management would applaud more frequent powder burnings among the patrons," but added: "There is no denying that the Brown derives a certain cachet of rich disorder from the assassinations. They establish a continuity with the Old West which is getting to be a commodity in great requisition."

Management of the Brown passed through several hands after Maxcy Tabor lost control, finally coming under the aegis of Denver sugar and cement millionaire Charles Boettcher and his son Claude. Claude Boettcher's second wife, the former Edna McElveen, was the reigning queen of Denver society in the 1920s and 1930s, and the Brown was in all respects a worthy setting for her fashionable court.

A more genuine, if less lustrous, representative of royalty was entertained in the hotel in 1926. Queen Marie of Rumania arrived in Denver in a private railroad car and traversed the lobby of the Brown on a red carpet laid beneath a specially constructed canopy. Less glamorous but more important visitors were Presidents Herbert Hoover and Franklin D. Roosevelt; the latter held political receptions in the hotel in 1932 and 1936.

Roosevelt's rise to political power owed much to the ravages of the Great Depression, an economic crisis that struck Denver as severely as other American cities but was little noticed by regulars of the Brown. Evalyn Walsh McLean's first return to Colorado in more than thirty years took place toward the end of the Depression. One Sunday at noon the grand dame summoned Lucius Beebe to her suite in the hotel. The journalist later recalled that Mrs. McLean was "waving the Hope diamond on its necklace like a yo-yo" when she explained the purpose of her summons. "I want a dinner for 100 here in this hotel this evening," she said. "Full dress. Get everybody, hire some bands, caviar and champagne, three or four wines, lots of flowers. You know. Lots of the best and all my old friends." To arrange a state dinner for one hundred persons, starting from scratch on a Sunday afternoon, was a formidable task, but not beyond the staff of the

A show of Arabian horses in the Brown Palace's main lobby, November 1970 (Courtesy of the Denver Public Library, Western History Department)

Brown Palace, who were used to filling extravagant demands. They set about the task in earnest and, by eight o'clock, an even one hundred diners sat down at a great horseshoe table in the hotel's banquet room. Men in tails and women in tiaras enjoyed quail in aspic, fresh beluga, lobster thermidor, and *faisan en cocotte Perigordino*. The wine was Bollinger's, the dessert fresh wood strawberries and *crème d'isigny*. A major-domo in knee breeches with a white wand and a corps of liveried footmen in frogged coats stood nearby as two bands played from an orchid-covered gazebo.

Mrs. Eleanor Roosevelt entertained more simply when she visited the Brown, as did Miss Margaret Truman, who received guests informally when she visited the hotel in the late forties. The Democratic women were greeted cordially, but not warmly, by the Brown and its staff, for the hotel was a bastion of privilege and a more congenial center of Republican rather than Democratic party intrigue. Dwight D. Eisenhower and his wife, formerly Mamie Doud of Denver, were warmly welcomed when they arrived at the Brown in 1952 to open the general's national presidential campaign headquarters. After the election the Brown became one of President Eisenhower's favorite vacation retreats.

There were changes in the wind at the Brown in the 1950s and 1960s. In 1959 the owners completed the Brown Palace Tower, a structure of twenty-two stories, across Tremont Street from the original building and connected with it. The Emerald

Room and Coffee House were converted into the San Marco Room, where two bronze horses, modeled after the steeds atop St. Mark's Cathedral in Venice, were displayed. The Prospector Suite and the Brown Palace Club were opened in 1962 and 1963.

But, for all the changes, the hotel remained remarkably faithful to the tradition of its builders. It was still a bastion of privilege, still frequented by men in tall boots and broad-brimmed hats and women with diamond brooches, still the scene of full-dress banquets and balls, still occasionally adorned with red carpet and specially built canopies. Carpenter Henry Brown thought the hotel would last a thousand years. In this age of perpetual change, when all that men create seems fragile and transient, the boast may be regarded with suspicion. But the dream it represents is credible. The granite and marble and onyx will fall before the millennium, but the spirit of the place—like the flame of the Old West—will certainly survive the destruction.

A Riviera in the Rockies

THE BROADMOOR, COLORADO SPRINGS

Colorado Springs, Colorado is one of America's most strikingly beautiful cities, a handsome community of tree-lined streets and wooded parks set at the edge of a spreading plain more than six thousand feet above sea level. To travelers, the city and its environs offer many attractions: the weirdly twisted sandstone formations of the nearby Garden of the Gods; the snake-like highway that scales the steep face of nearby Pike's Peak; the campuses of Colorado College, the University of Colorado, and the United States Air Force Academy. But the town is also noted as the home of one of America's great palace inns—a sprawling complex of buildings clustered around a lake in the shadow of wooded mountains south of the town. The Broadmoor Hotel was built in the early years of the twentieth century, but the history of the site and of the men who planned and executed the hotel is more venerable, nearly as old as that of Colorado Springs and, for students of the American epic, as fascinating.

Two things lured settlers to Colorado Springs in the last decades of the nineteenth century: the clear mountain air of the Rockies, and the promise of easy wealth from the gold and silver mines that abounded in the area. They came from all parts of the East and Midwest—refugees from the soot-clogged streets of Chicago and New York, from marshlands of the tidewater South, from bottom lands along meandering rivers in the Ohio and Mississippi valleys—men and women and children united in a single quest for health and wealth.

Founded in 1871 by Civil War hero and railroad promoter General William Jackson Palmer, Colorado Springs gained fame as a health resort after an English physician, Dr. Edwin Solly, took up residence there in the 1870s. Suffering from a mild case of consumption, Solly experienced a remarkable recovery in the dry mountain air of Colorado Springs. With another doctor, Virginia-born Boswell P. Anderson, Solly set out to publicize the town's remarkable restorative powers. He and Anderson were enterprising men, and their efforts to establish a health resort at Colorado Springs soon produced results. From all over the United States victims of consumption trekked across the western Great Plains to the Colorado town. Solly's and Anderson's practices flourished, as did the sanatoriums they established for the care and treatment of patients. Colorado Springs, in turn, was transformed from a tiny huddle of stores and houses into a prosperous community of banks, schools, and tree-lined avenues.

But the promise of health was not the only honey that lured settlers to the springs. From the 1850s onward there had been mineral strikes on the high plateau and in the nearby mountains—lodes of silver and lead and occasional pockets of gold. Towns had appeared overnight on precipitous mountain slopes, only to disappear as soon as the ore that gave them life was exhausted. But sourdough prospectors stayed on in the mountains to comb secluded valleys and canyons in search of telltale specks of silver or gold, traces of

The Broadmoor, Colorado Springs. Maxfield Parrish completed this idealized panorama in 1921. (Courtesy of the Broadmoor)

mineral wealth that would signal the start of yet another rush. One of the biggest and most lucrative discoveries ever made in the Colorado mountains was that uncovered in the fall of 1890 by an itinerant herdsman and part-time prospector named Bob Womack. Womack's discovery was in high pasturage around Cripple Creek on the southwestern slope of Pike's Peak, about eighteen miles from Colorado Springs.

Womack celebrated his find in typical frontier fashion with a night of riotous drinking and carousing in Colorado Springs. He awoke the next morning in jail insisting he had made a "big strike" in the mountains and waving a hefty bag of gold dust to prove his claim. Old mining hands were skeptical. There had been many strikes on Pike's

Peak, and the chance that any substantial lode of gold remained undiscovered was slight. Doubts about the discovery continued well into the following year, when a picturesque Prussian count appeared in Cripple Creek and offered to pay eighty thousand dollars for a single claim. Overnight the skepticism vanished, and a new gold rush was on.

By 1891 the count, one James Pourtales, was a familiar figure on the high plateau. A handsome man with a trim beard and pointed mustache, Pourtales had come to Colorado in 1884 from his native Silesia. Seeking profitable investments in the area, he purchased a half interest in a tract of land south of Colorado Springs, 1,600 acres then operated as a dairy. The count's partner, William Wilcox, lived in a rambling house on the property, which he called Broadmoor. The dairy was a modest enterprise, but Pourtales was taken with the beauty of the land—a wide plateau that rose out of the plain surrounding Colorado Springs and commanded sweeping views of the town and Pike's Peak. Behind the plateau lay Cheyenne Mountain, a mass of blue and purple shadow that was gnarled with rocks and mantled with forests of pine and cedar. Rivulets bubbled down from the mountain to water fields of wild flowers that spangled the plain with brilliant colors.

Though he returned at intervals to his Prussian home, Pourtales spent much of his time at Broadmoor supervising workmen, breeding cattle, building barns, irrigating oats and alfalfa. The dairy was a thriving business, but not grand enough to suit the ambitious count. With its vistas of mountain and meadow and its nearness to Colorado Springs (the center of town was only five miles away), the property seemed an ideal site for a more extensive development. Colorado Springs was expanding, and homesites in its vicinity were growing expensive. Pourtales believed Broadmoor could be developed into a handsome suburb. With Wilcox and a local judge as partners, he began in 1889 to lay out a subdivision. Damming a creek, he created an artificial lake, 300 feet wide and 1,500 feet long, that he named Cheyenne Lake. He laid out streets and parks and persuaded the owner of a Colorado Springs street railway to extend his tracks to the new lake. A country club was built, a race track laid out, and the streets lined with electric lights.

Impressive though these improvements were, they did not satisfy Pourtales. He obtained additional capital in New York—a loan of two hundred thousand dollars—with which he planned to build a casino like those that grace the great resorts of continental Europe. Many Colorado Springs residents, mindful of the disastrous Johnstown, Ohio flood of 1889, were reluctant to live anywhere near Pourtales' dam. To allay their fears, the count announced that he would build his casino at the summit of the dam, facing the lake and the wooded slopes of Cheyenne Mountain.

An architect from Philadelphia was commissioned to draw plans for the casino. It would be a handsome building two hundred fifty feet long, in Georgian style with white gables, columns, verandas, and multi-paned windows that would command grand views of the lake and mountains.

Construction began in the spring of 1891. Residents of the town watched intently as troops of workmen descended on the site and carloads of lumber and stone and glass were unloaded. The walls, verandas, and roof rose quickly. By July 1, Pourtales' birthday, the building was ready for its grand opening.

The interior of the casino was a profusion of salons and lounges, along with a large dining room, a combination ballroom and concert hall, and an elegantly appointed barroom. Liquor was nearly unknown in Colorado Springs, for the town fathers, mindful of the city's reputation as a health resort, had long before banned the sale and manufacture of alcohol. Local drug stores did a thriving business in wine-and-iron tonic, but they were not able to slake the thirsts of everyone in town. Pourtales reckoned that the casino barroom, safely beyond the city limits, would do a booming business, and he stocked his cellar heavily with fine wines and spirits.

On opening day 1,500 guests arrived at Broadmoor. Crowded carriages, coaches, and streetcars lined the graveled concourse that led to the main entrance of the casino. Inside, an orchestra of ten musicians, dressed in the colorful uniforms of Hungarian Hussars, played melodies of Brahms and Strauss. Coloradans were dazzled by the grandeur of the casino and its surrounding grounds. At night they crowded the restaurant and bar. In the afternoon they rowed on Cheyenne Lake. On weekends they watched cowboys and Indians race horses on the track and gasped in awe

James Pourtales. (Courtesy of the Broadmoor)

The original Broadmoor Casino. (Courtesy of the Broadmoor)

as a daring young woman ascended in a hot air balloon and floated to the surface of the lake in a parachute. When Pourtales contemplated the beauty of his creation, he was well pleased. "Here the greatest luxuries were unfolded," he remembered a few years later; "here could be found French cooking, with good wine on the table; here there was a lake on which one could row and sail, and the lake itself was stocked with mountain trout which those in the boats might catch and have cooked in the Casino restaurant by a French cook; here there were two fine concerts given daily, and twice a week there was dance music, and, in addition, there were other attractive presentations by imported artists each week."

Despite its many attractions, Broadmoor was without a hotel. There had, of course, been hotels in Colorado Springs from the early days. General Palmer had built the Colorado Springs Hotel in 1872—a three-story frame structure that was modestly advertised as "the most elegant hostelry between Chicago and San Francisco." The town's first settlers took rooms in the Springs Hotel while they waited turns to draw lots in the town, and tourists visiting Pike's Peak and the Garden of the Gods made it their vacation headquarters. But Palmer's business soon outgrew the three-story structure and, in 1883, he erected a new and larger building nearby. Called the Antlers, the new hotel

boasted hydraulic elevators, central heating, and pile carpets imported from New York. The Antlers drew throngs of pleasure-loving millionaires to Colorado Springs, among them the Michigan iron-ore king, James G. Hagerman, and the mattress manufacturer, Zalmon G. Simmons. In 1887 Hagerman built an extension of his Colorado Midland Railroad up nearby Ute Pass to the town of Aspen. Simmons, in turn, built a cog railroad up the side of Pike's Peak to the mountain's shivering summit 14,110 feet above sea level. The Antlers Hotel burned in 1898, but it was promptly replaced with a new and even grander structure, a palatial building with a marble staircase, Gobelin curtains, two telephones on each floor, and wing-collared waiters.

To complete his own development of Broadmoor, Pourtales made plans for a grand hotel. His palace inn would rise at the edge of Cheyenne Lake opposite the casino. It would be a building in the grand style, with loggias and colonnades, sweeping terraces, and a soaring, flag-topped dome. The hotel would be connected with the casino by two long galleries that, between them, would completely encircle the lake.

Before the structure could be built, Pourtales had business to attend to in Cripple Creek. Studying the men who frequented his Broadmoor casino, the count noticed that those who had the most money to spend were miners or men who had invested in mines. When a judge from the town of Pueblo appeared at Broadmoor in the fall of 1891 boasting of the marvelous discoveries at Cripple Creek and inviting the count to visit the district, Pourtales was not reluctant to go. When the German arrived at Cripple Creek, the only structures in a community crowded with dozens of unwashed prospectors were two rude cabins. A few holes had been dug in the neighboring hills, where sourdoughs claimed there were rich lodes, but it would take capital to excavate the claims. Pourtales was persuaded to invest in one of the mines—a vein of mixed marble and granite on the slope of a nearby mountain. He paid only two thousand dollars in cash for his claim, called the Buena Vista, but agreed to put up an additional seventy-eight thousand dollars within a year. News of the count's investment was not long in getting to local newspapers, and a mad rush to Cripple Creek began.

Soon a boom town nestled in the high pasture where Pourtales had found two log cabins. Stores and saloons and bordellos lined a rutted main street crowded with prospectors, investors, gamblers, and perfumed and painted ladies of the night.

To develop his mine, Pourtales organized a corporation and sold shares to any who would buy. James Hagerman, showing a little interest in the venture, put up a few thousand dollars for a substantial share of Pourtales' claim. Other lodes were discovered in the neighborhood, and carloads of ore were soon being dredged from the mountains and hauled to refineries in Denver. By 1899 Cripple Creek was the United States' most productive operating gold field, yielding more than twenty million dollars worth of bullion each year. Forty thousand men worked in the mines, and the town was a thriving city. A former Colorado Springs carpenter, Winfield Scott Stratton, struck it rich at Cripple Creek, rising overnight from the humble

Interior of the shaft house of the C.O.D. mine at Cripple Creek, photographed in 1894. Charles L. Tutt, Sr. is shown seated on barrel at right; Spencer Penrose, on lumber at left. (Courtesy of the Broadmoor)

The second Broadmoor casino, built in 1897. (Courtesy of the Broadmoor)

station of a three-dollar-a-day laborer to that of a multimillionaire investor and philanthropist. James Hagerman also did well. By wily maneuvers he obtained complete control of Pourtales' claims and added the millions of Buena Vista to his already substantial fortune. The claims for which Pourtales paid $80,000 in 1891 were eight years later worth more than $3,000,000. But the count was not able to enjoy them.

As miners and investors flocked to Cripple Creek, a general depression had settled over much of the United States. Stock prices had plummeted in New York, and business in Chicago and St. Louis had nearly ground to a halt. Crowds no longer came out from Colorado Springs to the Broadmoor casino, and the restaurant and bar were often empty. Pourtales' resources were drained by the expenses of his Buena Vista mine, and interest on the two-hundred-thousand-dollar loan used to build the casino could not be paid. Sadly, the count turned over the property to the New York investors who held the mortgage and headed south for Arizona.

Plans for the lakeside hotel at Broadmoor were

abandoned, though the casino was kept open, and a small hotel was put up nearby. In 1897 a fire swept through the casino, reducing it to ashes. A new building went up in its place, smaller and less imposing, a pale reminder of Pourtales' splendid palace.

Broadmoor greeted the new century with little gusto. A sprinkling of cottages had risen in the subdivision, and a few guests were housed in the little hotel. On summer afternoons sails dotted the surface of Cheyenne Lake, and occasional horse races were held on the country club track. In 1909 the syndicate managers who held title to the property sold it to the heirs of Winfield Scott Stratton, who built a home for the poor at the eastern end of the plateau. The casino and hotel were used for a while as a girls' school. In 1915 the hotel was reopened. Dances were held three nights a week, and Cheyenne Lake was opened to fishing. The place was handsome enough, but it suggested little of the splendor once envisioned by James Pourtales.

The count did not profit from his Cripple Creek investments, but he did very well in Arizona. By investing in mines near the town of Pearce he was able, by the turn of the century, to retire to his home in Prussia with a comfortable fortune. Others found fabulous wealth in the Colorado strike. Besides Hagerman and Stratton, there was Charles Tutt, a Philadelphian who parlayed an investment in Cripple Creek real estate into a sizable fortune; Tutt's childhood friend and business partner, Spencer Penrose, was another.

Penrose was a member of a prominent Philadelphia family, one of six brothers who traced their ancestry back to a partner of William Penn. Spencer's brother Richard was a distinguished geologist. Of his other brothers, Charles was a surgeon and gynecologist; Boies a United States Senator from Pennsylvania. All three had graduated with honors from Harvard. Spencer, tall, good-looking, and strong, had barely squeaked through the school, where he was remembered chiefly for drinking a gallon of beer in the record time of thirty-seven seconds. When he tried to match the skill of his brother Dick as stroke of the Harvard crew, he suffered a detached retina, and his left eye had to be removed.

He was still an imposing figure when he arrived in Cripple Creek in 1891 to join Charles Tutt in his real estate and mining business. What Penrose lacked in scholarly aptitude, he more than made up for in business acumen. Most of his financial successes were the result of luck, but his luck was backed up with a shrewd sense of values and the instincts of a disciplined gambler. Cripple Creek was good to Spencer Penrose, but Utah was even better. In 1902 he took a flier on a low-grade copper mine at Bingham Canyon. The mine, one of the richest copper deposits in the history of the United States, became the major asset of the Kennecott Copper Corporation, and Spencer Penrose became Kennecott's largest individual stockholder. By 1914 he was a fabulously wealthy man with a permanent, tax-free income of at least two hundred thousand dollars a month.

In his Cripple Creek days Penrose had often visited the Broadmoor, where he had admired the rambling casino, strolled with his wife along the graveled streets, paused to rest on benches at the edge of the sail-dotted lake. With his new-found wealth he traveled widely throughout the world—to Honolulu and Delhi, to Biarritz and Baden-Baden, to fashionable resorts in Switzerland and Germany and France. Everywhere he went, he compared the beauties of the local spas with those of Colorado Springs.

The high plateau did not have beaches or medieval castles, but it had attractions of its own. Pike's Peak was near, as was the Garden of the Gods. The air was clear and dry, and there were spectacular mountain views. Wild flowers dotted the plain in spring, and in summer the scent of pine and spruce and cedar perfumed the air around Cheyenne Mountain. Snow came occasionally, but its mantle was light and not unwelcome. Though scarcely a generation had passed since Colorado Springs was a rough frontier settlement, it had won a reputation as a social center of some elegance and polish. Many wealthy families lived in the town, and they prided themselves on their genteel manners and the leisurely pace of their lives. Traveling through the United States in 1914, the writer Julian Street met an Englishman who insisted there were only two civilized places between New York and San Francisco.

"What places do you mean?" Street asked.

Spencer Penrose, left, and his partner, Charles Tutt, Sr. (Courtesy of the Broadmoor)

"Chicago," the Englishman answered, "and Colorado Springs."

"But Colorado Springs is a little bit of a place, isn't it?" Street asked.

"About thirty thousand."

"Why is it so especially civilized?"

"It just *is,* y'know," he answered. "There's polo there."

"But polo doesn't make civilization," Street answered.

"Oh, yes, it does," the Englishman insisted. "I mean to say wherever you find polo you find good clubs and good society and—usually—good tea."

Intrigued, Street made a visit to the springs. Arriving at the train station, he immediately sensed the charm of the place. "One goes to the most delightful parties there," he wrote in *Collier's* magazine, "in the most delightful houses, and meets the most delightful people." The writer was a guest at some of the local clubs—the El Paso in the center of town and, farther out, the country club at Broadmoor. He found Broadmoor entirely to his liking—"a real country club," he said, "run for men and women who know what a real club is."

With his formidable wealth Spencer Penrose was sure he could make Colorado Springs one of the world's great resorts, a spa that would rival Biarritz and Monte Carlo, match the brooding beauty of Cheyenne Mountain, and complement the civilized society of Colorado Springs.

The millionaire had many ideas for Colorado Springs. He gave the town a public swimming pool and bought and modernized a cable car line that ascended a mountain west of the town. He looked for ways to promote automobile traffic on the high plateau and finally settled on a bold plan to build a motor road to the top of Pike's Peak. The highway was completed in the fall of 1915. To celebrate its opening, Penrose announced the Pike's Peak Hill Climb—a sensational auto race up the steep face of the mountain. The competition drew a troop of ace drivers, among whom none was better known than Barney Oldfield, famed as the first man in history to drive a car at sixty miles per hour on a circular track. But Oldfield's French Delage was not accustomed to running at fourteen thousand feet above sea level, and his race time, twelve miles in twenty minutes, was only good enough to place him twelfth in the competition.

The Pike's Peak Highway completed, Penrose looked for property in Colorado Springs that might be developed as a hotel. He tried to buy the Antlers, but he and the owners could not agree on a price. In 1916 with Charles MacNeill, a mining associate, as partner, he made an offer for the Broadmoor property. The heirs of Winfield Scott Stratton, who had done little to develop the tract, were pleased to sell it. At once the mining king made plans for his new domain.

The casino built in 1898 was moved from its site at the edge of Cheyenne Lake and converted into a golf club. Warren and Wetmore, New York architects who had designed Grand Central Station, were hired to draw plans for an elaborate new hotel at the edge of the lake. The building would rise nine stories above the water and be executed in a neo-Mediterranean style, with arches at the entrance and red tile on the roof. The walls, inspired by hotels Penrose had seen in Madeira, would be faced with delicate pink stucco. Inside, the bedrooms would have touches of Honolulu and Aix-les-Bains. The ballroom would suggest a salon in the Royal Palace at Peking. There would be suites in the style of Louis Quinze, others that would recall the imperial grandeur of Pompeii.

Construction began in May 1917 on the lakeside site of Count Pourtales' old casino. An army of artisans, many imported from Italy, worked feverishly to raise the walls, finish the graceful arches, apply decorated mouldings, columns, and frescos. Under the direction of the Olmsted Brothers, landscape architects who had conceived New York's Central Park and the grounds of the Chicago World's Fair, trees were planted, concourses graded, lawns seeded, and large flower beds planted. An eighteen-hole golf course was laid out near the lake and a little theater fitted up for theatrical presentations. Penrose decided to name his hotel for Count Pourtales' casino, the Broadmoor. When he discovered that the word had become part of the public domain and could not be registered as a trade name, he adopted the ingenious device of spelling the word with a raised, small capital "A"—BRO^ADMOOR. Thus the name was registered, and thus it has been spelled in all the hotel's promotional literature since.

The building was ready for a gala opening on June 29, 1918—a formal dinner-dance hosted by Penrose, his wife, his associate Charles Tutt, Jr., and Mrs. Tutt. More than two hundred guests sat down to a dinner of Broadmoor Trout au Bleu, Braised Sweetbreads aux Perles du Perigord, Boneless Royal Squab, and Souffle Glace, Comtesse de Cornet. Ladies in long gowns floated through the halls and salons, lavishly decorated with roses, lilies, and sweet peas. Couples assembled for dancing in the ballroom, where two orchestras played, then drifted out to the terrace to enjoy a breath of Colorado mountain air, wafting cool and fresh across the surface of Cheyenne Lake.

Spencer Penrose lived until 1939—all the while watching closely over his palace inn, continually updating and improving it. A private airplane hangar was built on the property. A stone tower and carillon were erected on a shoulder of Cheyenne Mountain and dedicated to America's beloved humorist, Will Rogers. A second, then a

The Broadmoor in 1918, as illustrated by Vernon Howe Bailey. (Courtesy of the Broadmoor)

The new Broadmoor complex. The nine-story Broadmoor South stands beside the main Broadmoor Hotel. (Courtesy of the Broadmoor)

third, golf course, a zoo, a chapel, two outdoor swimming pools, a race track and stadium, a large convention center, and an ice arena that twice played host to the World Figure Skating Championships were built. New buildings were added to the hotel complex—a nine-story Broadmoor South and a five-story Broadmoor West.

The Broadmoor became a popular rendezvous for celebrities from around the world—Arab kings and Indian maharajas, senators, governors, actors, actresses. Penrose was happy to greet Herbert Hoover and the Archduke of Austria, Helen Keller and Igor Stravinsky, the King of Siam and Shirley Temple, Jack Dempsey and Ignace Paderewski. Artists were among the first and best-known visitors to the hotel. Vernon Howe Bailey, who attended the opening in 1918, made a series of sketches of the Broadmoor that were widely reproduced in succeeding years. The celebrated illustrator, Maxfield Parrish, came a while later.

Penrose entertained Parrish lavishly, then urged him to immortalize the Broadmoor on canvas. The promise of a handsome fee, more than two thousand dollars, persuaded the artist to undertake the job. He made sketches and photographs, then returned to his studio to work on a grand canvas. Penrose was delighted with the finished work, an idealized panorama of the Broadmoor in which the artist moved the glimmering waters of Cheyenne Lake from the rear to the front of the hotel to heighten the picture's theatrical effect.

Of the thousands of celebrities who were greeted at the Broadmoor only one is known to have strained Penrose's equanimity. When Franklin D. Roosevelt, then a presidential candidate and already suspected by the social elite as a "traitor to his class," arrived at the hotel for a short stay, the Broadmoor's proprietor conveniently arranged to be out of town.

Half a century after its opening, nearly a century

after Count Pourtales' arrival in Colorado Springs, the Broadmoor remains one of the world's great hotels—a citadel of style and good taste in the midst of one of America's most beautiful natural settings. But style and beauty are not the only attributes of the Broadmoor. The spirit of Spencer Penrose is never far away, nor is the memory of the boom-and-bust days at Cripple Creek. Even today it is not hard to imagine the redoubtable Penrose, tall and erect, striding through the corridors of the palace inn. It is only a little more difficult to picture Count James Pourtales galloping over the high plateau, selecting the site for Cheyenne Lake, watching as workmen raised the lofty gables and columns of his casino. The Broadmoor today survives as a monument to both men.

11

Guardian of the Straits

GRAND HOTEL, MACKINAC ISLAND

One of America's best surviving examples of late nineteenth-century architecture sits high on a wooded island overlooking northern Michigan's historic Straits of Mackinac. Five stories tall, nearly nine hundred feet long, the mansion looks out from its pillared porch on one of the most spectacular views to be found anywhere in the Great Lakes region. Wooded slopes and grassy swards lead down from the building to a narrow beach that borders the northernmost reaches of Lake Huron. Less than a mile to the southeast the stone ramparts of Fort Mackinac, built in the eighteenth century by troops of King George III, look down on the streets and wharves of the storybook City of Mackinac Island. To the southwest the twin towers of the sleek Mackinac Bridge, a giant suspension span that links highways of Michigan's Upper and Lower peninsulas, rise from the windblown waters of Mackinac Narrows. "Grand Hotel," its builders called it when they raised the mansion's lofty pillars and soaring roof in the middle of the 1880s. Grand Hotel it remains today—one of the most notable waterfront landmarks in the United States, a monument as familiar to ferry boat passengers of the twentieth century as it was to steamboat captains and yachtsmen in the nineteenth.

Built in an era of Victorian flamboyance, when gingerbread adorned the humblest bungalows and cottages, Grand Hotel was notable for its clean lines and simple decoration. A long building with a lofty colonnade overhung by a hip roof, it looked more like a Mississippi River plantation house or a Brobdingnagian version of Mount Vernon than a summer hotel in northern Michigan. Uncluttered, without filigree or fretwork, the building's architecture was classic and timeless. Because it was built of wood, the hotel could easily be modified to suit the needs of future generations. In its nearly one hundred years of life Grand Hotel has been enlarged, modernized, and renovated many times, but its simple appearance has not been substantially altered.

The Mackinac region (for such the area, which includes straits, islands, and several towns, is properly called) is one of the most spectacular meetings of land and water in the world. West of the straits is Lake Michigan. East of them are Lakes Huron, Erie, and Ontario. Lake Superior lies to the north and west. Beneath the Mackinac Bridge the waters that connect the lakes narrow to a deepwater channel about four miles wide. The city of St. Ignace hugs the northern shore of the straits; Mackinaw City the southern. Fifteen miles from the soaring bridge Mackinac Island, three miles long and two miles wide, raises its humped profile above the shimmering expanse of lakes and straits.

"Mackinac," originally "*Michilimackinac*," is an Indian word that was adopted by the French, then shortened by the British and Americans. In the days of the earliest European settlers the word was commonly translated as "great turtle." Indeed, the humped island resembled a giant turtle, and local

126

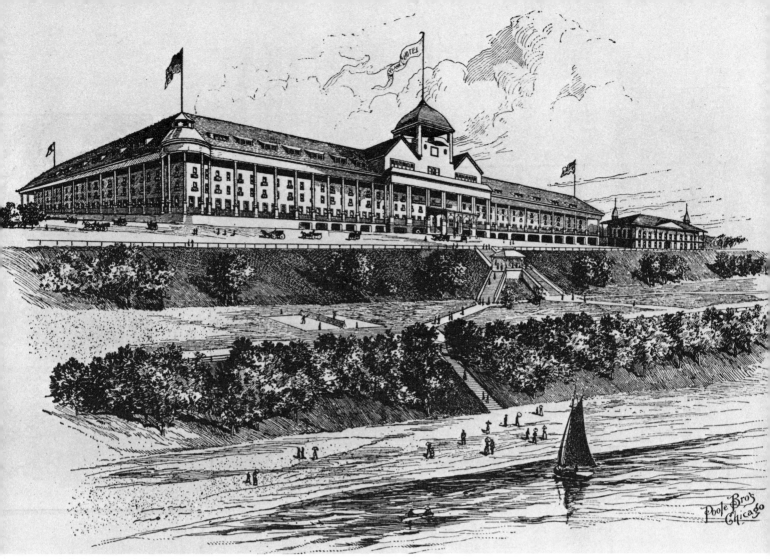

Artist's view of Grand Hotel, Mackinac Island. From Frank Leslie's Illustrated Newspaper, *June 1890. (Library of Congress)*

Indians held both turtles and the island in reverence. But ethnologist Henry R. Schoolcraft, who lived on the island through much of the 1830s and studied the native languages closely, concluded that it properly meant a place of dancing spirits. Historians have recorded more than sixty different spellings of the word, but only two survive in modern usage. "Mackinaw" is the city which clings to the southern shore of the straits, and the name of the popular coats, blankets, and boats originated in the area. The straits, the narrows, the bridge, and the island are all "Mackinac." The difference is only one of spelling. All are properly pronounced "Mack-uh-naw."

French missionaries explored the region early in the seventeenth century, and in 1671 Father Jacques Marquette established a mission at Fort de Buade near St. Ignace. The post was abandoned in the 1690s, but by 1715 the French had returned to establish a Fort Michilimackinac near present Mackinaw City. The British took over the fort in 1761 and twenty years later moved it from the southern mainland to the heights of Mackinac Island. As the highest mass of land in the region, the island commanded broad views to the west, south, and north and permitted defenders to spot approaching enemies as far as twelve leagues away.

Following the Revolution, boundary lines of the new United States were drawn to include Fort Mackinac. But George III's redcoats still lusted for the citadel. British troops recaptured Mackinac during the War of 1812, but a treaty of peace again returned it to the United States. Wary of their British neighbors in Canada, American troops strengthened the outpost in the 1820s and '30s, while French, American, and half-breed fur traders built a huddle of cottages, warehouses, and wharves along the southern shore.

For twenty years the island was headquarters for the vast, continental operations of John Jacob Astor's American Fur Company. Astor's biographer, Washington Irving, described the settlement during Astor's day as "a mere village, stretching along a small bay, with a fine broad beach in front of its

The British fort on Mackinac Island (Courtesy of Mackinac Island State Park Commission)

principal row of houses, and dominated by the old fort, which crowned an impending height." "The beach," said Irving, "was a kind of public promenade, where were displayed all the vagaries of a seaport on the arrival of a fleet from a long cruise."

Here voyageurs frolicked away their wages, fiddling and dancing in the booths and cabins, buying all kinds of knick-knacks, dressing themselves out finely, and parading up and down, like errant braggarts and coxcombs. Sometimes they met with rival coxcombs in the young Indians from the opposite shore, who would appear on the beach painted and decorated in fantastic style, and would saunter up and down, to be gazed at and admired, perfectly satisfied that they eclipsed their palefaced competitors.

By the 1840s the economy of the island had changed dramatically. Astor had sold out his interests, and the beavers which supported the Mackinac traders had all but disappeared from the Great Lakes. Seeking new ways to make their livings, the English, French, and Indian inhabitants of the island turned to the fish that abounded in the surrounding waters. Hoists were built on the island's wharves and nets stretched out to dry on the beach, as tons of whitefish and lake trout were hauled into the sheds of the waterfront to be dried and salted.

Spurred by the fishing trade, the old fur village acquired the appearance of a prosperous New England port—with clapboard houses with verandas and salt-box packing houses beside the wharves. The island was the principal processing and shipping center for fishing grounds up to 150 miles distant. In 1870 Mackinac County led all others in Michigan in fishing activity, with no less than fifty fisheries employing 167 men, who together shipped more than 10,000 barrels of fish. But the fish, like the beavers, were a finite resource. By the 1880s most of the trout and whitefish had disappeared, and the townspeople had begun to put away their nets and look for new ways to make their livings from the island.

The search was not difficult. From early days, visitors to Mackinac had praised its rugged beauty and healthful climate. The straits froze over in the winter, and snow piled high in the streets of the little village, but in spring the woods and meadows blossomed into a sylvan paradise. If residents of Chicago, Detroit, and Cleveland sweltered miserably in summer, Mackinac Islanders basked in cool breezes. At least since the 1820s a steady stream of visitors had clambered ashore at the Mackinac wharf eager to inspect the fort and appraise the views that spread out from the lofty east and west bluffs. In 1819 the first steamboat on the Great Lakes, a side-wheeler picturesquely named *Walk-in-the-Water*, stopped at the island on her maiden voyage, which ushered in the age of steam travel on the lakes.

The English novelist and essayist Harriet Martineau visited the island in 1836 and pronounced it "the wildest and tenderest piece of beauty" she had ever seen. Her countryman, the novelist Captain Frederick Marryat, who put ashore the following year, seconded her judgment. "It has the appearance of a fairy isle floating on the water," Marryat wrote, "which is so pure and transparent that you may see down to almost any depth; and the air above is as pure as the water, so that you feel invigorated as you breathe it. . . . I might have imagined myself transported to the Shetland isle, had it not been for the lodges of the Indians on the beach, and the Indians themselves either running about, or lying stripped in the porches before the whisky stores." Noting the healthy, well-fed appearance of the European residents, the Englishman asked an islander if they lived to a "good old age." "I guess they do," the islander answered. "If people want to die, they can't die here—they're obliged to go elsewhere."

By 1846, when the American poet William Cullen Bryant visited the island, it was apparent to many that a flourishing tourist trade lay in Mackinac's future. "I cannot see how it is to escape this destiny," Bryant wrote. "People already begin to repair to it for health and refreshment from the southern borders of Lake Michigan. Its climate during the summer months is delightful; there is no air more pure and elastic, and the winds of the south and southwest, which are so hot on the prairies, arrive here tempered to a grateful coolness by the waters over which they have swept. The nights are always, in the hottest season, agreeably cool, and the health of the place is proverbial. The world has not many islands so beautiful as Mackinaw. . . ."

With press agents as voluble and articulate as Martineau, Marryat, and Bryant (all of whom published their praises of the island), it was little wonder that the tide of summer visitors swelled. Steam packets from Detroit and Cleveland began to make regular trips to the island in the fifties and sixties, and railroad magnate James J. Hill launched massive lake steamers which plied a route between Buffalo in the east and Chicago in the west. The railroads followed close on the heels of the steamers. By 1881 the Grand Rapids & Indiana and the Michigan Central lines had reached Mackinaw City, where ferries waited to transport passengers over the water to Mackinac Island.

On shore, accommodations for guests were less inviting than they were in either the ships or the trains. The Mission House, once a school for Indians and half-breeds, was one of the oldest and largest of the island's inns. A rough frame structure with a long porch that faced the waterfront, it was converted to hotel use in 1852, the same year that Charles O'Malley built the box-like Island House, which accommodated up to 150 guests. In the 1860s the former headquarters of the Astor fur company was opened as a hotel by Ronald McLeod, who operated it as the McLeod House until the 1870s, when new owners named it the John Jacob Astor House. Nearby were the St. Cloud Hotel, "furnished in Queen Anne style," which advertised a corps of colored servants and a "Famous String Band," and the comfortable Mackinac House, which stood at the head of the island's main dock. Burned in 1887, the Mackinac was promptly rebuilt as the New Mackinac. A circular issued by its proprietor shortly after its reopening announced unusual attractions:

> **This hotel was built for the special comfort of summer boarders.**
> **On arrival each guest will be asked how he likes the situation, and if he says the Hotel ought to have been placed upon Fort Holmes or on Round Island, the location of the Hotel will be immediately changed. . . .**
> **Meals every minute, and consequently no second table.**
> **Every guest will have the best seat in the dining hall.**
> **Our clerk was specially educated for the "New Mackinac," he wears the original Koh-i-noor diamond, and is prepared to please everybody. He is always ready to sing, match worsted, take a hand at draw-poker, play billiards, sharpen your pencil, take you out rowing, lead the german, amuse the children, make a fourth at whist, or flirt with any young lady, and will not mind being cut dead when Pa comes down. . . .**

The Mackinac House circular may have led some prospective visitors to wonder how cordially they would be welcomed at the island, but the red carpets laid out for them on the steamships could not have aroused such doubts. The 300-foot *City of Mackinac*, operated by the Detroit and Cleveland Steam Navigation Company, was a splendid ship which cost $350,000 to build and required a crew of fifty to run. Hill's *Northwest* and its sister ship the *Northland* were widely praised "floating hotels" with spacious lounges, attractive dining rooms, and staterooms furnished with wicker chairs, Persian rugs, and the latest in "wire and hair mattresses." The boats which ferried passengers from Mackinaw City to the island were less pretentious, but not less comfortable. The *Algomah,* one of the most famous of the Mackinac ferries, was powered by steam engines personally installed by a young Detroit mechanic named Henry Ford.

Tourist interest in Mackinac was heightened in 1875 when Congress passed legislation creating Mackinac Island National Park, the country's second. (Only Yellowstone, created in 1872, predated it.) Placed under the control of the commandant of Fort Mackinac, the park embraced acreage above the ramparts and along the east bluffs. When, twenty years later, the Army decided that British Canada was no longer a military threat to the Great Lakes, Fort Mackinac was abandoned, and its land, together with that of the adjoining national park, was turned over to the State of Michigan to be administered as a state park.

The tourist season at Mackinac was short, but the steamships, trains, and ferries were crowded to capacity during the summer months. Noting the throngs that clamored for rooms at the waterfront hotels of Mackinac village, investors in Chicago and Detroit sensed that there was big money to be made on the island. Francis B. Stockbridge, a businessman and Michigan politician who had extensive interests in lumber, sawmills, and railroads, was one of those who saw a rosy future for Mackinac. Inspecting the lofty west bluffs of the island in 1882, Stockbridge purchased a plot of land that overlooked the straits and the old cow pasture of Fort Mackinac. Passing the word among his friends in Detroit and Chicago that he proposed to build a grand hotel on his property, Stockbridge attracted a host of attractive proposals from investors. In 1886 three transportation companies that served the island—the Michigan Central, the Grand Rapids & Indiana, and the Detroit and Cleveland Steam Navigation Company—joined to form the Mackinac Island Hotel Company. Stockbridge's political fortunes were rising (he was elected a United States Senator in 1887), and he decided to turn over the property to the new investors, each of whom took a one-third interest in the project.

Plans for the structure were impressive. A broad flight of steps would lead up from the cow pasture to a colonnade of pillars three stories high and more than six hundred feet long (the plans allowed for eventual expansion to nearly nine hundred feet). A soaring roof above the colonnade would be pierced by dormers and topped with two gables and a cupola. Clear white pine, the legendary

"Wood Eternal" of the Michigan forests, would be used throughout the building. To minimize the danger of fire, the dining hall would be separate from the main building but connected to it by a covered walkway. When finished, the hotel would loom boldly above the west bluffs and be plainly visible from both Mackinaw City and St. Ignace.

Raising the hotel's timbers and girders was a massive undertaking that required the assistance of workmen from miles in every direction. In April 1887, with the snow of the previous winter hardly off the ground, more than thirty wagons and teams of horses assembled on the island to haul lumber, nails, and brick over the rutted road that led from the docks to the west bluffs. Scores of carpenters, masons, tinsmiths, and painters worked feverishly through the spring and early summer to ready the hotel for an early season opening. By the beginning of July finishing touches were being put on the building as steamships and private yachts crowded with a throng of opening guests assembled in the harbor.

More than a thousand people were on hand for the opening, which took place on July 10, 1887. From Chicago came the Potter Palmers, the Marshall Fields, the meat-packing Armours and Swifts. From Detroit came the Algers, the Newberrys, the Whitneys. Adolphus Busch and his family came from St. Louis. Charles Warren Fairbanks, later to be Theodore Roosevelt's vice-president, brought his family from Indianapolis. Michigan's Governor Cyrus G. Luce and his family put up in the spacious Governor's Suite, which they liked so well that they decided to remain in it throughout the summer.

Operation of the hotel was entrusted to an experienced New England hôtelier and resort manager named John Oliver Plank. Plank had acted as an advisor during construction of the hotel and, after it was completed, the directors named him as its lessee-proprietor. At Plank's insistence the hotel was opened under the name of "Plank's Grand Hotel."

A train of horse-drawn breaks, carriages, and hacks lined up at the ferry docks to transport passengers from the village to the doors of the hotel. Fine meals were served in the spacious dining hall, while string orchestras played in the salons and ballroom. Tennis courts laid out on the greensward invited athletic guests to exercise. A stable of horses was available for rides through the woods. Children enjoyed the hayrides that regularly departed from the front porch, as well as the fleet of bicycles available for excursions through the

Approaching the Grand. To minimize the danger of fire, the dining hall (right) was separate from the main building, but connected to it by a covered walkway. (Courtesy of Mackinac Island State Park Commission)

streets of the old village and fort. Indians, who still pitched tepees on the southern beach, spread blankets on the ground, where moccasins, miniature birchbark canoes, baskets, and maple sugar were offered for sale. Visitors enjoyed browsing in shops along Market Street and hiking up the long ramp that led to the entrance of the fort. Tour guides led them through the island's many natural attractions—the sandy northern beach where British invaders landed in 1812, the seventy-five-foot cone of limestone called Sugar Loaf that towered above the forest northeast of the fort, and the spectacular natural bridge, Arch Rock, that hugged the island's eastern shore.

Lured by Mackinac's beauty, wealthy families from Michigan and Illinois bought land along the bluffs northwest of the hotel on which they began to build large summer homes. Towered, porticoed, and cupolaed, the homes were more ornate than Grand Hotel, but they blended well with its massive grandeur. To build homes at Mackinac, Henry Duffield, S. B. Grummond, and Ransom Hawley came from Detroit; Delos Blodgett and Crofton Fox from Grand Rapids; George Cass, David Hogg, Walter Newberry, and John and Michael Cudahy from Chicago. Many of the wealthiest homeowners traveled to the island in large private yachts, freshly painted and gaily sailed, while others came more conventionally in steamers or on ferries.

Whatever their mode of travel, they all arrived well-equipped for the summer months with families, servants, pets, and steamer trunks following behind.

The only things the summer inhabitants could not bring to the island were automobiles. In 1901, when there were less than two hundred "horseless carriages" in all of Michigan, Chicago's wealthy John Cudahy asked the State Park Commission for permission to bring over a spanking new "machine." Pondering Cudahy's request at length, the commissioners finally decided to deny it—for the "safety of visitors within the park." The rule forbidding automobiles was to remain permanently in force, sparing Mackinac from the noxious fumes and spreading asphalt roadways that in time were to blight most of the rest of the country.

Despite the popularity of the island, operators of the hotel encountered difficulties. Because it was open only two months of the year, the Grand produced disappointingly meager revenues. Expenses during the height of the season were high—so high that John Oliver Plank soon despaired of balancing his books. He withdrew from Mackinac in 1890, and directors of the hotel company signed a new, ten-year lease with James J. Hays of Detroit. Hays took up his duties with rosy expectations. But his optimism, sorely tried by the depression of the 1890s that severely thinned the ranks of

Early brochure advertising the many attractions of Grand Hotel (Courtesy of Mackinac Island State Park Commission)

island visitors, soon turned to defeat. A third lessee, Henry Weaver, took charge in 1900. Owner of the famous Planters Hotel in St. Louis, Weaver was a dynamic hôtelier with a keen instinct for profit. When revenues of the Grand fell below his expectations, he persuaded directors of the hotel to give him a fifty percent interest in the property and, a little while later, to sell him the other fifty percent.

The hotel was enlarged. A golf course was laid out on the old cow pasture of Fort Mackinac. The colonnade was extended nearly three hundred feet, and a fifth story of rooms was added where the old roof dormers had been. Despite the improvements, Weaver could not make the hotel show a profit. When in 1910 he announced plans to raze the building and sell its site, islanders were shocked. Led by Frank Nagel of St. Louis, who owned a summer home at Mackinac, a new group of stockholders bought the hotel and operated it

until 1917, when J. Logan Ballard of West Baden, Indiana became the new owner.

Spending heavily, Ballard commenced an extensive program of improvements. A patio garden and swimming pool were built on the green in front of the hotel. Rooms were enlarged, plumbing modernized, carpets replaced, walls repainted. The hotel was doing a thriving business in the season of 1919 when a young college student from Indiana took a job at Grand Hotel as a desk clerk.

As a boy in Greensburg, Indiana, W. Stewart Woodfill had suffered from summer attacks of hay fever and asthma. To relieve his condition, his parents had taken him to northern Michigan, usually to Mackinac Island, where the lake-washed air was free from irritating pollen. Fascinated by the old village and fort and by the majestic hotel that stood guard over the straits, Woodfill returned to the island in 1919 and took a summer job. At the desk of Grand Hotel he impressed his superiors with his intelligence, industry, and willingness to work long hours at low pay. He was asked to return again the following summer, and again the next.

When Ballard died in 1923, executors of his estate asked Woodfill to become manager of the hotel. Acquiring a partnership interest, he ordered the staff to change their costumes. The dock porter was attired in the uniform of an admiral. Guests who entered the lobby were greeted by a gray-haired black butler, resplendent in scarlet cutaway, black silk stockings, knee breeches, and silver-buckled pumps. At the lobby desk, rooms were assigned by a smiling assistant manager dressed in black cutaway, striped trousers, and pearl-gray spats. Waiters and bellmen throughout the hotel wore colorful uniforms and spotless white gloves.

Acquiring full ownership of the Grand in 1933, Woodfill nursed it through the rigors of the Great Depression and into the prosperous years of the post-World War II boom. Dressing in smart double-breasted sport jackets, always carrying a walking stick, Woodfill ruled his island domain with a firm hand. As chairman of the Mackinac Island State Park Commission, he led a corps of historians, archeologists, and architects who restored the buildings of the old village and fort to their eighteenth- and nineteenth-century appearance. Under his leadership Grand Hotel emerged as one of the United States' most successful summer resorts. The building itself was widely advertised as the world's largest summer hotel—a claim which the large crowds of visitors who regularly passed through its doors did little to refute. By the

1950s more than 350,000 tourists came to Mackinac each summer—a large part of them taking rooms in Grand Hotel.

Woodfill had definite ideas about how a resort hotel should be run. To accommodate the increasing numbers of visitors, the season was extended to six months, opening in May and closing in October. Informal resort attire was permitted on the long porch and hotel grounds, but decorum was demanded—and received—inside the building. During the day men were required to wear shirts with collars and, after six, women dressed and men wore jackets and neckties. Tipping was forbidden—a flat service charge being added to all bills instead. Waiters, clerks, doormen, and coachmen were brilliantly costumed.

Leaving the lake ferries at the village docks, visitors arriving at the island stepped suddenly out of the twentieth century and into a storybook recreation of the nineteenth. Sparkling in their coats of fresh white paint, buildings restored by the State Park Commission stood cheek-by-jowl with old hotels, Victorian houses, and quaint shops. On the bluff immediately above the town the lime-

stone walls of the restored Fort Mackinac gleamed in the sun. Boarding carriages pulled by teams of rosette-adorned horses and driven by coachmen in beaver top hats, the visitors ascended the sloping road that leads to Grand Hotel. On every side were breathtaking vistas—the blue waters of the Straits of Mackinac, the grassy expanse of the hotel golf course, gardens bright with masses of geraniums, pansies, petunias, and marigolds. Below the road was a serpentine swimming pool, tennis courts, and a sandy beach. From the porch, longer than the length of two football fields, guests entered a red-carpeted lobby where bellmen and clerks in colorful coats took their bags and showed them to their rooms.

When England's Queen Elizabeth II passed through the straits on her historic 1959 cruise of the St. Lawrence Seaway, her yacht *Britannia* passed within two hundred feet of the island shore. The Queen waved from the deck as the ship passed Grand Hotel, and three cannons on shore thundered a twenty-one-gun salute. Nearly two centuries earlier Elizabeth's ancestor, George III, had lost the island and the straits in a war with

Birdseye view of Grand Hotel and its golf course, serpentine swimming pool, and beach (lower left). (Courtesy of Grand Hotel)

Grand Hotel's porch, longer than the length of two football fields. (Courtesy of Grand Hotel)

American revolutionaries. In the interval the bitterness of that long-ago struggle had been forgiven, if not forgotten. But the gesture was still significant. A wave from a British monarch might have signaled a call to arms at Mackinac in the last years of the eighteenth century. In the twentieth it was a welcome, even coveted, gesture of friendship.

Ninety years after its 1887 opening, Grand Hotel continued under the stewardship of Stewart Woodfill. There was no talk, as there had been in 1910, of razing the hotel, which was earning record profits with its new, lengthened operating season. The hotel had outlived hundreds of its late nineteenth-century comtemporaries. Its remarkable durability was due in part to the simplicity of its design, in part to the malleability of the Michigan white pine with which it was built. In a speech delivered in 1969 Woodfill himself explained the advantages of a wood structure over one of brick or stone. "Masonry hotels become obsolete," he explained, "because little can be done to change them. However, frame hotels such as the Grand can always be modernized and altered by carpenters at the direction of good architects and decorators. Wood yields to the artisan's hands while masonry materials do not. Such has been the course of change at Grand Hotel."

In midsummer, evening comes slowly to Mackinac. The sun sinks behind the towers of Mackinac Bridge casting fingers of golden light across the straits. Shadows lengthen on the long porch of Grand Hotel, and the great halls glow with the warmth of thousands of lamps. Below the porch wooded slopes and grassy swards lead down to the beach that borders the straits. A decade short of its hundredth anniversary, the hotel remains Mackinac's grandest landmark. At least in the foreseeable future, it is not likely to relinquish that distinction.

12

Flagler's Florida

THE BREAKERS, PALM BEACH

He was born in 1830 in New York's Hudson Valley and spent most of his boyhood on a farm near Lake Ontario. He left New York when he was fourteen to seek his fortune in Ohio. There he worked as a store clerk, as a grain merchant, and finally as an oil refiner. Through forty long, freezing winters in Ohio and New York, Henry M. Flagler suffered miserably from the cold. When he was fifty-five years old and one of the richest men in the United States, he decided to warm his cold-wracked bones on the palm-fringed eastern shore of Florida. His discovery of the undeveloped southern state changed him, but it changed the state even more.

Flagler spent half his life making money and half spending it, and in both occupations he was notably successful. Anticipating the great hotel chains that were to be established in the twentieth century by Ellsworth Statler and Conrad Hilton, Flagler built a series of resort inns along the Florida coast from St. Augustine to Miami, each more elegant, more lavish, more flamboyantly extravagant than the last. He spent money with determination, even inspiration; yet, when his spending spree was ended by death in 1913, the cold-wracked boy from New York's Hudson Valley still had one hundred million dollars left.

In the 1860s he had been a partner in John D. Rockefeller's fledgling oil refining business in Cleveland. In 1870 he became one of the five original stockholders of the Standard Oil Company. A close friend and business associate of the ambi-

tious Rockefeller, Flagler was himself no shrinking violet in the business world. Years later Rockefeller was asked how he had gotten the idea of Standard Oil. "I wish I'd had the brains to think of it," the billionaire answered. "It was Henry M. Flagler."

As an officer of Standard, Flagler took the lead in buying up small, competitive refineries in the Cleveland area, where he struck hard, even "brilliant" bargains that never failed to warm the stony cockles of John D.'s heart. Flagler was instrumental, too, in obtaining secret rebates from railroads which transported Standard products, an achievement that added immeasurably to Standard's wealth and John D.'s esteem. By 1879 the Rockefeller-Flagler interests controlled no less than ninety-five percent of the petroleum industry in the United States. From 1870 to 1882 Standard's capital increased from one million dollars to more than fifty-five million dollars. By 1882, when the Standard Oil Trust was formed, Rockefeller's and Flagler's refining partnership had become the biggest—and one of the most hated—businesses in the world.

After Standard moved its offices to New York City, Flagler set himself up in a sumptuous mansion on Fifth Avenue and a forty-room summer house at Mamaroneck on Long Island Sound. He piloted stylish yachts along the coast and entertained important guests in his Manhattan mansion. But he still suffered painfully from the cold of winter. When, late in the seventies, his invalid wife was advised by her doctor to spend some time

The new Breakers Hotel, Palm Beach, 1926. (Courtesy of the Henry Morrison Flagler Museum)

in Florida, Flagler jumped at the opportunity to visit the southern state.

Florida was little known to most Americans in the 1870s. Modern railroads had been built as far south as Savannah, but passage from the Georgia port into the peninsula state was difficult and dangerous. A writer for *Harper's Weekly* in 1870 reported that there were two ways of getting from Savannah to Jacksonville, Florida's principal city. "Whichever way you choose," the writer said, "you will be sorry you had not taken the other. There is the night train by railroad, which brings you to Jacksonville in about sixteen hours; and there is the steamboat line, which goes inland nearly all the way, and which may land you in a day, or you may run aground, and remain on board a week." Though Jacksonville was Florida's most important settlement, it had only fifteen thousand residents in 1880, and only one hotel of consequence, the wood and brick St. James.

Flagler enjoyed his sojourn at the St. James, but business commitments forced him to return to New York before he could explore the surrounding country. More than anything else he saw in Florida, the millionaire was impressed by the weather—warm and deliciously balmy when most

of the rest of the country was blanketed by snow and ice. His wife died in 1883. When he took his second bride on a honeymoon two years later, they headed straight for Florida. The newlyweds remained only a few days in Jacksonville, soon moving south to the seaside village of St. Augustine, oldest permanent settlement in the United States. When Flagler first saw it, the old Spanish town was small and dilapidated, with no large hotels and little in the way of business. But it faced a breathtaking expanse of sea and shore and was surrounded with acres of orange trees. The weather was if anything even milder than that of Jacksonville. As Flagler and his bride basked in the sun at St. Augustine, a cold wave of unusual intensity settled over most of the United States. On January 4, 1884, the temperature in St. Louis dropped to twenty-three degrees below zero; in Cleveland to fourteen. In St. Augustine, on the palm-shaded eastern coast of Florida, the skies were clear, the sun shone brightly, and flowers bloomed in profusion. For once in his life Henry Flagler felt comfortably warm.

The millionaire was impressed by St. Augustine, but he was equally struck by its deficiencies. Transportation routes to the town were primitive and unreliable. There were no docks, railroads, or tourist hotels to lure winter-weary New Yorkers and Ohioans from their snow-banked northern lairs. St. Augustine's backwardness was only symptomatic of the general drowsiness of Florida. Of the 270,000 people who lived in the state in 1880, 40,000 were crowded into the northeastern corner, most in the small area between Jacksonville and St. Augustine. The principal transportation route for both freight and passengers was the meandering St. Johns River, which connected Jacksonville with marshy Lake George, a few miles west of Daytona Beach. There were half a dozen rail lines in the northeastern counties, but the roads had varying gauges and maddeningly unpredictable schedules. Few of the rivers in the area had been bridged, and travel from any point to another was at best slow and uncertain.

On his return to New York Flagler purchased a luxurious private railroad car to return to the south in February 1885. This time he came not as a casual tourist to admire the tropical foliage and bask in the winter sun, but as a man with a mission.

The millionaire's arrival in Florida in 1885 has been likened to the Spanish explorer Ponce de Leon's discovery of the peninsula in 1513. The Spaniard came in search of the legendary Fountain of Youth. Flagler, nearing the age when many men dream of finding such a fountain, did not seek youth in Florida, but he entertained many of its ambitions. Nine years older than Rockefeller, he was a handsome man of fifty-five years, with a shock of silvery hair and a long face that was lightly though unmistakably etched with wrinkles. Age had marked the man, but it had not dimmed his vision or softened the determination in his cold, gray eyes.

He had retired from Standard Oil, though he was still one of its largest shareholders and retained his seat on its powerful board of directors. The great oil trust was no fountain of youth, but it was a fountain of money, a seemingly bottomless well from which Flagler and its other owners could draw lucre enough to satisfy their every whim.

Flagler was aware that he was one of the United States' most hated men when he came to Florida in 1885. In its short fifteen years of life, Standard Oil had fought, clawed, and (some said) cheated its way to a position of awesome economic power. The "Robber Barons" of the trust were cursed by competitors, vilified by trade unionists, praised by bankers, feared by politicians. Flagler's unsavory reputation preceded him to Florida, but if Floridians had apprehensions about his decision to invest in their state, they kept them well con-

cealed. Standard Oil money seemed "dirty" to many, but it was money, and money was desperately needed to awaken Florida from its centuries-old torpor.

If a reliable railroad could be built into the peninsula, its wonders could be made accessible to thousands of Americans who had previously only dreamt of them. If tourists in large numbers were to come, suitable lodgings would have to be available. Hotels and railroads—the two were inseparable. Though Flagler had little thought of building an empire when he came to Florida in the mid-eighties, he was determined from the first to build on a large scale.

His attention focused first on St. Augustine. A group of New England investors had opened a small but attractive hotel in the town in the interval between Flagler's first and second visits, and a narrow-gauge railroad had been built from Jacksonville. But these improvements only

Henry Morrison Flagler, 1909. (Courtesy of the Henry Morrison Flagler Museum)

scratched the surface of St. Augustine's potential. In March 1885 Flagler bought several acres of land in the center of town and in May summoned New York architect Thomas Hastings to inspect it. The land was low and marshy, but Hastings thought it could be drained, filled, and made suitable for building. Conscious of St. Augustine's Spanish heritage, Flagler proposed to build a massive Spanish-style inn on the property. Back in New York Hastings and his partner John Carrere studied photographs, drawings, and books showing types of Spanish architecture, then began to draw blueprints for Flagler's inspection.

The only stone available in the vicinity of St. Augustine was a marine limestone known as coquina, which was too soft to support a structure as large as that envisioned by Flagler. Consulting with the millionaire's builders, McGuire and McDonald, the architects hit on the novel idea of mixing crumbled coquina with cement and pouring the combination into wooden forms. Excavation for the building began on December 1, 1885, with the majority of St. Augustine's two thousand inhabitants on hand to watch. When stories of Flagler's project filtered back to New York, many

businessmen raised their eyebrows skeptically. A friend asked Flagler why he was undertaking such a risky project at his age, and the millionaire replied with a story.

"There was a good old church member," he said, "who had always lived a correct life. One day when he was very old he went on a drunken spree. While still drunk, he met his pastor, who soundly upbraided him. 'Up to now,' the old man said defiantly, 'I've been giving all my days to the Lord. Now I'm taking one for myself.' That's the way it is with me. Up to now, I've devoted all my time to business. Now I'm pleasing myself." In the months ahead, Flagler was to find his Florida venture more and more pleasing.

Work continued on the hotel in St. Augustine throughout 1886 and 1887. As the walls of coquina and cement rose above their heavy foundations, the bold outlines of the building became apparent. In all, the hotel covered nearly five acres. Its arched front gates were flanked by covered walkways or arcades paved with tiles and edged with pillars. Inside the gates was a large court, 150 feet square, with a tiled floor, formal gardens, and a large fountain. Broad steps led from the court into

The Ponce de Leon Hotel, St. Augustine, as it was nearing completion. (Courtesy of the Henry Morrison Flagler Museum)

Front view of the Alcazar, St. Augustine. (Courtesy of the Henry Morrison Flagler Museum)

the main lobby, a spacious rotunda decorated with mosaics, surrounded by oak pillars, and surmounted with a soaring dome. A maze of parlors, salons, corridors, and dining halls led from the rotunda into the adjoining wings. Four hundred fifty guest rooms and suites occupied the upper floors. Atop the building was a heavy tile roof and a profusion of towers, cupolas, turrets, chimneys, and domes. Had the great inn been built on a hillside in Granada facing the ramparts of the Alhambra, it could not have been more convincingly Spanish. Remembering the explorer who sought eternal youth in Florida, Flagler named his great hotel the Ponce de Leon.

Before the structure was completed, Flagler made preparatons to improve rail lines into Florida. He bought the narrow-gauge road that connected Jacksonville and St. Augustine and immediately tore up the old rails and replaced them with standard-gauge track. Branch lines to Palatka and Tocoi were added to the system, and in 1883 a new line was built south through San Mateo and Ormond to Daytona Beach. While construction

crews worked along the route, trains continued to run on regular schedules. A new station was built in St. Augustine and standard-gauge tracks laid over the entire route from Jacksonville to Daytona.

Admiring the sprawling splendor of the Ponce de Leon, the millionaire determined to build more in St. Augustine. Acting on orders from Flagler, Carrere and Hastings drew plans for a companion to the first hotel, a Spanish Renaissance castle to be called the Alcazar. Construction on the new hotel began in 1887 and was completed in 1889. The Alcazar was not as large as the Ponce de Leon, but it was a worthy neighbor. With a central court, arched arcades, towers, cupolas, and balconies, it rose four stories above the street. Its façade was a replica of the celebrated Alcazar in Seville. Inside, the hotel was equipped with sulphur and saltwater baths, steam rooms, and a complex of game courts. Outside, its walls of coquina and cement were banked with palms and spreading beds of flowers.

When the Alcazar was finished, Flagler added a third hotel to his St. Augustine holdings. Like the

Ponce de Leon, Casa Monica was a soaring Spanish castle, with an entrance inspired by the main portal of the Puerto del Sol in Toledo and balconies copied from iron galleries in Seville. The hotel was erected by a rival developer, one Franklin Smith, but purchased by Flagler soon after its completion. Renamed the Cordova, it became the oilman's third hotel in 1889. Visting St. Augustine soon after Flagler began his developments there, a reporter for *Harper's Weekly* marveled at the city's overnight metamorphosis from a sleepy village into a throbbing resort. ''It was but yesterday,'' the reporter noted, ''that in order to seek the most charming of retreats the whole of our continent had to be crossed, the objective point being the Pacific Ocean. To-day, perpetual summer can be had in a twinkling. You leave Boston or New York on a Monday morning, and by Wednesday you can gaze at the Ponce de Leon, the Alcazar, and the Casa Monica, and believe in Aladdin's palaces.''

Impressive though his St. Augustine developments were, Flagler's appetite for building was only whetted in the town. South along the ocean, the east coast of Florida was a vast and seemingly limitless expanse of sandy shore scarcely touched by human hands. When the state government offered his railroad, renamed the Florida East Coast Railway, handsome incentives to move farther south (including grants of as much as eight thousand acres of land per railroad mile), the millionaire ordered his construction crews to push south.

The railroad reached Ormond Beach, about fifty miles below St. Augustine, in 1890. There Flagler purchased the Ormond Beach Hotel, put up by northern investors a few years earlier. He enlarged it, built a golf course nearby, and added it to his chain of resort inns. South of Cape Canaveral, the railroad paralleled the long coastal lagoon known as the Indian River. In April 1894, nearly 250 miles south of St. Augustine, Flagler's tracks reached the shore of Lake Worth. Really a narrow arm of the sea rather than a lake, Worth divided the marshy mainland from a snake-like spit of sand and trees called Palm Beach. Extending for some fourteen miles along the coast, ranging in width from five hundred yards to three-quarters of a mile, Palm Beach was the site of a small huddle of houses and shacks when the Florida East Coast Railway reached it. Even before the railroad's arrival, Flagler had begun to develop the lagoon's two shores. In the spring of 1893 he laid out on the mainland side of the lake a town called West Palm

Beach, in which he hastily erected tents and cottages for construction workers. On the Palm Beach side he began to put up a large hotel.

Unlike his St. Augustine hotels, the Palm Beach inn was built of wood. Six stories tall, with a large central rotunda that served as the nexus of a labyrinth of hallways and verandas, it was conceived on a larger scale than any of the millionaire's previous hotels. Because it was started before the railroad reached Lake Worth, most of the materials for its construction were brought in by sea, and a formidable list of materials they were: no less than 5,000,000 board feet of lumber, 360,000 shingles, 500,000 bricks, 1,200 windows, 1,300 doors, and 1,400 kegs of nails. When completed, the hotel included 540 guest rooms and a dining room capable of seating nearly 800. Running out from the rotunda were spacious drawing rooms, lounges, parlors, and porches. The exterior of the building was painted a soft banana yellow with white trim and green shutters. One of the largest resort hotels in the world, the new structure was opened in February 1894 as the Royal Poinciana.

If anything, Flagler was even more impressed with Palm Beach than St. Augustine. Determined to make the coastal village one of the world's great resorts, the millionaire began to put up a second hotel a short distance east of the first. Built of wood like its massive neighbor, the new inn faced the ocean beach, where long breakers rolled incessantly on the sun-baked sand. Smaller than its neighbor, the ocean-front hotel matched the Royal Poinciana's elegance and style. Opened as the Palm Beach Inn, its name was soon changed to the Breakers.

A vast park spread over the beach between the Royal Poinciana and the Breakers. Acres of lawn were etched with curving walkways, spreading beds of flowers, and rows of nodding palms and Australian pines. A miniature railway, with cars pulled by donkeys, transported lazy guests between the two hotels. For those who wished to enjoy the sea air without the slightest physical exertion, wicker chairs with bicycles attached—called ''Afrimobiles'' in allusion to their black operators—crawled along the walkways and roads. Between the Breakers and the Poinciana was a large golf course.

Though his state permits allowed him to extend his railroad south of Lake Worth, Flagler did not think seriously about further development. He was pleased by his hotels at Palm Beach and by the rapid growth of its mainland neighbor, West Palm

The Royal Poinciana Hotel, Palm Beach. (Courtesy of the Henry Morrison Flagler Museum)

Beach. He continued to lavish affection on St. Augustine, where he built his own winter home and a vast, Venetian-style Presbyterian church, in which he reserved a mausoleum for his own remains. But his complacence was soon changed by a quirk in the weather.

A freeze of unexpected intensity struck the northern counties of Florida in the winter of 1894, burning grass and flowers, devastating thousands of acres of oranges. As citrus production, a mainstay of freight shipments on the Florida East Coast Railway, dropped from 5,500,000 boxes to only 150,000, Flagler sent out men to inspect the damage and devise ways to recoup losses. A small contingent of the millionaire's men strayed into the southern half of Florida and stopped for a rest in Miami. A widow named Julia Tuttle, who owned 640 acres of land near the junction of the Miami River and Biscayne Bay, was on hand to meet them. Miami was a small, isolated community of farmers and merchants in 1894, but Mrs. Tuttle believed it could be developed into a major resort—possibly the largest in all Florida—

if Flagler's railroad were brought to Biscayne Bay. Speaking with one of the developer's men, Mrs. Tuttle handed him a box of fresh orange blossoms carefully packed in dampened cotton. "Take them to Mr. Flagler," she said.

When the millionaire received Mrs. Tuttle's offering—proof that southern Florida had been untouched by the massive freeze—he quickly decided to move south. Acquiring a little more than half of the widow's land, he promised to extend the railroad to Miami and to build a terminal, streets, and a municipal water system. As his tracks moved south from Palm Beach, Flagler began to acquire more land on Biscayne Bay and to make plans for his inevitable hotel. Foundations for the building were laid on a plot of fifteen acres where the river met the bay. Called the Royal Palm, the new inn was five stories high, 680 feet long, and 267 feet wide. From its upper verandas breathtaking views spread out in all directions, northward and westward to the marshy expanse of the Everglades, eastward to Biscayne Bay and the sandy island called Miami Beach, southward to

Seaside view of the first Breakers Hotel. (Courtesy of the Henry Morrison Flagler Museum)

Key Biscayne and the silver Atlantic. Palms, growing in profusion about the hotel, shaded the maze of walks and roads that laced the property and swayed gently when trade winds blew in from the ocean.

The Florida East Coast Railway reached Biscayne Bay in April 1896. In July the city of Miami was incorporated and in January 1897, eleven months after foundations for the Royal Palm were laid, the inn was opened for business.

Miami grew rapidly after Flagler's arrival, attracting trainloads of determined sun-seekers, travelers from Pennsylvania, New York, and New England. When Miami Beach was opened to development, it, too, mushroomed. Flagler was pleased by developments in the southern city (which narrowly missed being named for him at the time of its incorporation), but he admitted he felt more at home in the placid surroundings of Palm Beach. Aspiring industrialists, ambitious speculators, parvenu millionaires, all found congenial surroundings in the bustling city on Biscayne Bay.

An older aristocracy, more sedate, more dignified, more discreet in its display of wealth and power, gravitated to Palm Beach. Wanamakers, Carnegies, Wideners, Phippses, and Stotesburys were often seen on the long verandas of the Royal Poinciana or rolling idly in "Afrimobiles" along the beach trail in front of the Breakers. Large private homes were built along the spit of sand between Lake Worth and the ocean—mansions with sheltered courts, heavy roofs, and lush tropical gardens. Lavish cottages, nestled here and there in the park that surrounded the Poinciana and the Breakers, were reserved for wealthy families who did not care to build private homes. Flagler himself spent much of his time at the hotels before his third wife persuaded him to put up Palm Beach's greatest mansion on a choice plot of land south of the Poinciana.

The second Mrs. Flagler had exhibited troubling signs of mental illness fifteen years after their wedding. Nurses were hired to watch her around the clock, and specialists were consulted for diagnoses. Sporadic periods of hospitalization seemed to do little to better her condition. After 1896 she was permanently confined to an institution in New York. Despite the fact that he had been separated from his wife for more than four years, Flagler's critics raised a storm of protest when he sought to divorce her in Miami in 1901. An amendment to Florida law that established for the first time incurable insanity as a ground for divorce in the state was derisively dubbed the "Flagler Divorce Law," since it had been passed only a few months before the decree was rendered. The fact that the millionaire provided handsomely for his spouse (her settlement was worth nearly three million dollars) eased some of the criticism, but his marriage to the thirty-four-year-old Mary Lily Kenan a week later rekindled the controversy. At the age of seventy-one Florida's Flagler was embarking on a third—and some thought scandalous—marital adventure.

If lavish wealth was what Mary Lily craved, her silver-haired husband did not disappoint her. A few months after they were married, ground was broken for Flagler's Palm Beach mansion.

The house was designed by the same New York architects who sixteen years earlier had drawn the plans for the Ponce de Leon. "Build me the finest home you can think of," the millionaire told Carrere and Hastings, "and don't waste time doing it." Already past his "allotted" three-score-and-ten, Flagler was concerned that he might not live to occupy a house that took several years to build. The architects did not disappoint him. Eight months after ground was broken for the mansion called Whitehall, the house was finished. Visiting Palm Beach in March 1902, a reporter for the *New York Herald* described the mansion as "more wonderful than any palace in Europe, grander and more magnificent than any other private dwelling in the world."

It was a dazzling villa of white marble with long columns, soaring arches, broad steps, and a heavy tile roof. In front it faced a long walk edged with coco palms and marble benches. In back it looked over a sun-splashed beach and the blue expanse of Lake Worth. Its entrance was marked by massive bronze doors poised so delicately on cylindrical hinges that the slightest pressure from a child could open them. Behind the doors was a foyer or lobby a hundred feet long and forty feet wide, with walls and floors finished in seven shades of delicately veined marble. Cavernous salons, gaping corridors, a vast ballroom, a library, music room, and dining room surrounded the tiled central court. Twin stairways led from the foyer to the second-floor bedrooms, which numbered no less than thirteen. Throughout the house ornate sculptures, gilded medallions, rare tapestries, glittering chandeliers set off the rich walls and floors. In the foyer a nine-foot rosewood clock was installed to remind Flagler of the month, year, and day as well as the hour. But the great bronze doors were equipped neither with locks nor bells, for liveried doormen were on duty at all hours to greet visitors or see departing guests to their carriages. Estimates of the cost of the mansion varied from $2,000,000 to $5,000,000. Judged conservatively, Whitehall could not have cost its owner less than $2,500,000. Surveying the broad halls and soaring columns of her own Taj Mahal, the thirty-five-year-old Mary Lily declared herself well satisfied with her accomplishment.

But her septuagenarian husband still harbored ambitions. Below Miami a string of palm-ringed coral islands swept in a long arc to the south and west, extending 150 miles from Biscayne Bay to Key West, ninety miles from Havana. As early as 1831 newspapers in the Florida Keys had written longingly of a railroad that would someday connect the islands with the mainland. But great ex-

The Palm Beach Inn, later renamed the Breakers Hotel. (Courtesy of the Henry Morrison Flagler Museum)

panses of open sea constituted formidable barriers to any such road. By the 1890s those who still believed the Florida Keys could be spanned by a railroad centered their hopes on Flagler. He was the only man in the state who might successfully undertake and complete such a vast project.

The developer showed a little interest in the idea. He bought land in the keys and sent engineers and surveyors south to inspect the islands and the ocean straits that divided them. Much of his fortune had been invested in his developments in St. Augustine, Palm Beach, and Miami, and he was more than a little reluctant to undertake a larger and even more speculative project. But his marriage to Mary Lily had fired him anew with vigor. Perhaps more important, a recent balance sheet of the Standard Oil Trust convinced him that he need not trouble himself with costs.

Flagler was seventy-five years old when he gave the order to begin construction of the "Overseas Railroad" to Key West. It was a vast engineering project. Trestles, causeways, and bridges had to be built across hundreds of keys and hundreds of open stretches of sea. As the first year of construction passed, then the second and third, Flagler fidgeted. Would he live long enough to see the vast project completed? Would engineers successfully solve the many difficult technical problems? Millions of dollars were sunk in the sea as four thousand men worked feverishly to push the ribbon of iron rails toward Key West. Mosquitoes were a constant hazard, and hurricanes occasionally forced abandonment of work, but the crews pushed on. Flagler's eightieth birthday passed, and still the road was not finished—but the end was growing closer. It was January 22, 1912, twenty days after the millionaire's eighty-second birthday, when a special train of the Florida East Coast Railway at last pushed into Key West and a crowd of spectators greeted it with a chorus of cheers. Bursting with pride, Henry Flagler waved frailly from an observation car.

The millionaire died fourteen months after the road was completed. His passing left a void, but not an unfillable void, in Florida. The institutions he left were durable, if not imperishable, monuments to his energy and vision. Trains still sped along the polished rails of the Florida East Coast Railway from Jacksonville in the north to Key West in the south, a route that was probably the longest stretch of rails in the United States ever financed by a single man. The complex of Flagler hotels at St. Augustine still threw open their doors to flurries of winter vacationers, some of whom now and

then strayed into the neighboring Presbyterian church to admire the marble sarcophagus of Henry Flagler. Miami grew rapidly, soon becoming Florida's most popular seaside resort and a major commercial center as well. Palm Beach, which had supplanted St. Augustine as Flagler's favorite Florida development, settled into comfortable opulence as the single richest community in the United States—possibly in the world (its several hundred families, according to the Florida Development Commission, controlled three-quarters of the wealth in the country).

Palm Beach reached its zenith in the 1920s, the frenzied decade of flappers and bathtub gin, stock market speculation and jazz, Warren Harding and Calvin Coolidge, Billy Sunday and Al Capone. Mrs. E. T. Stotesbury of Philadelphia was the reigning queen of island society in those days, though she had more or less hopeful rivals in Mrs. Isabel Dodge Sloan, Mrs. James P. Donahue, Mrs. Harrison Williams, Mrs. Joseph P. Kennedy, Consuelo Vanderbilt Balsan, and Marjorie Merriweather Post (alternately Mrs. E. F. Hutton and Mrs. Joseph E. Davies).

Flagler's personal wealth lived long after his death, though some of his institutions did not. Most of his estate was put in the hands of trustees, though Mary Lily was well provided for, and there were numerous charitable bequests. Mary Lily lived only until 1917. Flagler's second wife, still hopelessly institutionalized, did not die until 1930, by which time her 1901 marital settlement had grown from $3,000,000 to more than $15,000,000.

After Mary Lily's death Whitehall was converted into a private club. In 1925 a three-hundred-room, ten-story tower was added to the west side of the mansion, which was opened as Palm Beach's newest luxury hotel.

St. Augustine's development had been hampered by its harbor, shallow and strewn with treacherous sandbars, and the town did not develop as Flagler had hoped. The great hotels in the center of the city remained dark and empty for many years until new uses could be found for them. The Alcazar and Cordova became city and county office buildings, and the Ponce de Leon was converted into Flagler College. On Labor Day, 1935, the "Overseas Railroad" to Key West was whipped and torn by an angry hurricane that twisted rails, tumbled causeways, and toppled bridges along a major part of the route. Directors of the Florida East Coast Railway declined to rebuild the road, so the State Road Department took over the chain of bridges and used them as the foundation for a spectacular Overseas Highway to Key West that was completed in 1938.

The Ormond Beach Hotel became a retirement home, while the Royal Palm in Miami and the Royal Poinciana in Palm Beach were eventually leveled to make way for other more modern developments. In 1959 the tower extension of Whitehall was demolished and the mansion restored to its 1902 appearance. At a gala ball given for the elite of Palm Beach society the house was dedicated as the Henry Morrison Flagler Museum.

Alone among the many inns and resorts built by Flagler along the east coast of Florida, the Breakers continued to operate as a hotel. Its survival was the ironic result of a tragedy which might have spelled its death but instead gave it a new lease on life. On the afternoon of March 18, 1925, a small fire kindled in one of the bedrooms spread rapidly· through adjoining bedrooms and halls. Water pressure in the old building was inadequate to the task of containing the flames. Guests fled as the fire roared hungrily through the lobbies, parlors, and dining rooms. Embers blown by the wind settled on the roof of the Royal Poinciana, threatening for a time to set it afire, but firemen dashed water on the building in time to save it. When the flames were finally extinguished, the Breakers lay in a twisted, blackened rubble.

Some personal property had been removed from the building before it was finally destroyed. An army of millionaires and millionairesses spent most of the following day rummaging through the mountain of luggage hurriedly deposited in the Poinciana ballroom. Mrs. D. S. Culver of St. Paul, Minnesota, bemoaned the loss of a trunk containing sixty thousand dollars worth of jewels. Mrs. M. G. Wendt of New York tearfully reported a loss of more than two hundred thousand dollars. Some tears were dried when the vault of the ruined hotel was found to be intact and it yielded up a treasure of jewels and other valuables worth three hundred thousand dollars. But the recovery did little to soothe the concern of the directors of the Florida East Coast Railway, which held title to the property. Their own loss had exceeded two million dollars.

Fearful that the disaster` might destroy the tourist business of Palm Beach, the directors hurriedly met in the Royal Poinciana to announce that the Breakers would be rebuilt. Work would start as soon as plans could be finished, and the new structure would open in time for the next season, scheduled to begin January 1, 1926.

But the directors' predictions were too optimis-

tic, and construction was not finished until nearly a year after the projected completion date. When, on December 29, 1926, the hotel finally threw open its doors to guests, Palm Beach regulars were satisfied that the wait had been worthwhile.

Designed by Leonard Schultze of the New York and California architectural firm of Schultze and Weaver, it was a soaring structure of concrete and stucco, with nine stories, twin towers, and more than five hundred guest rooms. Its façade was inspired by the Palazzo of the Villa Medici in Rome; its delicate, sculptured central fountain by that of Florence's Bobli Gardens. Inside, the dining rooms and salons were redolent with memories of the Rome of the Borgias, the Milan of Duke Lodovico. The grand lobby, with vaulted and frescoed ceilings, captured the atmosphere of the Piazza Carega in Genoa. The ceiling of the Gold Room was copied from one in the Doge's Palace in Venice. The domed dining room was perhaps the hotel's most beautiful chamber—ornately carved and inlaid like that of the Florentine Palace Davanzate. Opened on December 29, 1926, the new Breakers satisfied fastidious Palm Beachers that the resort had a future as well as a past.

Fearful that fire would engulf the Royal Poinciana as it had the old Breakers, railroad directors ordered that the wooden hotel be demolished. Regulars of the resort grieved when the great inn disappeared, but their grief was quickly forgotten in the luxury of the Breakers. Through the thirties, forties, and fifties the seaside hotel remained the queen of Palm Beach hostelries. Cadillac limousines lined up beneath its entrance canopy as industrialists, bankers, and investors, accompanied by stiff-lipped, fur-wrapped dowagers, were helped into the lobby by liveried doormen. Quiet games of bridge occupied the ladies in the vaulted card room while their husbands chased golf balls on the nearby Poinciana links.

"The trouble with Palm Beach," said American Broadcasting Company President Robert Kintner early in the fifties, "is that by the time you can afford it you're too old to enjoy it." Frazier Jelke recalled that his parents paid $3,000 a month for four rooms at Palm Beach's Everglades Club and, when they moved to the Breakers, they paid $6,000 a month—but this time meals were included. The first secretary of the Palm Beach Bath and Tennis Club summed up the atmosphere of the resort when he declared emphatically, "Nobody should come to Palm Beach who doesn't have money."

But nothing in the world is immune from

change—not even staid Palm Beach. High-rise apartments began to crowd Worth Avenue in the 1960s and '70s. The flow of Cadillac limousines at the entrance to the Breakers declined to a trickle. The cadre of jeweled dowagers, their ranks seriously depleted by the graduated income tax, retired to private chambers. During the spring and summer of 1969 the Flagler heirs, who still owned the hotel, began an extensive expansion program. A new Venetian ballroom was built overlooking the ocean. An intimate lounge was decorated in Moorish style and named for Flagler's Alcazar in St. Augustine. New wings of guest rooms were built, a new Breakers Beach Club opened, and a West Golf Course added to the existing Poinciana golf links.

Visiting the hotel in the seventies, a writer for *Holiday* magazine heard Palm Beachers complain, "It isn't what it used to be." "Of course it isn't," the writer answered. "Nothing is. . . . But only yesterday's society is gone. Preserved for us and generations that follow is one of the world's most exceptional resort hotels. . . . America's answer to European criticism of American taste."

The Breakers is, of course, more than an exceptional resort hotel. It is a reminder of the days when modern Florida was being carved out of a waste of sand and palms. It is a direct link with the silver-haired "Robber Baron" who poured millions into the sun-washed peninsula and watched it emerge from obscurity into glamour and prosperity. The Breakers, as much as its neighbor Whitehall, is a museum—vaulted, towered, arched, frescoed—the last of Henry Flagler's great hotels, but evidence enough that the millionaire's tradition of hospitality still lives.

13

On the Great Sky Top

MOHONK MOUNTAIN HOUSE, LAKE MOHONK

A spectacular natural setting combined with the gentle art of "friendly persuasion" made the rambling Mountain House at Lake Mohonk one of New York State's most popular summer resorts in the last years of the nineteenth century. Suceeding generations of Mohonk owners, kinsmen of the determined Quaker schoolmaster who founded the resort in 1869, have maintained the great hotel much as it was a century ago—a fairy-tale castle of wood and stone balanced on the rocky lip of a lake more than a thousand feet above the nearby Hudson River Valley.

The Shawangunk Mountains have often and unfairly been confused with their more celebrated northwestern neighbors, the Catskills. Rising precipitously from the Hudson Valley near Kingston, the mountains run southwesterly through Ulster and Orange counties into northwestern New Jersey, where they merge with the Kittatinny range.

Bounded on the southeast by the Wallkill Valley and on the northwest by the valley of the Rondout Creek, the Shawangunks rise at their highest levels to something over 1,800 feet above sea level. The Catskills are a loftier range, embracing at least two peaks which exceed four thousand feet in elevation. Viewed from a distance, the heavily wooded Catskills are soft and round, warm and inviting, lying on the horizon, as their biographer Alf Evers has written, "blue and mysterious." The Shawangunks are more rugged, more arrestingly spectacular mountains. Their spine is a narrow ridge of tumbled rock wooded with tenuous stands of white pine, red maple, oak, chestnuts, and hemlock. Unlike their neighbors, the Shawangunks are hard and angular, glistening like diamonds in the white light of morning, shimmering in the yellow luster of afternoon, casting black and jagged profiles against the western horizon when sunset turns the sky to crimson.

Unlike most mountain lakes, Mohonk does not rest in a secluded vale guarded by wooded slopes, watered by freshets of rain or icy, snow-fed creeks. Like its southern neighbor, Lake Minnewaska, it perches precariously in a cleft of rock near the crest of the mountain ridge, facing on one side the peak known as Sky Top, and on the other the broad expanse of the Rondout Valley. Beyond the Rondout, blue and misty in the distance, the Catskills float lazily on the horizon. The Mountain House, occupying a ledge of land at the northwestern corner of the lake, is so close to the water that canoes occasionally bump against its timbers, so high above the valley that its cupolas and turrets loom like watchtowers and its windows, catching the afternoon sun, send beams of light miles into the Catskills.

A little less than half a mile long, an eighth of a mile wide, and sixty feet deep, the lake was formed by a succession of geological accidents. Hundreds of millions of years ago vast sheets of shale were raised and twisted by Herculean forces to form a rugged range of hills. Above them a harder layer of white sandstone conglomerate raised the hills to the elevation of mountains. Glaciers

The Mohonk Mountain House, Mohonk Lake, New York (Courtesy of Mohonk Mountain House)

coming down from the north pushed boulders before them, scoured the sides of the peaks, and carved deep rents in the summits. Near the northern end of the Shawangunks two faults in the crust of conglomerate were filled with the waters of natural springs. Lake Minnewaska was a long sheet of water that formed near the crest of the mountains 1,600 feet above sea level. Mohonk, seven miles to the northeast, was a smaller, more intimate lake that rested at an elevation of just over 1,200 feet. Centuries of erosion softened the layer of shale that formed the base of the mountains, an effect that caused the harder conglomerate on top to crack and splinter so that cliffs tumbled and boulders and monoliths piled up like the playthings of some race of giant children.

The Algonquin Indians who inhabited the Hudson Valley made no settlements in the mountains, though they visited them frequently and bestowed imaginative names on many of their most prominent features. "Shawangunk" (Pile of White Rock) referred to the glistening cliffs of the mountains, "Minnewaska" (Floating Waters) to the large lake that straddled the mountain ridge, "Mohonk" (On the Great Sky Top) to the knob of rock that loomed above the other and smaller lake. Dutch settlers from the Wallkill and Rondout Valleys and Huguenots from the nearby village of New Paltz, on the eastern slope of the mountains, made picnic and camping excursions into the hills, where they marveled at the profusion of weirdly tumbled rocks and the panoramic views that spread out from the highest peaks. Artists from New York City occasionally strayed into the mountains determined to brave the rutted roads and precipitous trails to catch some part of the Shawangunk beauty on canvas.

In the 1850s a farmer named John Stokes, who

lived at the northern base of the mountains, began to buy land in the vicinity of Lake Mohonk. Picnic parties had become increasingly popular in the area, and Stokes shrewdly anticipated that the mountain crest would soon become valuable. Adding gradually to his holdings, he acquired title to the whole of the lake and a generous expanse of surrounding land. Primitive roads were built westward from New Paltz. A house with a barroom, a large ballroom, and ten guest rooms was put up near the northern end of the lake. Stokes' principal business was in liquor, which he dispensed with the help of a wizened woman and a muscular young Irishman. When guests at the house demanded dinner, the Irishman caught a chicken, killed it in front of the house, and passed it to the woman to cook. When denizens of the barroom drank too much (which was often), Stokes banished them to the rocky shore of the lake. Despite its rough-and-ready atmosphere, Stokes' business flourished. Campers came into the mountains and pitched their tents near the lake. Canoes and boats appeared on the water, and a long list of vacationers waited for rooms in the tavern.

Albert Keith Smiley was forty-one years old and content with his life as a schoolmaster when, in the late summer of 1869, his twin brother Alfred set out from his home in Poughkeepsie to explore the nearby Shawangunks.

The brothers had been born in March 1828 to Quaker parents in Kennebec County, Maine. Graduating from Pennsylvania's Haverford College in 1849, Albert commenced a distinguished career as a teacher and schoolmaster in Pennsylvania and Maine. With Alfred he founded the English and Classical Academy at Philadelphia and in 1860 became principal of the prestigious Friends' School at Providence, Rhode Island.

Both brothers were devout Quakers who abhorred all forms of drinking and carousing, and Alfred was more than a little scandalized by John Stokes' tavern. But the wild beauty of the mountains and lake made up for the bad impression given by the house. When Stokes hinted that his craggy domain might be for sale, Alfred wrote to his brother, urging him to come west and inspect the property.

With the innkeeper as their guide, the Smileys walked along the lakeshore. Stokes was a shrewd businessman, but the Quakers thought he had little feeling for the natural beauty that surrounded him. "I suppose," he said sourly, snatching a leaf from a bush, "that the Creator made everything

for some use; but what in the world he ever made this pizen laurel for I can't see. It never grows big enough for firewood, and the cattle won't eat it."

Stokes told the Smileys that he owned three hundred acres on the mountain top and showed them a map to prove it. As the men climbed upward through the rocks, they found a trail that led to the jagged summit of Sky Top, nearly three hundred feet above the water. Below them, nestled in its cleft of rock like a giant sapphire in a setting of gold, was Lake Mohonk. On every side magnificent views revealed themselves—the Rondout, Wallkill, and Hudson valleys, quiet and velvety green; the Catskills, blue on the horizon; the white water of the Hudson at West Point, clear and bright in the sun; the Kittatinnies of New Jersey looming on the southern horizon; the Taconics of Connecticut to the east; and far to the north, the Berkshires of Massachusetts and the Green Mountains of Vermont, rolling, wave on wave, seemingly to the end of the earth.

In the evening at the tavern the men talked business. Stokes was willing to sell his mountain

Albert Smiley and his twin brother Alfred (Courtesy of Mohonk Mountain House)

domain for forty thousand dollars. It was not an inconsiderable sum, but the brothers thought it worthy of consideration. Albert had saved fourteen thousand dollars, which he believed would be enough to bind any transaction. Leaving for Providence the next morning, he instructed his brother to bargain with Stokes, to get a lower price if he could but, if not, to agree to the figure asked. Back in his Rhode Island schoolhouse, Albert received a happy letter from Alfred advising that Stokes had finally agreed to a price of twenty-eight thousand dollars.

"I bought Mohonk with the idea of making it a home," Albert remembered years later, explaining that he hankered for a summer retreat where he could enjoy pure mountain air and forget his schoolhouse duties. A manager was employed to operate the tavern for a year of two; then Alfred agreed to move to the lake and manage the property for his brother. The old building was repainted, remodeled, and enlarged to make room for about forty guests. Under the Smileys' management, the inn was dramatically different than it had been when Stokes owned it. Drinking was

Lake Mohonk, 1890 (Guide-Book to Mohonk Lake)

forbidden, as were such other un-Quaker vices as dancing, smoking, and card playing, and prospective visitors were solemnly cautioned not to arrive or depart on the Sabbath. Despite its austerity, the Smileys' "genteel summer boarding house" attracted visitors from near and far.

Albert continued to work in Rhode Island until 1879, all the while sending money to Alfred to help with improvements at Mohonk. A continuing program of additions enhanced the building's beauty and greatly increased its size. New guest rooms, parlors, large dining rooms, docks, boat houses, and dozens of summer houses doubled, tripled, then quadrupled the inn's facilities. Profits from the business were used to buy nearby tracts of land, additions vastly increasing the Mohonk holdings. As the inn was enlarged, roads were built around and about the lake and through the adjoining wilderness of rocks and trees. A woodland drive was laid out at the base of Eagle Cliff and through a neighboring forest of chestnuts. A scenic road was built along the eastern edge of the lake. In quick succession other roads were extended to Cope's Lookout, North Lookout, and Sky Top. The roads made the principal points of interest accessible to carriages and stages, but trails and paths invited visitors to explore less approachable recesses—rock-walled fissures, tree-clogged labyrinths, vales tangled with brambles and vines.

The soil on the mountain ridge was thin and rocky. Lichens and ferns flourished among the rocks, and trees clawed at the cliffs with sinewy roots, but flowering shrubs and vines found the hard earth inhospitable. Albert Smiley was determined to grow flowers at the lake and, after 1880, when he left the Friends' School to live permanently at Mohonk, he worked diligently to cultivate gardens. Soil was hauled in from miles away. Special containers were built around the edges of the hotel. A large garden northeast of the lake was laid out. Soon azaleas and rhododendrons, roses, geraniums, and delphiniums painted the mountain with brilliant colors.

When in 1880 Alfred Smiley left Mohonk to develop a resort hotel at Minnewaska, Albert asked his younger brother Daniel to help him with the management of the Mountain House. By 1892 Daniel had assumed full control of the hotel.

Albert, meanwhile, was busy with other projects. Corn and hay were raised on lower slopes of the Mohonk tract, while on others dairy cows were grazed. There were horses to be fed in the stables and milk and butter to be hauled up the slopes to the Mohonk kitchens. When horse-drawn stages carrying passengers from the train station in New Paltz clattered over the wooden bridge, the proprietor scrambled down the front steps to greet them.

Albert's interest in social and cultural affairs continued unabated after his retirement from teaching. In 1875 he became a member of the Board of Trustees of Providence's Brown University. A little later he took a similar post on the board of Bryn Mawr College. In 1884, when a State Normal School was established in New Paltz, he became first president of its Board of Trustees. Albert, interested in the life and history of the native Americans, collected artifacts, studied languages and dialects, and exchanged letters with students of Indian lore throughout the country. Recognizing his interest in the original Americans, President Rutherford B. Hayes named him to the United States Board of Indian Commissioners in 1879. Meeting with his fellow commissioners, Smiley was surprised to discover that they had little understanding of the Indians' problems. "Come to my house," he said, "and we'll talk it over."

The first meeting of Indian commissioners, held at Mohonk in 1883, was so successful that Smiley invited the commissioners to return the next year—and again the next. In 1885 he organized a Conference of Friends of the Indians that brought experts on Indian problems from all over the country to the Mountain House. The conferences were repeated each year, making Mohonk one of the nation's leading conference centers. As he expanded his humanitarian horizons, Smiley turned his attention from the Indians to other pressing social concerns. The problems of black Americans were the subject of Mohonk conferences in 1890 and 1891, and in 1895 Smiley organized the first of a series of Conferences on International Arbitration to promote the cause of the peaceful settlement of international disputes.

By the turn of the century Mohonk was a vast wonderland of natural and recreational beauty. Smiley's total holdings had increased to about five thousand acres, and the hotel had grown to more than three hundred rooms. It was a vast building, nearly one-eighth mile in length, a soaring mass of towers and turrets, balconies, verandas, and gables—built in some parts of wood, in others of brick or stone—surrounded by lawns and broad beds of flowers. If King Ludwig had built the Mountain House on a slope of the Bavarian Alps, the pile would have been taken as evidence of royal dementia. If Hans Christian Andersen or

Summer vacationers at Mohonk in the 1890's (Courtesy of Mohonk Mountain House)

the Brothers Grimm had described it in one of their fairy fantasies, it would have been regarded as the handiwork of literary genius. At Mohonk in the Shawangunk Mountains of southeastern New York, it was accepted for what it was—a resort hotel of grandeur, imagination, and surpassing comfort.

In summers the lake was typically crowded with boats, some with fishermen aboard, others with men in starched shirts and bowler hats, with pink-cheeked women lolling lazily beneath parasols. Bathers relaxed on the lakeside beach, and hikers swarmed over the nearby mountain slopes. The season ended in mid-October, when the chill winds of autumn blew down from the north, rustling dead leaves in the roads, whipping the surface of the lake into angry waves. Only a few hardy souls remained on the mountain after the first snows fell. They gathered wood to burn in the hotel's fireplaces, skated on the surface of the lake, and rode sleighs on the snow-banked roads. After 1889, when Smiley bought a large ranch in southern California, he, too, left the mountain in winters. His California property, near the town of Redlands southwest of Los Angeles, was devel-

oped into a private park with lavish plantings of shrubs, trees, and tropical flowers.

Part of the profits of Mohonk went into the California land, but an even larger part was used to continue development of the New York resort. Additional acreage was purchased, new roads were laid out, and old ones repaired. Observation towers were built at points of vantage in the mountains, and a large golf course was planted. A dining hall capable of seating five hundred diners at a single meal was finished in the 1890s, and a huge parlor, forty-five feet by sixty feet, was completed in 1899. In 1907, to honor the golden wedding anniversary of Albert Smiley and his wife Eliza, two thousand loyal guests of the Mountain House joined to put up a stone gateway at the entrance to the Mohonk grounds. Christened the Smiley Testimonial Gateway, the structure, an impressive towered arch, was evidence of the widespread affection felt for the schoolmaster who had built Mohonk into one of the world's great resorts.

The Mountain House changed little after Albert Smiley's death in 1912. Daniel managed the hotel and estate until his own death in 1930, after which Daniel's sons and grandsons took charge of the property. Two thousand acres were added to Albert's holdings, bringing the total Mohonk acreage to 7,500. Though the inn's appearance remained much as it had been in the early 1900s, significant changes were made in its operation. After 1933 the hotel remained open in winter for the benefit of skiers and other winter sports enthusiasts. The prohibition against dancing was rescinded. Drinking was permitted in the private rooms, and cocktails were served in the dining room, though there was no bar, and smoking was still forbidden in the dining halls.

The automobile came slowly to Mohonk. Through the 1910s and '20s "horseless carriages" were shunned by Mohonk regulars, who regarded the puffing machines as an affront to the inn's traditional surreys and buggies. It was not until 1930 that automobiles were allowed to approach the hotel, and then only under the supervision of Mohonk drivers. When the roads were improved with dividers, painted arrows, and directional signs, private motorists were permitted to pilot their own vehicles in and out of the mountain estate.

Despite its resistance to the encroachments of twentieth-century life, the Mountain House found itself threatened by the commercial development of neighboring land, the advent of high-speed throughways, the creeping growth of towns and cities in the nearby valleys. After 1930 the estate was operated as a partnership of the sons of Daniel Smiley. In 1963 the Mohonk Trust was established to administer land surrounding the Mountain House as a natural preserve. As defined by its charter, the principal goals of the trust were to preserve the wildlands of Mohonk in perpetuity for recreation, inspiration, and scientific research, and to promote international understanding and peace through conferences and informal exchanges of ideas in the inspiring Mohonk setting. By 1977 the trust had acquired more than five thousand acres of the Mohonk estate. The Mountain House was owned and operated by Smiley Brothers, Inc., successor to the old Smiley partnership.

Mohonk entered its second century of operation in 1969. It was a dowager queen of hotels, but a hale and healthy dowager that still enjoyed the

The spacious parlor at the Mohonk Mountain House (Courtesy of Mohonk Mountain House)

Riding horse-drawn sleighs on the snow-banked roads of Mohonk, winter 1970 (Courtesy of the Mohonk Mountain House)

patronage and affection of hundreds of thousands of vacationers. The lake was crowded in summers, as it had been in the days of Albert Smiley, and hikers still swarmed over the maze of mountain trails. In winter skiers and skaters warmed themselves beside the hotel's great fireplaces, and horse-drawn sleighs glided over the snow-banked roads. Christmas was a time of festivity. After a dinner of roast goose with sugarplums and fresh chestnut dressing, guests gathered in the great parlor to decorate a huge tree and sing traditional carols. The celebration was a pretty sight—a perpetuation of old values, an expression of conti-

nuity in a world badly disjointed by the rush of time and events.

To traditionalists, Mohonk's fidelity to the ways of a century past is reassuring. It demonstrates that the hotel's ideals transcend the narrow limits of time and mean profits, that the best of the old can survive in a world nearly overwhelmed by the new. More than anything else, it proves the enduring quality of Albert Smiley's vision. If the old Quaker were alive to see his Mountain House today, there is little doubt that he would be pleased by the sight.

14

A Paragon of Grandeur

THE PLAZA, NEW YORK CITY

The plaza that nestles beneath tall buildings and leafy trees at the wooded southeastern corner of Central Park is one of Manhattan's last and grandest concessions to urban civility. It was a treeless expanse of brick and cobbles in the 1880s and '90s, veined by the polished steel rails of the Fifty-ninth Street horse-trolley and crowded on afternoons and holidays by the sleek carriages of millionaires who entered and exited the nearby expanse of green. In winter, snow mantled the pavement, and the wheels of hansom cabs drew delicate lines in the blanket of shimmering white, as mufflered and mittened skaters crowded the frozen surface of a diminutive lake called The Pond. In 1908 the plaza was decorated with an equestrian statue of General William Tecumseh Sherman, the work of Augustus Saint-Gaudens. In 1912 it was further ornamented with a spectacular marble and bronze fountain financed by the estate of Joseph Pulitzer and designed by Thomas Hastings, Henry Flagler's St. Augustine architect and the designer of the New York Public Library. Trees planted at the edges of the expanse unfolded in spring and summer into umbrageous canopies of green, ripened in fall to rich red and gold, and in winter raised thin fingers of leafless wood into the storm-darkened sky. Manhattanphile Ed Sullivan thought the square, officially denominated Grand Army Plaza, "the most beautiful sight in New York." Others called it "America's Place de la Concorde," a sobriquet that aptly described its noble character, if it exaggerated its physical dimensions.

It was one of Manhattan's most welcome sanctuaries, a refuge from the turmoil of crowded streets, looming skyscrapers, and murky subways. But it was more than a haven, more than a sheltered port for harried denizens of the city. It was the setting for one of New York's—and the world's—great caravansaries: a palace inn in many ways as notable as the square and park together. When the Plaza Hotel opened its doors in the first decade of the twentieth century, it was acclaimed as America's greatest hotel, the ne plus ultra of commercial hospitality. Nearly three-quarters of a century later, many still accord it that honor.

The Plaza's opening date—October 1907—qualifies it as one of the country's oldest hotel structures. In its life of seventy years, it has seen dozens of lesser inns rise from the bedrock of Manhattan, blossom into citadels of fashion, then decline into obscurity or, worse, bow to the inexorable summons of the wrecker's ball. The Plaza is, as hotels go, an old hotel, but its tradition is even more venerable, dating back to the flickering eighties and nineties, when the forward-looking social and financial leaders of New York were laying foundations for the great new century to come.

Fifth Avenue above Fiftieth Street was an avenue of millionaires' mansions in the last years of the nineteenth century, lined on either side by looming chateaux, gaping castles, neo-Renaissance palazzos, villas, and townhouses that bulged with expensive paintings, exotic tapestries, and rare antiques. On the west side of the avenue,

The Plaza Hotel from Central Park, 1907. Photograph by Byron. (Courtesy of the Byron Collection, Museum of the City of New York)

The Grand Army Plaza in spring, as depicted on canvas by Howard B. Spencer, 1953 (Courtesy of the New York Historical Society, New York City)

between Fifty-seventh and Fifty-eighth, the one-hundred-room French Renaissance chateau built by Cornelius Vanderbilt in 1895 looked down on the cobbled plaza that bordered the park. West of the square stood the New York Skating Club, a fashionable rink that drew its water from The Pond and its coterie of polite winter sportsmen from the elite society that swirled around Manhattan's reigning social queen, Mrs. William Astor.

Long before the Vanderbilt mansion was built, the parkside rink was threatened by the rapid increase of property values in the neighborhood. Nine blocks to the south the looming spires of St. Patrick's Cathedral, completed in 1879, gave impetus to the northward march of fashionable society. In 1883 John Charles Anderson sold the skating club property—approximately one and a quarter acres facing Grand Army Plaza between Fifty-eighth and Fifty-ninth—to John R. Phyfe and James Campbell for the grand sum of $850,000.

The property was not bought as the site for another mansion. Its new owners—ambitious investors rather than posturing magnificoes—sensed the vast economic potential of the parkside oasis. Gathering half a million dollars of their own money, Phyfe and Campbell borrowed an additional eight hundred thousand dollars from the New York Life Insurance Company and made plans to build a large hotel on the property. Their bankroll was impressive, but it paled beside the splendor of the projected inn. The building would occupy the entire block between Fifty-eighth and Fifty-ninth streets, rise eight stories above the surface of the plaza, and include accommodations for more than five hundred persons. Construction was already under way when, in November 1887, the investors realized the inadequacy of their financing. They failed to make their mortgage payments, and New York Life foreclosed on the property. But construction continued under the insurance company's aegis, and by October 1, 1890, the building was ready for a formal opening.

"A sumptuous bed of rich red roses," wrote a *New York Times* reporter, "marked the centre of one of the largest oval tables ever set in New York at the new Plaza Hotel last evening. Around the table sat nearly half a hundred influential well-wishers of the new enterprise." Taken on a tour of the inn, the reporter noted the mahogany furniture and finishings, the delicately tinted parlors and bedrooms, the mosaic bathrooms, the gold and white dining room with stained glass windows and arched ceilings threaded in gold. "The hotel probably cost $1,500,000," the reporter continued,

"and the furniture will cost $500,000. The management of the new establishment have selected the lion as their 'trade mark,' and a remarkably fine specimen of the king of beasts forms the central feature of the mosaic tiling in the main entrance hall. The figure of a lion is woven in the lace curtains at each window, and the head of the same stalwart beast adorns each piece of silver and each piece of china on the table."

With the opening of the Plaza, traffic on Fifth Avenue increased dramatically. Now carriages and cabs crowded Fifty-ninth Street and Grand Army Plaza mornings and weeknights, as well as on the usual afternoons and holidays, disgorging cargoes of silk-hatted millionaires and jeweled dowagers at the hotel's Fifth Avenue portico. The success of the Plaza attracted envious eyes to neighboring properties, which seemed as likely for hotel development as the former skating club site developed by Phyfe and Campbell.

Following quickly on the heels of the Plaza, ground was broken on the east side of Fifth Avenue for two new hotels. At the southeastern corner of the Avenue and Fifty-ninth Street Judge P. Henry Dugro put up the limestone Savoy. Across from it, at the northeastern corner of Fifth Avenue and Fifty-ninth Street, William Waldorf Astor erected a fifteen-story brownstone fortress which he called the Netherland Hotel. "For at least twenty years past," reported *Frank Leslie's Weekly* in March 1892, "Madison Square has been what might be called the hotel centre of the metropolis. . . . But in a little while this centre will have moved still farther up, and probably stop at Fifty-ninth Street and Fifth Avenue, at the entrance to Central Park. There it will probably linger as long as it did in Madison Square."

The Plaza was leased for a term of fifteen years to David and Frederick Hammond at a rental of $125,000 a year, a handsome sum that was guaranteed to yield the insurance company a healthy return on its investment. But the value of upper Fifth Avenue property was increasing more rapidly than even the most starry-eyed speculators could dream. By 1902 New York Life found itself considering a torrent of proposals to buy the property. The successful bidder was the aggressive George Fuller Construction Company, builder of New York's first skyscraper, the Flatiron Building at Fifth Avenue and Twenty-third Street. Newspaper readers were shocked when they read that the Plaza had been bought by Fuller for three million dollars, said to have been the largest sum ever paid for a single parcel of Manhattan real estate. Their

The first Plaza Hotel. (Courtesy of the Plaza Hotel)

shock turned quickly to disbelief when Fuller announced its intention to raze the twelve-year-old Plaza and build a new hotel in its place. Demolition would begin in 1905, the buyers announced, when the Hammonds' fifteen-year lease expired. Work would immediately begin on a mammoth new building expected to cost no less than twelve million dollars.

Guiding spirits of the audacious enterprise were a group of men whose enviable records in business and finance had shown that grandiose schemes could be matched by ability to perform. Canadian-born Harry St. Francis Black had been a successful banker in Washington State before he came to New York, took a job with the Fuller Company, married the boss's daughter, and in 1900 succeeded to the company presidency. Through a series of innovative mergers Black organized the United States Realty and Improvement Company with himself as president and the Fuller Company as its prime asset. Black's friend, Bernhard (Ben) Beinecke, was a German immigrant who had come to New York in 1864, taken a job in a butcher shop, and in a few years become New York's most successful wholesale meat merchant. Parlaying his ownership of large stockyards into several pieces of Manhattan hotel property—

notably the thousand-room Terminal Hotel at Broadway and Thirty-second Street—Beinecke became a force to be reckoned with in the city's financial life.

Black and Beinecke lured other plungers into the new Plaza venture: Kansas-born Paul Starrett, who had succeeded Black as president of the Fuller Company; Walter Clough, who with Black and Starrett had recently built a new Willard Hotel in Washington, D. C.; and John W. Gates, an Illinois-born barbed wire salesman who had pyramided a thirty-dollar-a-month salary into a fifty-million-dollar fortune and earned the colorful sobriquet by which all New Yorkers knew him, "Bet-a-Million." Black, Beinecke, Starrett, and Clough readily agreed to take part in the building of the new Plaza. "Bet-a-Million" Gates was willing to plunge, but only if Fred Sterry, the highly admired manager of the Homestead resort in Hot Springs, Virginia and Henry Flagler's Royal Poinciana and Breakers at Palm Beach, was chosen to head up the new Plaza. "Get Fred Sterry to manage the hotel," Gates thundered, "and you can count on me for all you need." Black and the others knew Sterry and shared Gates' high regard for his abilities. With a hearty shaking of hands, the coterie of capitalists sealed their agreement.

To design the new hotel, the promoters selected Henry Janeway Hardenbergh, a New Jersey-born architect who had distinguished himself with designs for the Astor's Waldorf-Astoria, the Manhattan Hotel at Forty-second Street and Madison Avenue, Boston's Copley Plaza, and Washington's Willard (the last two United States Realty Company properties). Perhaps most distinguished of Hardenbergh's pre-Plaza projects was his design for the Dakota Apartments, a landmark that still stands at Seventy-second Street and Central Park West amid hundreds of newer and less graceful urban warrens.

Hardenbergh planned the new hotel in the style of the French Renaissance, believing it would complement the neighboring Vanderbilt chateau yet lend itself well to the massive dimensions and lofty scale required of a large metropolitan hotel. To take optimum advantage of the neighboring open spaces of park and plaza, he designed the building so that it could be viewed to advantage from close at hand or more distant points. The hotel was to rise eighteen stories above the plaza, and its basements would plunge three floors beneath the surface of Fifth Avenue. To give solidity to the soaring structure, Hardenbergh planned three stories of marble with broad balconies and stout pillars. The next eight floors were to be sleek and free of ornamentation. Above that, the hotel would blossom into a profusion of balconies, gables, dormers, towers, and turrets, all crowned with a soaring French roof. Inside there would be 800 rooms and 500 baths, two floors reserved exclusively for public functions, and dozens of suites ranging in size from fourteen to seventeen rooms each.

The old Plaza was demolished in record time, as Starrett and Clough, working for the United States Realty Company, supervised the assembling construction crews that would build its successor. Excavation was impeded by pockets of quicksand and spongy bogs that lurked in the ground beneath the old hotel, but the architects and builders were determined. They tore out the old pilings, drained pockets of moisture from the rock-clogged soil, and sunk new pillars of steel deep into the earth. "The new foundation," said Hardenbergh, "was not completed until it became part and parcel of the eternal anchorage of Manhattan."

While the foundation was being laid, manager-designate Fred Sterry was busy arranging for decorations and acquiring furnishings. Vast quantities of linen were bought in Ireland and shipped to New York; embroidered organdy for bedroom curtains was ordered from Switzerland; the ateliers and boutiques of France were tapped for precious stores of crystal, tapestries, brocades, Savonnerie rugs, and rare Louis XVI furniture. Closer to home, gold-encrusted china was ordered from L. Straus & Sons, and W. & J. Sloane was commissioned to weave custom carpets. Silver flatware was imprinted with two P's, back to back, on every piece. As the hotel neared completion, Sterry breathed a sigh of satisfaction, confident that its furnishings would do ample justice to the building.

The structure itself was a paragon of grandeur. There were five grand staircases, each lined with veined and tinted marble; ten hydraulic elevators with gilded cages and cavernous subterranean shafts that plunged 200 feet below the main floor of the building; thirteen dumbwaiters, powered by electricity and subject to instantaneous push-button control; a water filtration system capable of supplying 1,500,000 gallons a day; hundreds of marble fireplaces; and no less than 1,650 crystal chandeliers. The Palm Court, a magnificent tearoom that faced the Fifth Avenue side of the building, was finished in Caen stone and Breche violet marble and crowned with a high dome of Tiffany glass. The ballroom was perhaps the hotel's greatest attraction. Finished in white and gold, with wall panels of yellow silk and huge crystal chandeliers, the room was ringed on all sides by a resplendent white and gold balcony, one section of which could be lowered in only five minutes to form a commodious stage for musical and dramatic presentations. Watching the great urban chateau rise above Grand Army Plaza, newspaper reporters hinted that its cost would exceed the original estimates by several million dollars—totaling perhaps as much as seventeen million dollars. No so, the promoters snapped. They might be plungers, but they were certainly not wastrels. The Plaza would be finished for twelve million dollars, no more and no less.

The splendors of the new hotel were matched only by the coterie of well-heeled magnificoes who, it was announced, would become permanent tenants. Unlike most other luxury hotels, the Plaza was to be the home of men and women of wealth and substance, no mere way station for transient ostentation. The press reported the roster of projected Plaza tenants with a kind of breathless wonder. The *Times* listed the first apartment lessors, not alphabetically or in the order in which they had signed their leases, but according to the

The Plaza Hotel Palm Court, 1907. Photograph by Byron. (Courtesy of the Byron Collection, Museum of the City of New York)

size of their personal incomes.

The *Journal*, which accorded the Plaza "the assured distinction of sheltering as permanent guests the largest millionaire colony in this city, or as a matter of fact, in the entire world," printed a cutaway picture which showed eight suites at the corner of Fifth Avenue and Fifty-ninth Street overlooking the park. The suites were occupied, said the *Journal*, by Mrs. James Henry Smith, who had briefly been married to Wall Street's "Silent" Smith; John W. "Bet-a-Million" Gates; Mrs. Young-Heyworth; Alfred Gwynne Vanderbilt, whose mother still lived in her mansion on the south side of Grand Army plaza; George J. Gould, son of Jay Gould; John Drake; Cornelius K. G. Billings, who had a "country home" on the Hudson River at 193rd Street and a fleet of twenty chauffeur-driven automobiles; and Mrs. Oliver Harriman, whose husband was the scion of one of the country's largest railroad fortunes.

It was Tuesday, October 1, 1907—seventeen years to the day after the old Plaza opened its doors—when the first guests began to arrive at the new hotel. The first day's register, preserved in later years as a semi-official roster of the reigning kings and queens of New York society, revealed appropriately impressive names: Mr. and Mrs. Alfred G. Vanderbilt and servant of New York; Mrs. and Mrs. William G. Roelker and maid of Newport; Mrs. and Mrs. B. Beinecke of Newport; Mrs. and Mrs. Young-Heyworth of Chicago; and so on, seemingly ad infinitum. Carriages lined up at the Fifty-ninth Street entrance added to the continuing parade of notables: "Diamond Jim" Brady, resplendent in top hat and tails, with a diamond-and-ruby-headed cane in hand and a buxom actress named Lillian Russell on his arm; Philadelphia department store tycoon John Wanamaker; tobacco magnate Benjamin W. Duke; impresarios Oscar Hammerstein and David

Belasco; actor John Drew; actresses Billie Burke and Fritzie Scheff; and a fierce-miened, tousle-haired scribbler known as Mark Twain.

Ninety percent of the Plaza's guest rooms and suites were occupied by permanent tenants, thus assuring the hotel a steady and lustrous income. Reporters speculated wildly about the rentals, saying that "Bet-a-Million" Gates was paying $42,000 a year for his rooms and that rates for transient rentals ranged up to $500 a day. One starry-eyed writer estimated that "when sleep time came to the Plaza each night . . . $387,000,000 worth of slumber would be represented."

The hotel's first large public function was a state dinner given on October 15 to honor the Rt. Rev. Arthur Foley Winnington, D. C., Lord Bishop of London and spiritual adviser to King Edward VII. Despite the bishop's disapproval of alcohol, the four hundred guests who gathered in the grand ballroom drank to his health in champagne when Columbia University President Nicholas Murray Butler rose to propose a toast and Senator Chauncey M. Depew, whiskers bristling, began to orate.

From the day of its opening the Plaza was a kind of public court for the moneyed elite of New York, a capitalist palace whose activities were as eagerly and minutely reported as those of the great royal palaces of Europe. Reporters, pencils and pads of paper in hand, eager to record the comings and goings of the aristocracy, clogged the lobbies and dining rooms. Guests from abroad enjoyed the ambience of the parkside citadel as much as the millionaires of midtown Manhattan, knowing that it was the best place in America to get one's name in the papers.

When Mrs. Patrick Campbell, George Bernard Shaw's favorite correspondent, arrived from England for a theatrical engagement, she went directly to the Plaza, where she and her monkey-spitz poodle were put up in a suitably elegant suite. Concerned that her presence in the hotel might not in itself assure a front-page story, Mrs. Campbell repaired to the tearoom, where she alarmed the busboys and waiters by lighting a slender Russian cigarette and puffing on it with evident satisfaction. Manager Sterry was hurriedly summoned to inform the lady that, while Americans abroad did not object to the sight of women smoking in public, "to try it here is another matter. The Plaza does not want to be the first to permit the custom." Mrs. Campbell extinguished her smoke, but not before newspaper reporters had breathlessly recorded every detail of the scandalous event for their readers.

More celebrated than the British actress, and even more newsworthy, was the Metropolitan Opera star Enrico Caruso, a connoisseur of hostelries from Vienna to San Francisco and, as it turned out, a very difficult guest for the Plaza to please. Practicing in his room one day, Caruso was interrupted by the novel and annoying buzz of an electric alarm clock. Armed with a knife, the singer proceeded to attack the offending timepiece. He quickly silenced it, but in the process also decommissioned hundreds of other clocks in the hotel, which were connected to his own through the medium of a master magnetic clock.

Prospecting for heiresses, as much as publicity hunting, was the impetus behind many foreign visits to the Plaza. The courts of Edwardian Europe were thronged with droves of titled but impecunious gentlemen who sought to better themselves financially and who properly looked upon the Plaza as a likely place to do so. If American society did not bend its collective knee before the European visitors, hostesses competed eagerly for the honor of entertaining them. Hungarian Count Laszlo Szechenyi wooed and won Gladys Vanderbilt in the Plaza's Tea Court. Lord Decies came there in successful pursuit of Vivien Gould, daughter of George J. Gould, and the lord's best man, Lord Camoys, fell in love with Mildred Sherman, a Newport heiress. The Earl and Countess of Castlevart came often to visit her parents, Mr. and Mrs. Solomon R. Guggenheim, who occupied a luxurious Plaza apartment.

When a panic on Wall Street in the fall of 1907 temporarily thinned the ranks of permanent Plaza guests, Sterry asked Frederick Townsend Martin, a bachelor socialite who had recently succeeded to Ward McAllister's old position as *arbiter elegantarium* of New York, to take on the duties of social organizer for the hotel. The dapper Martin put on a series of balls, banquets, and related convocations that quickly restored the Plaza to fiscal and social integrity. Perhaps most notable of Martin's promotions was a special theatrical performance given in the grand ballroom in 1908. The play chosen for the event, *Mrs. Van Vechten's Divorce Dance*, was of doubtful artistic merit, but the appearance in the title role of Mrs. George J. Gould, the former Edith Kingdon of the New York stage, assured that it would have a capacity audience. Publicity for the event was predictably lavish. The New York *World* reported the doings in an eight-column headline that read: "A $20,000,000 ACTRESS POINTED A $100 PISTOL AT A $1,000

ACTRESS AND A $100,000,000 AUDIENCE APPLAUDED. THE ACTORS SAT ON AN $18,000 SOFA, LEANED ON A $4,000 BUREAU AND WALKED ON A $3,000 RUG." All in all, said the *World,* the affair was truly "swell."

In surroundings of great wealth, where obsequious servants vastly outnumbered the masters and mistresses who employed them, where dazzling jewels and expensive furs were commonplace, where money was "no object," but the *spending* of money was the only object, it was inevitable that ostentation should be elevated to cult, that extravagance should turn quickly and easily into indulgence, that eccentricity should be not merely tolerated, but cultivated, and exorbitance looked upon as a social, if not moral, virtue. Thus Mrs. Julia Watts Curtis demurely explained to reporters when she took one of the Plaza's most elegant suites that she was not extravagant, but a "sense of duty" made her spend two hundred dollars a day. "An income is like a reputation," she reminded the reporters. "One must live up to it." Thus ten-year-old George A. Fuller, Jr. drove his boy-size electric automobile at twelve miles per hour on a speedway one-seventh mile long, erected for his personal use in the Plaza basement. Thus Princess Vilma Lwoff-Parlaghy of Berlin and Vienna arrived at the Plaza with her own complete service of crested dinner plates, her own supply of fine Irish linen, and a personal staff of five butlers, two footmen, and a bodyguard, all attired in crimson satin liveries, black satin breeches, silk hose, and silver-buckled pumps.

It was duty of a different sort than that felt by Mrs. Curtis that drew Henrietta Howland Green to the Plaza in 1908. Alternately hailed as the world's richest woman and condemned as its most miserly, Hetty Green's income for the year 1900 was estimated at about seven million dollars. Despite her great wealth, she lived in a broken-down tenement in Hoboken and wore a black frock so old and worn it had turned green at the edges. The newspapers were appropriately delighted when the "Witch of Wall Street" and her daughter Sylvia, thirty-seven years old and still unmarried, unexpectedly checked into a Plaza suite. Sylvia's advancing spinsterhood did not bother her mother, though it clearly troubled her friend, Annie Leary, a socialite spinster who later received the papal title of countess for her work in Roman Catholic charities.

At Miss Leary's prodding Hetty agreed to give one of the most sumptuous dinners ever held in the Plaza and to prepare for the event by first checking in to Mme. Le Clair's Fifth Avenue beauty salon for a cosmetic rejuvenation. The dinner was given in the suite occupied by mother and daughter and served from gold plate lent by Miss Leary. The food, as expensive as the Plaza chef could contrive in only ten courses, was accompanied by three wines and served against a background of flowers and fine music. Among the guests was a sixty-five-year-old bachelor named Matthew Astor Wilks, a great-grandson of the original John Jacob Astor. Wilks and Sylvia Green shared an immediate attraction—an attraction which soon blossomed into romance.

At the end of a month Mrs. Green checked out of the Plaza, explaining that she had paid off "Sylvia's social debts." Reporters speculated that Hetty had paid fifteen dollars a day for her suite, though that figure was revised downward when they learned that the total bill for her month's rental did not come to more than three hundred dollars. Wilks and Sylvia were married in 1909, but not before the miserly "Witch" extracted from the groom a written promise that in return for five thousand dollars he would waive any claim to the Green estate.

There was eccentricity, extravagance, and ostentation at the Plaza, to be sure, but the hotel was saved from overweening vulgarity by a quality of urbane civility that pervaded the place, a sense of style and grace that moderated the worst manifestations of posturing and display. It was a preserve of millionaires, but not exclusively so. Actors and writers found the restaurants and bars of the hotel as much to their liking as the homelier cafes and bistros of lower Broadway. Playwrights dallied in the dining rooms with comely chorus dancers, and painters and sculptors displayed their works in the ballrooms and corridors. When sojourning in Manhattan, governors and presidents found the Plaza dining rooms suitable settings for state dinners and diplomatic tête-à-têtes over brandy and cigars.

Count Aponyi of Hungary was honored by New York's Mayor Gaynor and Mrs. Andrew Carnegie at a Plaza banquet. Earl Gray, Governor General of Canada, was entertained in the hotel by Mr. and Mrs. Theodore Roosevelt. President and Mrs. William Howard Taft were frequently in residence with members of the president's cabinet and their wives. Thomas G. Masaryk, first President of Czechoslovakia, was in the hotel for a series of meetings with Woodrow Wilson when the Czech Republic was declared in October 1918, and the Plaza became the first building in the world to fly

Streetside view of the Plaza Hotel, 1913. (Courtesy of the Bettmann Archive)

the Czechoslovakian flag.

British art dealer Lord Joseph Duveen held spectacular sales of rare and valuable paintings in the Plaza, as did his rivals Hiram H. Parke and Otto Bernet. Solomon R. Guggenheim kept a fabulous collection of modern French paintings in his first floor suite. Architect Frank Lloyd Wright took up residence at the hotel while working on a museum to house the Guggenheim collection. The Renaissance splendor of the hotel contrasted sharply with Wright's own architectural style, but he found much that pleased him in the Plaza. "It's

genuine," he said. "I like it almost as much as if I'd built it myself."

Broadway's "Yankee Doodle Dandy," George M. Cohan, probably the most versatile entertainer in the history of the New York stage, was a regular in the Plaza's Oak Bar, where he appeared promptly at five each afternoon to share cocktails and spirited talk with a company of actors and producers. F. Scott Fitzgerald wandered in and out of the hotel as frequently as the characters in his jazz-era novels, a habit that prompted Ernest Hemingway to suggest that when Fitzgerald died he should will his liver to the Princeton museum and his heart to the Plaza. Maurice Maeterlinck and Ferenc Molnar were among the many foreign-born writers who put up in the hotel when war forced them to abandon their European homelands.

The Plaza's cuisine was a paragon of delicacy, though it was served in quantities large enough to supply an army in the field or both of the opposing sides in a medium-sized sea battle. The first chef, Andre Lapperuque, had supervised the kitchens of the French Rothschilds and Delmonico's fabled Manhattan restaurant before Fred Sterry put him in charge of the Plaza's cooking staff. Lapperuque's successors were worthy inheritors of his tradition. The Terrace Restaurant, the hotel's formal dining hall, was the most notable of its early culinary salons, though the Plaza Restaurant, a high-windowed cafe at the corner of Fifty-ninth Street, had a circle of loyal supporters. Several distinctive dishes were invented in the Plaza kitchens, among them Chicken Soup à la Plaza, Crab Meat Remick (named for New York Stock Exchange President William H. Remick), and Eggs Melba, a concoction of poached eggs on artichoke bottoms and mushrooms covered with hollandaise sauce and foie gras (created and named for Australian diva Nellie Melba).

The repeal of Prohibition was celebrated in the Plaza in 1934 with the opening of a cocktail lounge and supper club called the Persian Room. Occupying space which had formerly housed the Rose Room, the new club was decorated with lavish draperies and elaborate frescoes of Persian scenes. The frescoes would have delighted the tentmaker Omar had he been alive to see them; they did, in fact, dazzle the eyes of the Persian Shah of Shahs, His Highness Mohammed Reza Pahlevi, who made a point to inspect them on one of his visits to the Plaza. The Persian Room was a favorite rendezvous of diners and dancers and the scene of glamorous shows headlining such entertainers as Tony and Renee De Marco, Emil Coleman, Eddie Duchin, Paul Draper, and "The Incomparable" Hildegarde. The last was a favorite of Persian Room patrons during the early years of World War II, when she wrung tears from most and dollars from many by combining a misty-eyed rendition of "The Last Time I Saw Paris" with an appeal for the purchase of war bonds. Before the hostilities were over, the Persian Room chanteuse had delighted both New York and Washington by selling more than one million dollars in bonds.

The Plaza weathered the crises of the two world wars, the lean years of the Great Depression, and the thirsty years of Prohibition with remarkable aplomb. There were Red Cross cots in the ballrooms during both great conflicts, and enlisted men as well as officers were welcomed in the bars and restaurants. The number of permanent Plaza residents was seriously reduced in the thirties, though many millionaires and millionairesses stayed on, their only concessions to the financial crisis being token reductions in the numbers of their butlers, valets, and maids. The Volstead years caused less discomfiture than temperance advocates might have hoped. The Oak Bar was converted into a brokerage office for E. F. Hutton and Company, and alcoholic beverages were banished from the hotel's cafes and restaurants, but the private suites, where champagne still flowed, were more often "extra dry" than "dry."

In the eyes of Plaza regulars a more serious crisis than war, depression, or prohibition was the sale of the hotel in 1943 to the flamboyant collector of hotels and publicity, Conrad Hilton. Hilton's previous hotel acquisitions had not matched the Plaza's elegance or prestige, and devotees of the parkside palace were sure the outsider would hopelessly commercialize the hotel. To make matters worse, Hilton had bought the hotel for a song—$600,000 down against a total price of $7,400,000, less than it had cost to build in 1907. In return for a forty percent interest in the hotel, Floyd Odlum's wheeling and dealing Atlas Corporation agreed to put up all the cash necessary to close the deal. Why had the Plaza, the paragon of Manhattan's fiscal conservatism, been sacrificed in a shoe-string sale to a brace of parvenu financiers? The answer was that the United States Realty Company had seriously overexpanded during the late twenties and thirties by putting up hundreds of buildings and at least one luxury hotel, the Savoy-Plaza, that directly competed with the Plaza. Bonds which came due in the early forties had to be redeemed, and the only way to do so was to raise cash. Thus did the dowager queen of Fifth Avenue hotels become the brightest jewel in the ever-brightening crown of Conrad Hilton.

In his memoirs, *Be My Guest,* the hotel magnate admitted that Plaza regulars at first regarded him as a sort of Genghis Kahn, "or, at the very best, Tom Mix about to shoot his guns off in the lobby." To assuage their fears, he wrote personal messages to all permanent tenants, then proceeded cautiously to undertake a program of restoration and renewal. E. F. Hutton's office was moved to a mezzanine, and the historic Oak Bar was reopened. Recapturing the ambience of Edwardian days, ladies were forbidden to enter the woody sanctum of the adjacent Oak Room until after the daily close of the stock exchange. At night while millionaires slept, marble was restored, tapestries cleaned, plumbing unclogged and rearranged. Before his work was done, Hilton had put about six million dollars into Plaza refurbishing, but he considered the money well spent. The rate of occupancy quickly rose from sixty-one percent to one hundred percent, and income grew accordingly. When late in 1945 Hilton's roving eye settled on Chicago's queen of hotels, the Palmer House, he was able to use his Plaza success to secure financing for yet another breathtaking acquisition.

Continuing his efforts to mollify long-time Plaza admirers, Hilton commissioned artist Everett Shinn to paint three nostalgic murals for the Oak Bar, re-creating views of the hotel and Grand Army Plaza during Edwardian days. Hoping to revive the spirit of the palmy days of dukes and duchesses, the hôtelier hired White Russian Prince Serge Obolensky as Plaza public relations director. Married at one time to a Romanov, later to an Astor, Prince Serge had learned the ins and outs of the hotel business in the Astor-owned St. Regis at Fifth Avenue and Fifty-fifth Street. With his aide-de-camp, Count Vasilli Adlerberg, at his side, Obolensky set out to recapture the era of Frederick Townsend Martin by organizing a series of lavish parties and banquets. Notable among his productions were celebrations of Russian Easter and Orthodox Christmas, which soon became regular Plaza events. He also transformed the old Grill into a new chamber of gustatory delights called the Rendez-Vous, which quickly acquired a wide circle of admirers.

Hilton, who bought and sold hotels with the good-humored nonchalance of a Monopoly player, transferred title to the Plaza to A. M. Sonnabend of Boston in 1953, realizing a handsome profit on the deal. But he retained management and control through a long-term lease. When the lease expired in 1960, Sonnabend's Hotel Corporation of America (later Sonesta Corporation) took over the building. In 1974, completing yet another transfer of title, the hotel was sold to the United Airlines-owned Western International Hotel Company. In just under three-quarters of a century the value of Ben Beinecke's, Harry Black's, and "Bet-a-Million" Gates' parkside palace had doubled. The price paid by Western for the Plaza was a round twenty-five million dollars.

The frequency with which Plaza deeds were shuffled seemed to have little effect on the hotel's health. The great building throbbed with a life of its own, a rhythm and pulse attuned more to its long-time admirers and the great city that surrounded it than to its changing managers. Staff members survived successive administrations, some remaining in their positions as long as fifty years, and many tenants, nearly as durable, came to be regarded as permanent fixtures. Clara Bell Walsh, the Kentucky-born widow of Royal typewriter tycoon Julius Walsh, was the most steadfast of Plaza regulars. From the hotel's opening in 1907 until her own death in 1957, Mrs. Walsh held forth in her seventh floor suite surrounded by an unchanging collection of overstuffed furniture, china dolls, Edwardian bric-a-brac, and hunting prints.

Following the example of Hilton's six-million-dollar facelift in the forties, there were periodic campaigns of renewal. Hotel Corporation of America committed four million dollars to Plaza refurbishing in 1961, and in 1975 Western International announced that it would spend between eight and ten million dollars once again to revive the hotel's Edwardian luster—renewing copper window frames, steamblasting marble, installing new carpets, and replacing faded paint.

There were successive anniversary celebrations. At a fortieth birthday party in 1947 speeches were made by Conrad Hilton and Ben Beinecke's son Edwin, and guests were presented with a souvenir program containing a nostalgic history of the Plaza by Lucius Beebe. In 1957, with Hilton still in charge, a Golden Ball was held that attracted the attention of much of New York. The sixtieth anniversary was marked by the publication of a book-length history of the hotel penned by society columnist Eve Brown, one-time "Cholly Knickerbocker" for Hearst's New York *Journal-American*.

In 1947 Lucius Beebe expressed satisfaction that the lights of the hotel, gleaming across Grand Army Plaza and the sidewalks and pavement of the wealthiest avenue in America, had shone so long undimmed. Spurred by the memory of what had been and the rosy expectation of what might yet be, Beebe hoped that the hotel's lights would continue to shine "for many and many a year." A generation after the wish and more than a decade after Beebe's own death, the Plaza that he and others loved so well still towered above the southeast corner of Central Park, still dominated the expanse of Grand Army Plaza, "the most beautiful sight in New York." If ever a wish was father to reality, it most probably was at the Plaza.

15

Ghosts of Peacock Alley

THE WALDORF-ASTORIA, NEW YORK CITY

The story of America's greatest palace inn began inconspicuously enough more than two centuries ago in a small village in the Rhineland Duchy of Baden, when the wife of a local butcher gave birth to a squealing baby boy named John Jacob Astor. Eighty-four years later and thousands of miles away, in the shadowed sanctum of a four-story brownstone on lower Manhattan Island, the same John Jacob Astor succumbed to the accumulated debilities of a long and unremittingly acquisitive life. Just before he gave up the ghost, the redoubtable "Landlord of New York," who owned more Manhattan real estate than any man before or since and who is thought to have been the richest man in the United States, if not in the world, uttered a lament: "I should have bought more uptown."

Whether or not the story of Astor's "last words" is true, the sentiment it expresses is wholly characteristic of the man, who grasped for pennies, dollars and, above all, acres, to the very end of his long and fabulously successful life. John Jacob's failure to "buy more uptown" was a sin his son, William Backhouse Astor, was determined not to repeat. Among William Backhouse's many real estate purchases in Manhattan was a plot of several acres of farm land which bordered Fifth Avenue where Thirty-third and Thirty-fourth streets were later cut through. The younger Astor bought the plot in 1827 for a reported $20,500. Years later his descendants thanked him many times for the wisdom of his acquisition. In 1929, when a part of

the land was sold as the site for the Empire State Building, it brought the healthy price of $13,500,000—more than 650 times the amount of William Backhouse Astor's original investment.

Long before that momentous transaction the Fifth Avenue property had been the scene of doings of note—the location of two of the most celebrated of Manhattan's many Astor mansions and the site of a curious but indubitably grand twin-hotel that, for over a generation, dazzled New York society and made the village of John Jacob Astor's birth synonymous with the word "hotel." That village, a few lazy kilometers from the medieval university-city of Heidelberg, was called Walldorf. Slightly condensed, its name was applied to the first half of the New York hotel that was officially denominated the Waldorf-Astoria. Unofficially the great palace was always "The Waldorf." The name was preserved for decades in the famous society dictum, "Meet me at the Waldorf" and, even longer, in the name-plates attached to hundreds of houses of hospitality from Hong Kong to Zanzibar. Some were marble palaces that recalled, if they did not duplicate, the splendor of the Fifth Avenue original. Others were shanty flophouses that parodied the New York tradition. But all dutifully and gratefully preserved the name of the obscure German village in which the whole story began so long ago.

In the 1870s the great mid-Manhattan brownstones were built, which for twenty years or so were to house the courts of two branches of the Astor

The new Waldorf-Astoria, New York City (Ezra Stoller © ESTO)

clan. John Jacob Astor III built his home at 338 Fifth Avenue, the northwest corner of the intersection of Fifth Avenue and Thirty-third Street. A well-kept garden separated it from its neighbor, an equally handsome house at 350, built by John Jacob's younger brother William. William's wife, formerly Caroline Schermerhorn, was a descendant of an old Knickerbocker family, a fact that, combined with her husband's wealth, inclined her to airs. It was Caroline who took to printing the name "Mrs. Astor" on her invitations, thus signaling her intention to be known as *the* Mrs. Astor. It was Caroline who installed the chivalrous South Carolinian Ward McAllister as New York's *arbiter elegantarium*; Caroline who inspired McAllister's famous (or infamous) dictum that the elite of New York society did not exceed four hundred (the number that could comfortably be entertained in the ballroom at 350 Fifth Avenue).

William Waldorf Astor, who inherited the house at 338 when his father, John Jacob III, died in 1890, was not fond of his Aunt Caroline—nor, indeed, was he fond of much in New York. He regarded Caroline's claim to be known as *the* Mrs. Astor as, at best, an affront to his mother and, at worst, a violation of the well-settled principles of primogeniture. His property in and out of the city made him a fabulously wealthy man. (Since he was an only child and controlled an undivided half of the original Astor estate, he was worth a good deal more than Caroline's son, his cousin, John Jacob IV.) Despite the tribute that the city annually paid him in rents, annuities, royalties, and the invisible but immensely valuable "unearned increment," William Waldorf Astor loathed New York and most of the land that surrounded it. His disenchantment sprang from a curious but deep-seated feeling that America was not a fit country for a "gentleman" to live in. The conviction became acute when New York voters twice rejected his lavishly financed bids for election to Congress.

Two years spent in Rome as American Minister to Italy gave him time to contemplate his country from a distance. When his father died in 1890, William Waldorf darkly pondered his future. Meditating at his mansion in Newport, he came to two startling decisions: First, he would raze the mansion at 338 Fifth Avenue and, to spite his Aunt Caroline, who lived next door, build a large hotel in its place. Second, he would put all his American property in the hands of agents, resign from his clubs, and move to England—a country that, unlike America, still appreciated the virtues of birth

William Waldorf Astor (Courtesy of the New York Historical Society)

and breeding and the etiquette of precedence.

It is impossible to determine which of William Waldorf Astor's decisions was most troubling to New Yorkers, though it is sure that both surprised them. Many must have welcomed the announced departure of a crusty patrician who derived much of his income from shabby tenements and disdained the ways of democratic society. More must have been alarmed by his plan to disrupt the well-heeled residential serenity of middle Fifth Avenue by planting a flaunting caravansery in its midst. There were no zoning laws in 1890 to tell a man where he could and where he could not build a skyscraper. If society in America did not appreciate birth and breeding, it still permitted a capitalist to do with his property whatever he pleased. For this, at least, William Waldorf Astor was grateful.

With his commercial counselor, Abner Bartlett,

offering advice, Astor hurriedly arranged the details of the projected hotel. Bartlett called on George C. Boldt, a German-born hotel manager who had made something of a name for himself in Philadelphia's Hotel Bellevue, and asked for his ideas. Boldt's enthusiasm for the Astor project was so great that Bartlett and the millionaire promptly signed him to a contract to run the new place. To design the hotel, Bartlett and Boldt called on Henry Janeway Hardenbergh, who was already known for his design of the Dakota Apartments and who would later achieve architectural immortality of sorts by supervising construction of the second Plaza Hotel. In September 1890 the disgruntled William Waldorf Astor sailed with his wife and family for England. In December, plans for the new hotel, to be called the Waldorf, were filed with the city.

The Waldorf was not the first, nor would it be the last, Astor-owned hotel in New York. Years before, William Waldorf's great-grandfather, the first John Jacob, had owned the City Hotel, the first building in America erected solely for hotel

George C. Boldt (Courtesy of the Waldorf-Astoria)

purposes and, in 1834, he had erected the palatial (for its time) six-story, three-hundred-room Astor House on lower Broadway. Modeled after Boston's Tremont House, the Astor House was still flourishing in 1890. From his new home in England William Waldorf would shortly add to his roster of American hotel properties by erecting the Netherland at Fifth Avenue and Fifty-ninth Street and the Astor Hotel at Longacre (later Times) Square. But the fame of the hotel on Fifth Avenue at Thirty-third was destined to eclipse all the rest of the expatriate's palace inns.

The site for the new hotel was a gaping hole in the ground when a twenty-four-year-old Swiss happened by on his way to church one Sunday morning. Oscar Tschirky had been a waiter in the celebrated Hoffman House on Madison Square and later at Delmonico's fashionable restaurant. In the latter establishment he had achieved an enviable reputation as the favorite table attendant of such regulars as "Diamond Jim" Brady, Lillian Russell, and the president of the Pennsylvania Railroad. Approaching Boldt with a petition signed by several hundred of his admirers, Tschirky persuaded the hôtelier to sign him to a contract as the Waldorf's head waiter.

While Boldt was busy signing contracts, ordering furnishings, linens, crystal, and flatware, construction of the hotel proceeded apace. By March 13, 1893, the building was completed and ready to open its doors for business.

It was a handsome building, in an overripe, late-Victorian way. Thirteen stories of steel, granite, and marble, it rose like a fortress from the corner of Fifth Avenue and Thirty-third—a row of Roman arches at street-level, tiers of slitted windows above, and on top a fairyland roof surmounted with towers, turrets, dormers, and massive Heidelbergian gables. Inside, the hotel was less forbidding, if not less imaginative: spacious lobbies carpeted with Persian rugs and crowded with forests of mahogany furniture; broad halls lined with marble and hung with fine tapestries; luxurious bedroom suites that seemed to observers to resemble museum galleries more than sleeping apartments.

At every turn the hotel revealed nooks of extravagance and beauty. The Marie Antoinette salon, an oval reception room for ladies, was paneled in mirrors and decorated with an elaborate ceiling painting executed by Will H. Low. The Men's Cafe, designed in the style of the German Renaissance, was paneled in oak and decorated with murals of Teutonic warriors. The grand

The Waldorf before it was joined by the Astoria. This drawing, based on architect's designs, appeared in Harper's Weekly, *March 14, 1891.*

ballroom, in Louis XVI style, was decorated with wall and ceiling paintings by Maitland Armstrong and Frank Fowler and with a massive mantel of pale green cipollino marble. One of the private supper salons faithfully restored the dining room that had graced the demolished Astor mansion, complete to oak wall panels, crystal chandeliers, oil paintings, furniture, and table service. Reporters who inspected the hotel were suitably impressed. Wrote *Harper's Weekly*: "To endeavor to give any adequate idea of the beautiful decorations of the Waldorf in a short sketch is almost as idle as to try to make marginal notes of the good things in the printed works of William Shakespeare." "Louis XIV," wrote a reporter for the *New York*

Sun, "could not have got the likes of the first suite of apartments set apart for the most distinguished guests of the hotel. There is a canopied bed upon the dais, such as a king's should be. Upon this dais shall repose the greatnesses and, looking about them, see many thousands of dollars' worth of fineries. Think of the joy of being great!"

George Boldt, who did not think he was great, and William Waldorf Astor, who was sure he was, were overjoyed at the hotel's opening. Though Astor was not in attendance, most of New York's self-anointed elite were there, lured by an ingenious ploy engineered by Boldt. It was not the habit of Manhattan society to display its finery in public, but few among them could resist an open appeal to charity. When Boldt announced that the first major event at the Waldorf would be a benefit for St. Mary's Free Hospital for Children, the resistance of the *grandes dames* was demolished. Mrs. W. K. Vanderbilt, a patron of the hospital, responded to the occasion by hiring the entire New York Symphony Orchestra to play. Tickets were offered at the then-considerable price of five dollars each but, from far and wide, socialites eagerly vied for the opportunity to attend. From Philadelphia came the Biddles, Drexels, Peppers, Lippincotts; from Boston, the Lowells, Sargents, Averys, Peabodys; from New York, the Vanderbilts, Carnegies, Oelrichses, Van Rensselaers, Westervelts, Stewarts, Choates, Delanos. The event was pleasing to those who attended, though it must have distressed War McAllister. From among the ranks of the old "Four Hundred," 1,500 very fashionable people had suddenly materialized.

If *the* Mrs. Astor was in attendance, the fact was not noted in the newspapers. More likely, she and her son, the twenty-nine-year-old John Jacob IV, now head of the American branch of the Astor family, arranged to be out of town the day of the celebration. Predictably, she and her husband William had been outraged by William Waldorf's hotel plans, knowing that shadows from the new building would effectively obscure the sun that warmed No. 350. In a pique, William threatened to demolish his own mansion and put up New York's biggest stables in its place. But William died in 1892 before he could carry out his threat, and his son John Jacob IV ("Jack" to his family) thought better of the idea. He would, indeed, demolish his mother's mansion, but not to create a Fifth Avenue mews. Instead, he would raise his own hotel— bigger and even grander than the Waldorf—and name it, for his mother, the Schermerhorn.

Whether the idea for a second hotel on Fifth Avenue originated with Jack Astor or with George Boldt, both men were delighted with it. Build a hotel on your land, said the hôtelier, and I will join it to the Waldorf to form a great twin-hostelry. Boldt would operate both hotels, though ownership of each half would remain with the feuding cousins. In England the crusty William Waldorf agreed to the proposition with certain reservations. The two hotels could be built so as to form a functioning unit, but he would reserve the right to wall up the passage between them in the event of any disagreement. Further, Jack Astor would have to choose a name other than Schermerhorn for his half. Jack thought awhile, then announced he would accept the conditions.

The prospect of having doors and hallways sealed off frightened Boldt, but he knew the stipulation was the price of William Waldorf's assent and agreed to it. The new hotel would be called the Astoria in honor of the original John Jacob Astor's historic fur-trading post in Oregon. Wreckers attacked the walls of *the* Mrs. Astor's brownstone in 1895. By November 1, 1897, the Astoria was ready to open.

It was a towering structure that stretched seventeen stories into the sky and cast long shadows on its thirteen-story neighbor. It had an indoor driveway on the Thirty-fourth Street side, the first in hotel history, a grand ballroom capable of seating 1,500, and a Grecian Roof Garden. Interior decorating was by the firm of Arnold Constable, whose buyer had spent three hundred thousand dollars in Europe picking up Continental treasures. Between them the two hotels had one thousand guest rooms, three floors of public parlors and salons, vast expanses of lobby and corridor, and one of the most imposing profiles of any building ever seen in New York—if not in the world.

The great twin-hotel lacked nothing but a common name. Ward McAllister's daughter is credited with having remedied the deficiency by coining the phrase, Waldorf-Astoria. If the coinage was not original, it was comfortable and rested well on the tongues of most New Yorkers. Wags of the day were delighted to tell their friends, "Meet me at 'The Hyphen.'" "Where's that?" the friends would ask. "Between the Waldorf and the Astoria," the wags answered, laughing. As a nickname for the hotel "The Hyphen" did not stick, but the Waldorf-Astoria did. Long after the stone and marble of the hotel had crumbled, the hybrid name survived as one of the most valuable intangible assets ever known to the world of American business.

The Waldorf-Astoria was a great public building but, to New Yorkers in the 1890s, it was more than merely a physical phenomenon. The idea that two feuding branches of one of America's wealthiest families should join to create a hotel was as fascinating as the pile itself. The spectacle of social leaders regularly trekking to its ballrooms and restaurants for evenings on the town was both refreshing and surprising. No longer would *grand dames* confine their soirees to the secluded recesses of brownstone ballrooms. Henceforth, as many debutantes would "come out" in the Waldorf as in private mansions; as many charity balls would be held in the Empire Room as in the salons of *the*

The carriage entrance of the Waldorf-Astoria on Thirty-fourth Street (Courtesy of the Waldorf-Astoria)

Mrs. Astor (whose new mansion was far away, at Sixty-fifth Street overlooking Central Park); as many millionaires would rest their polished boots on the brass rail of the Astoria's stand-up bar as would tipple in the gloomy recesses of private billiard rooms or dens. The Waldorf-Astoria was more than a large, elegantly appointed building in which to eat and sleep. It was a public court for the island of Manhattan, a palace of midtown hospitality, a glittering nexus for the best and the worst of fin de siècle society in the nation's largest city.

The success of the Waldorf was attributable to many things and many people. George Boldt was responsible for much of it. He ruled his twin-hotel with the proverbial iron fist in a velvet glove. A martinet who worked his staff nearly to the point of exhaustion, he was also suave, debonair, and unctuous in dealing with distinguished guests.

The rules he laid down for the conduct of waiters and bellmen—derived in large measure from his Old World upbringing—were stringent and unbending. Once, spotting an assistant manager dancing with a guest, Boldt reprimanded him by publicly slapping him across the face.

Although he sported a bristling mustache and an elegantly pointed beard, Boldt decreed that all male members of the Waldorf staff be clean-shaven. Against protests that his rule was unfashionable and blatantly inconsistent with his own hirsute adornment, Boldt answered that clean-shaven waiters presented a more hygienic appearance in the dining rooms. Grudgingly, the decree was complied with. But when the hôtelier attempted to apply the same rule to hack drivers who waited for rides outside the hotel, a storm of opposition erupted into a full-blown political

The old Waldorf-Astoria on Fifth Avenue between Thirty-third and Thirty-fourth streets (Courtesy of the Waldorf-Astoria)

storm. New York's Governor Roswell P. Flower, who had once defeated William Waldorf Astor for Congress, rushed to the defense of the cabbies. "It was not many years ago," the governor said, "that I was a servant myself, and I used to wear my beard as I pleased and my hair as long as I pleased. Had any man dictated to me that I should put a French twist to my beard or a Spanish curl to my hair I would have taken it as an insult. I will veto any bill regulating men's beards."

Once, when a guest about to depart the Waldorf complained about the amount of his bill, Boldt met him and, cooly tearing up the bill, announced that the guest need not pay it, nor need he return to the Waldorf, as the hotel was only for those to whom "cost is no object."

Despite his Prussian hauteur, Boldt introduced many innovations to the Waldorf that added immeasurably to the comfort and ease of hotel life. He installed a popular feature of European hotels called "room service" that enabled guests to indulge in the morally suspect but pleasurable French custom of breakfasting in bed. He relaxed rules that prohibited men from smoking in the presence of women, installed an orchestra in the hotel lobby, hired Turkish waiters to serve coffee, and placed plenty of ash trays at strategic locations among the potted palms. When important men appeared at his desk, he adopted a courtly, Old World manner that invariably impressed those he most wanted to impress. Prominent investors and industrialists became permanent guests at the hotel. Among the regular tenants one of the most notable was the self-made millionaire and big plunger, John W. "Bet-a-Million" Gates, who was later to become one of the backers of the Plaza Hotel.

If the Waldorf was recognized as a paragon of luxury, it was also known as a place where high livers indulged their whims, where display occasionally descended to ostentation, and where the minions of great wealth from time to time showed the unmistakable symptoms of an aristocracy gone haywire. One event above all others gave an aura of heady declension, if not dissolution, to the society that swirled in and out of the Waldorf.

The celebration was no sub rosa revelry or clandestine bacchanal, but a lavish ball advertised openly in the best Manhattan papers and covered by national magazines. Notwithstanding the bright lights that were shined on it, the Bradley Martin Costume Ball of 1897 struck many observers as darkly depraved. The event, which took place in February of that year, anticipated the

opening of the Astoria by a few months, but it soon came to be associated with both hotels and was not unfairly considered the most extravagant affair either half of the hyphenated palace had ever hosted. It was organized by Mr. and Mrs. Bradley Martin, parvenus from Troy, New York, who despite their humble origins, were well-heeled and generally well accepted in Manhattan society. Frederick Townsend Martin, who later became social organizer of the Plaza Hotel, was Bradley Martin's brother.

On the night of the Waldorf affair the ballroom was festooned with more than five thousand mauve orchids and draped with endless cables of asparagus vines. Satin bags filled with pink roses hung from the chandeliers. A doorman in the dress of a sixteenth-century French court attendant announced the arrival of each of the thousand or so guests and described the character and historical period of his or her costume. Mrs. Bradley Martin, dressed as Mary Queen of Scots, received on an elevated dais under a tapestried canopy. Two Hungarian orchestras played waltzes, while music for quadrilles was supplied by Victor Herbert and his Twenty-second Regiment Band. Mineral water, whiskey, brandy, and cases of Moët et Chandon champagne were available in abundance. Supper, served by waiters in royal livery with knee breeches and powdered wigs from midnight to 2:30, included whole roast English suckling pig and the usual trimmings. An ample buffet was available at all hours to assuage untimely attacks of hunger. Outside the hotel, special squads of police held back onlookers while four hundred two-horse carriages stood by to spare revelers the inconvenience of keeping their own coachmen up until all hours.

It was estimated that, directly and indirectly, the total cost of the ball was two hundred thousand dollars. In normal times, the figure might have raised eyebrows. In 1897, in the midst of one of the country's recurrent depressions, it raised blood pressure and even a few angry fists. The New York *World,* which deplored the showy affair, reported it in most uncharitable terms, describing Mrs. Bradley Martin as "a short, stout woman with cold blue eyes, a square, determined face and a nose that looked as though it intended to tilt but stopped short. She wore a train twenty feet long, a crown on her brow, and $100,000 worth of diamonds on her stomacher, which looked like a waistcoat." The *World* thought it "perfectly astonishing how Mrs. Astor managed to find a place for so many jewels; they covered her like a cuirass.

She was gowned as a Venetian lady in a dark-blue velvet costume. It was laden with $200,000 worth of jewels. The supper, at which the guests behaved like children afraid of mussing their clothes, consisted largely of champagne with a few things thrown in like bouillon, truffles, and duck. There was no stint in the champagne, like the usual stingy one quart to a person at most New York balls."

"God pity the shivering, starving poor these days," thundered a Brooklyn minister who heard of the affair, "and send a cyclone of justice upon the ball of selfishness." The Rev. Madison Peters, delivering a sermon on "The Use and Misuse of Wealth," warned darkly: "Sedition is born in the lap of luxury—so fell Rome, Thebes, Babylon, and Carthage."

The Bradley Martins had defenders, such as E. S. Martin of *Harper's Weekly* who pooh-poohed the uproar and said: "The ball was a great ball, an astonishing ball, but it was not really a great event. The money spent on it was much less than what is lost daily, without particular attention, by a big fire." Martin might have added that a big fire would not have been nearly as much fun.

Incensed by the popular disapproval of their soiree, the Bradley Martins—like William Waldorf Astor before them—decided to forsake America for England and Scotland. But, before boarding their steamer, they paused at the Waldorf long enough to give a farewell dinner for eighty-six persons that cost $116.28 per plate.

The excesses of the Bradley Martin ball may have been characteristic of the Waldorf, but they were not typical. No other event matched that revelry in cost or notoriety, and George Boldt was just as glad. The Waldorf thrived on a consistent diet of *sensible* extravagance and did not relish outlandish displays. There was not a night in a typical Waldorf week when men of substance and women of style did not cross the great Thirty-fourth Street lobby or pull up to a table in the Astor dining room. The Bradley Martins had left New York, but there were Vanderbilts enough—and Oelrichses,

Dancing in costume at the Bradley Martin Ball, February 10, 1897 (Harper's Weekly)

Van Rensselaers, Morgans, Schermerhorns, and Fricks—to assure the Waldorf undiminished luster.

The eagerness with which millionaires and millionairesses vied for opportunities to spend their evenings and their dollars in the hotel was due in large part to the suave and affable manner of Oscar Tschirky, who quickly rose from head waiter to *maître d'hôtel* and an unofficial position as chief lieutenant to George Boldt. A handsome man with a winning smile and an enviable ability to bow nearly to the floor while at the same time extending an upturned palm in a most supplicating manner, Oscar became known to hotel regulars, and eventually to the world, as Oscar of the Waldorf. The title was not patronizing. It signified elevation to a kind of American nobility—making him perhaps the only peer in the world to have a hotel in his title. Oscar was liked as much as he was admired, and newspapers often poked good-natured fun at him. Once when Boldt ordered all members of the hotel staff to be vaccinated for smallpox, the *World* commented wryly: "It was feared by some that the virus would make Oscar's arm so sore he would be unable to extend it for the customary gratuity. Rather than offend his friends, however, he gritted his teeth and took the tips."

Another stellar attraction of the hotel was a long corridor that ran through the Waldorf half connecting two of the most popular restaurants, the Palm and Empire rooms. It was a glittering hall with walls of veined marble, soaring Corinthian columns, mosaic floors, and fine sofas and chairs along the sides. Almost from the opening of the hotel, the corridor was a popular promenade for ladies of fashion who liked to show off their gowns and jewels, a display case for the exhibition of New York's gaudiest plumage. According to Oscar, it was the society editor of the New York *Tribune* who first called the corridor Peacock Alley. It mattered little that the fineries displayed there were feminine rather than masculine. The name, conjuring up images of strutting birds and sweeping plumes, was apposite, and it stuck. When, a few years after the hotel's opening, fashionable crowds showed a preference for parading in an even grander corridor on the Astoria side, the name of Peacock Alley was transferred to the new gallery. It was not unusual for twenty-five thousand people to stroll the length of Peacock Alley on a single day, and for nearly as many to take seats along the way to watch the strollers. Women who could not afford to join the parade loved to stare at it, noting frocks, admiring hats,

Peacock Alley at the old Waldorf-Astoria (Courtesy of the Waldorf-Astoria)

appraising wraps, and trying to guess the identities of the socialites who wore them. For social aspirants, Peacock Alley was the unworldly *summum bonum* of the good life. For those who had already arrived, it was a properly glamorous stage for strutting.

If the alley was the domain of ladies, the ornate, paneled bar was the preserve of gentlemen. The gallery of magnificoes who habituated the room were, in a somber way, as impressive as the women who paraded in the corridor, for together they accounted for much of the wealth and a good part of the power of the republic. Clouds of blue smoke swirled continuously in the masculine sanctum, as glasses were raised, gold coins clanked, and cigar ashes flicked nonchalantly on the floor. Mark Twain was there occasionally, usually in the company of his friend, Standard Oil executive H. H. Rogers. "Diamond Jim" Brady liked to frequent the room, more for conviviality than for refreshment, for the dude was better known as an eater than a drinker. Senators Charles Warren Fairbanks of Indiana, Edward O. Wollcott of Colorado, and Matthew Stanley Quay of Pennsylvania liked to drink together in the bar, though Quay's colleague, Senator Boies Penrose, preferred to take his refreshment alone.

Peter Fenelon Collier, an Irishman who founded a publishing empire in America and, with the profits, bought a great castle in his native land, was often there, as was Richard Harding Davis, a one-time newspaper reporter and magazine editor who won fame and fortune as the author of popular short stories and novels. Silver-haired Lieutenant General Nelson A. Miles was occasionally seen wiping his mustache in the bar, reminiscing about his days as an Indian fighter. Colonel William F. Cody, resplendent in Prince Albert coat, wide-brimmed hat, and long mustache, occasionally strolled in to talk with old friends who invariably invited him to "have one." It is not recorded that the colonel ever refused. Vying in sartorial elegance with the ladies of Peacock Alley was bar-patron Evander Berry Wall, known on three continents as "King of the Dudes," a veritable human peacock who had a wardrobe of five hundred complete changes and wore a minimum of six distinct outfits daily.

"Bet-a-Million" Gates and his bosom friend, Colonel "Ike" Ellwood, were sometimes seen in the bar, though they preferred to spend their time in the Men's Cafe or in a suite of club rooms on the fifteenth floor. True to his colorful sobriquet, Gates was an inveterate and passionate gambler. Much of his public betting was done at Caulfield's, a posh club on East Forty-fourth Street. More was done privately at the Waldorf.

Gates liked to play poker with Herman Frasch, a sulphur magnate; Herman Siecklen, a coffee tycoon; Judge Elbert H. Gary, president of the Federal Steel Company; and William Henry Moore, who founded the American Can Company and in his spare time dabbled in enterprises like the Diamond Match Company, the National Biscuit Company, and the Chicago, Rock Island & Pacific Railway. The limit at Gates' games was usually a sensible thousand dollars, though even at that rate it was possible for an enthusiastic player to take or drop one hundred thousand dollars in an evening. One all-night game of baccarat is said to have terminated at breakfast-time only after one million dollars had changed hands among Gates' guests.

Once Judge Gary, hankering for a game, appeared at the Waldorf and sent word to Gates that he would like to come up and take a hand. When the message was handed to Gates, the plunger told the bellboy: "Tell Judge Gary the game is going so high it will be over his head." The president of Federal Steel, soon to become United States Steel, bowed his head and sadly turned away.

The popularity of the Waldorf did little to enhance the fortunes of either of the Astors who built it. William Waldorf Astor is said to have been in the hotel only once, and that time he paced nervously through Peacock Alley, his eyes on the floor, as he hurried to an elevator. In England his heavy investments in newspapers and castles had stimulated the British economy so much that, in 1917, he was rewarded with a peership and the title of Viscount Astor of Hever Castle. Loathing America to the end, Lord Astor died in England in 1919. His cousin Jack was an occasional visitor to the hotel, but he was not the kind to draw attention. A pleasant man of no particular distinction, he was best known for the bravery he showed while a passenger on the stricken White Star liner *Titanic*. One of the many who did not escape from the crippled vessel, Jack Astor met his death in an icy north Atlantic sea in April 1912.

But the hotel made George Boldt a wealthy man. He plowed his considerable Waldorf earnings into shrewd investments in real estate. When he died in 1916, he was not in the Astor class, but he was a respectable millionaire.

Even before Boldt's demise, there had been unmistakable signs of change at the Waldorf. The value of property in the neighborhood of Fifth Avenue and Thirty-fourth Street had grown enormously in the twenty years since the hotel had opened. On all sides great towers of steel and glass rose into the soaring Manhattan skyline. New hotels like the Plaza, the Savoy, the Netherland, the Pierre, and Jack Astor's own St. Regis had drawn fashionable traffic north to blocks in the fifties and sixties. The Waldorf was inconveniently distant from the new row of luxurious mansions that faced the eastern edge of Central Park. After Boldt's death, the hotel seemed to many to bow its head and breathe a sigh of resignation and defeat.

New fortunes made in World War I had brought new faces to Manhattan, and many old ones—chastened if not destroyed by the imposition of the federal income tax—had been little seen of late. Two men who observed the decline in Waldorf patronage nevertheless believed it could be reversed. The first, Lucius Boomer, was an hôtelier

The bar, old Waldorf-Astoria (Courtesy of the Waldorf-Astoria)

who had been trained in Henry Flagler's Florida hotels and earned a reputation for efficiency and style in New York's McAlpin, a block from the Waldorf. General, later Senator, Coleman Du Pont of the Delaware Du Ponts, a man with wide business interests and a liking for hotels, was the second. "Boomer," Du Pont is supposed to have said one day, "I'll buy the Waldorf if you'll run it." The proposal was too good for the McAlpin manager to decline.

The firm of Boomer and Du Pont bought the Waldorf from the Astors in 1918 and immediately began a new regime. A perfectionist who could spot ashes on the carpet, sloppy tables, and soggy pastries, Boomer was also a dynamic business executive. With Du Pont he acquired Sherry's famous Manhattan restaurant, expanded it into a chain, and eventually combined it with William Waldorf Astor's old Netherland Hotel to form a fashionable "apartment hotel" called the Sherry-Netherland. Despite Boomer's vigorous operation of the Waldorf in the twenties, it was clear to many

observers that the days of the dowager were numbered. No quality of the hotel itself destined it to eventual destruction—but its site did.

As property values in the neighborhood assumed astronomical heights, taxes on the hotel became nearly unbearable. Rumors that the Waldorf would be razed circulated through New York as early as 1925, though Boomer regularly and dutifully denied them. By December 1928 he was through denying. Out went the Waldorf's mahogany furniture—the dainty china cuspidors that had replaced the usual brass, the canopied beds, the four-sided bar that had creaked under the elbows of Mark Twain and "Bet-a-Million" Gates—out the ghosts of Bradley Martin, Evander Berry Wall, Colonel William F. Cody, "Diamond Jim" Brady, and Lillian Russell. A new corporation proposing to erect the world's largest office building had offered $13,500,000 for the site on which the Waldorf stood. With only a twinge of regret, Lucius Boomer and Coleman Du Pont signed the necessary contracts and pocketed several million dollars in profits. An army of eager wreckers wrote the last page in the epic of the old Waldorf in May 1929.

The hotel was gone, but the ghosts of Peacock Alley would not sleep. When the Boomer-Du Pont Company was dissolved, Boomer shrewdly retained exclusive rights to use of the name Waldorf-Astoria. The hôtelier was at his winter home in Florida late in 1929 when he received a wire from a builder in New York asking if he would like to head up a new and greater Waldorf. Boomer, who relished the prospect of a sunny retirement in Florida, was of a mind to refuse, but his wife insisted that he return to New York and discuss the idea. Four days after he had left Manhattan, Boomer was back in the city and engaged in conversations with promoters and investors. The new hotel, he was told, would be built on Park Avenue between Forty-ninth and Fiftieth, occupying the whole block through to Lexington. Leonard Schultze of the firm of Schultze and

The old and the new Waldorfs. This perspective drawing, done to scale by architects Schultze and Weaver, shows the contrast in size between the old and new buildings. (Courtesy of the Waldorf-Astoria)

Weaver, who had recently designed the new Breakers Hotel in Palm Beach, was asked to submit drawings. His sketches showed a massive twin-towered hotel (one tower for Waldorf, one for Astoria) that rose forty-seven stories above the street. A few days short of the stock market collapse in October 1929, Boomer and his backers worked out details of financing for the world's greatest hotel.

The new Waldorf-Astoria was a vast undertaking joined in by many men and nearly as many corporations. Construction funds totaling forty million dollars were provided by a consortium of banks and railroads, including Hayden, Stone & Company, Hallgarten & Company, Kisser, Kinnicutt & Company, and the New York Central and New York, New Haven and Hartford railroads. The construction firm of Thompson and Starrett was hired to build the structure. On April 1, 1929, preparations were made to transfer a New York Central power station from the proposed site to a new location beneath the Commodore Hotel. On November 4 demolition of buildings already on the site began. Excavation commenced on January 6, 1930, and the first rivet in the steel frame of the new building was driven on March 24. On October 1, 1931, the new Waldorf-Astoria was opened to the public.

Describing the hotel was a little like attempting to portray the wonders of Hoover Dam or the Golden Gate Bridge—an exercise in ooh-and-ah statistics: The hotel extended 200 feet along Park and Lexington avenues, 405 feet along Forty-ninth and Fiftieth. Three thousand cubic feet of granite were consumed in its construction, as were 27,100 tons of steel, 76,700 barrels of cement, 1,000,000 square feet of metal lathing and furring, 2,695,000 square feet of terra cotta and gypsum blocks, 11,000,000 bricks, and 300 imported mantels of marble. The tracks of the Penn Central Railroad ran beneath the hotel, which was cushioned from vibrations by an elaborate steel carriage. From its sidewalk entrances to the top of its twin towers, the hotel soared 625 feet into the air. With just under two thousand rooms, it was the largest hotel in the United States, if not in the world.

On September 30, the night before the official opening, thousands of New Yorkers gathered in the great ballroom as Lucius Boomer raised his hands in a gesture of silence and a voice from far-away Washington squeaked through a radio loudspeaker. It was Herbert Hoover, the first President of the United States to speak at the opening of a hotel. "Our hotels have become community institutions," said Hoover. "They are the central

"Oscar of the Waldorf," Oscar Tschirky. Paul Trebilcock completed the oil painting on January 21, 1936. It now hangs in the Waldorf's fourth-floor lobby. (Courtesy of the Waldorf-Astoria)

maple cabinets fronted with glass in which leading New York merchants displayed their wares. It was a handsome corridor which captured the spirit, though it did not duplicate the appearance, of the fabled promenade in the old Waldorf. But it bore the same name, Peacock Alley, and that fact was enough to warm the hearts of nostalgics.

Despite Herbert Hoover's brave hopes, the Waldorf did little to help the sluggish economy of New York in the 1930s. The hotel employed 1,600 people, and hundreds of thousands of guests regularly rested their heads on its pillows, but costs of operation were unexpectedly high, equaling and sometimes exceeding revenues. The beginning of World War II marked a return to prosperity for the city and the hotel.

Even during the bleak years of the Depression, the Waldorf was widely acclaimed as the world's greatest hotel. Top-name entertainers appeared regularly in its Empire Room. Important balls and banquets were held in its ballroom. Hundreds of notables, ranging from European kings to Indian maharajas, bedded down in its luxurious tower suites. President Hoover, after his departure from the White House, made his home in the Waldorf, as did General of the Army Douglas MacArthur, the Duke and Duchess of Windsor, publishers Henry Luce and William Randolph Hearst, Jr., song writer Cole Porter, and a gallery of lesser celebrities.

In the summer of 1949 a writer named Thomas Ewing Dabney readied for publication a book-length biography of hôtelier Conrad Hilton. The book traced the story of Hilton's rise from obscurity in New Mexico, his entry into the hotel business in Cisco, Texas, and his celebrated purchases of Chicago's Palmer House and New York's Plaza. The book, titled *The Man Who Bought the Plaza*, was finished and in the hands of printers when the publishers suddenly ordered work to halt. Title pages were destroyed, dust jackets discarded, and the author called in to revise the text. Conrad Hilton was a good subject for a biography but, as Dabney had learned, a very poor sitter for a portrait. Hastily updated, the book was released to book stores in 1950 under a new title—*The Man Who Bought the Waldorf*.

Why had Hilton, who had already won hotel fame and earned enough money to live on comfortably for several lifetimes, decided to buy the Waldorf? There were many possible reasons—some that were even probable. It was a famous property with a lustrous history, a vast "city within a city" with nearly unlimited revenue-

points of civic hospitality. . . . The erection of this great structure," he continued, mindful of the awful Depression that had settled over the nation, "has been a contribution to the maintenance of employment, and an exhibition of courage and confidence to the whole nation."

Oscar was on hand for the opening, his smile as broad as ever, his palm still discreetly but unmistakably upturned. Those who remembered the old Waldorf were as pleased to see him as anyone, or anything, else in the new hotel—with the possible exception of a broad hallway which paralleled Park Avenue and was entered from the main foyer. Its walls were paneled with French burl walnut inlaid with ebony, its pilasters faced with French rouge marble and topped with capitals and cornices of nickel bronze. Along the walls, at intervals rested producing possibilities. It was a handsome structure that could profitably be operated in conjunction with Hilton's growing chain of hotels in other cities. All these reasons, and more, were summed up in a single phrase scrawled by the ambitious hôtelier across a photograph of the Waldorf-Astoria: "The greatest of them all." Because it was the greatest, Hilton was determined to own it. On October 12, 1949, the Waldorf became a Hilton hotel. More than a quarter of a century later, it continued to carry that designation.

As the new Waldorf approached the fiftieth anniversary of its 1931 opening, it was still New York's greatest hotel. Visiting kings and queens made it a regular stop on visits to New York, as did presidents of the United States. The United States Ambassador to the United Nations maintained a suite in the hotel, as did ambassadors from more than thirty other nations. One day in the early 1960s ex-President Eisenhower was in the Grand Ballroom for a banquet while then-President John F. Kennedy was attending a fund-raising dinner in the Empire Room. Past President Herbert Hoover received an award that day in the hotel. Six astronauts were checking out as the Duke and Duchess of Windsor, with ninety pieces of luggage, were checking in. Francis Cardinal Spellman attended a lunch honoring General Mark Clark, while future Presidents Lyndon B. Johnson and Richard M. Nixon wandered about in the halls.

With five American presidents and a former King of England in the building, it was not a typical day for the Waldorf, but it was not so far out of the ordinary as to cause any great consternation for the hotel.

The Waldorf, as Frank Crowninshield once wrote, is the "Unofficial Palace" of New York, a citadel of luxury, a center of power and wealth, and a living museum of Manhattan history. There are notes here and there that recall the old Waldorf on Fifth Avenue—portraits of hotel luminaries, including a handsome canvas of Oscar Tschirky, at whose death in 1950 all Waldorf flags were lowered to half-staff; the reconstructed Peacock Alley; a magnificent clock saved from the old hotel that has nine feet of bronze adorned with a miniature replica of the Statue of Liberty, four spread-winged eagles, a series of sports scenes, and the likenesses of Queen Victoria, George Washington, Ulysses S. Grant, and Benjamin Harrison.

But the grand tradition that lives in the building recalls the past even better than these relics—memories of the Astors, echoes of "Diamond Jim" Brady, "Bet-a-Million" Gates, and the Bradley Martin Ball; recollections of Coleman Du Pont, Herbert Hoover, and Douglas MacArthur. When night descends on New York and an air of respectful silence creeps through the great lobbies and corridors, the palace inn breathes deeply—but the ghosts of Peacock Alley do not sleep.

Sources

AMERICA INVENTS THE HOTEL

Jefferson Williamson's *The American Hotel, An Anecdotal History* (New York, 1930) is a comprehensive and always fascinating history of American hotels in the nineteenth century. *Fare Thee Well* by Leslie Dorsey and Janice Devine (New York, 1964) is a pictorial review of celebrated nineteenth-century hotels. *Hotel Life* by Norman S. Hayner (Chapel Hill, North Carolina, 1936) is a sociological study of the phenomenon of American hotel life, with frequent references to hotel history. In *Palaces of the People, A Social History of Commercial Hospitality* (New York, 1970), Arthur White broadly surveys the history of hotels throughout the world, briefly mentioning prominent hotels of nineteenth-century America.

THE WHITE FAÇADE THAT GLEAMS
ACROSS THE WAY

The Parker House, Boston

James W. Spring's *Boston and the Parker House* (Boston, 1927), written for the Whipple Corporation at the time of the opening of the new Parker House, devotes most of its space to a detailed history of the hotel property before Harvey Parker acquired it, though it briefly traces the history of the old hotel and describes the new building in detail. More informative, if less pretentious, is the thirty-nine-page historical report by Elizabeth R. Amadon titled *The Parker House*. Published in 1969 by Architectural Heritage, Inc., of Boston (but now available only in libraries), the report traces the ownership of the Parker House property, details the history of the successive Parker House buildings, and describes the owners from Harvey Parker through the Dunfeys.

Lucius Beebe's *Boston and the Boston Legend* (New York, 1936) is the source of valuable background and choice bits of Parker House lore. *King's Handbook of Boston*—especially the Seventh Edition (Boston, 1885)—describes the hotel and its competitors as they were in the seventies and early eighties. Dickens' activities in Boston and at the Parker House are meticulously chronicled in Edward F. Payne's *Dickens Days in Boston* (Boston, 1927), which also contains some interesting background material on the hotel. The story of the foundation and early years of the Saturday Club is told by Edward Waldo Emerson in *The Early Years of the Saturday Club, 1855-1870* (Boston, 1918). M. A. De Wolfe Howe's *Boston: The Place and the People* (New York, 1903) contains further references to the club and its members. The complete text of Oliver Wendell Holmes' "At the Saturday Club" appears in his *Before the Curfew and Other Poems* (Boston, 1888). Articles which appeared in the Boston *Globe* on June 21 and December 3, 1925, and on June 16, 1929, cover further aspects of the Parker House story.

MAGNOLIA DAYS

The Greenbrier, White Sulphur Springs

William Olcott's *The Greenbrier Heritage* (n. p., n. d.), available at the Assistant Manager's office of the Greenbrier, is a concise, informative, and reliable history of White Sulphur Springs from the 1750s through the early 1960s. William Alexander MacCorkle, Governor of West Virginia from 1893 to 1897, published a lengthy volume titled *The White Sulphur Springs: The Traditions, History, and Social Life of the Greenbrier White Sulphur Springs* (New

York, 1916), which preserves early descriptions of the springs and its social life.

Mark Pencil's comments are set forth in *The White Sulphur Papers* (New York, 1839). Civil War military operations at the springs are described by Boyd B. Stutler in *West Virginia in the Civil War* (Charleston, West Virginia, 1966). Lee's visits to the springs are recounted by Douglas Southall Freeman in his *R. E. Lee: A Biography* (four volumes, New York, 1934-5). Descriptions of the springs in the 1870s may be found in Edward King's *The Great South* (Hartford, Conn., 1879; reprinted Baton Rouge, La., 1972) and in John Esten Cooke's "The White Sulphur Springs," *Harper's New Monthly Magazine* (August, 1878), 337-356.

THE PRIDE OF STATE STREET

The Palmer House, Chicago

The history of Potter Palmer and the Palmer House is nearly inseparable from the history of Chicago. Among recent histories of the city, Finis Farr's *Chicago: A Personal History of America's Most American City* (New Rochelle, 1973) and Stephen Longstreet's *Chicago, 1860-1919* (New York, 1973) are recommended. Bertha Palmer is the subject of a biography by Ishbel Ross, *Silhouette in Diamonds* (New York, 1960). In *Give the Lady What She Wants!* (Chicago, 1952), Lloyd Wendt and Herman Kogan tell the story of Potter Palmer's early association with Marshall Field.

A short but informative account of the holocaust of 1871, amply illustrated, is *The Great Fire: Chicago 1871* (New York, 1971) by Herman Kogan and Robert Cromie. Personal recollections of the first and second Palmer Houses, with stories of the fire, are recorded in Henry Ericsson's *Sixty Years a Builder* (Chicago, 1942). Lady Duffus Hardy's impressions of the hotel are recorded in her *Through Cities and Prairie Lands* (London, 1881). Kipling's views of the hotel and city may be found in *From Sea to Sea: Letters of Travel*, available in various editions. Files of the *Chicago Tribune* yield many Palmer House references, as does a reference report titled *The Palmer House*, issued in March 1972 by the Chicago Historical Society.

A DREAM OF GOLD AND SILVER

The Palace, San Francisco

The definitive history of the pre-1906 hotel is *Bonanza Inn: America's First Luxury Hotel* (New York, 1939) by Oscar Lewis and Carroll D. Hall. Ralston's story is told by George Lyman in *Ralston's Ring: California Plunders the Comstock Lode* (New York, 1937) and by David Lavender in *Nothing Seemed Impossible: William C. Ralston and Early San Francisco* (Palo Alto, Cal., 1975).

The strange case of Sarah Althea Sharon is explored in *Sarah and the Senator* (Berkeley, 1964) by Robert H. Kroninger. The earthquake and fire are covered in *The*

Earth Shook, The Sky Burned (Garden City, N. Y., 1959) by William Bronson and in *The San Francisco Earthquake* (New York, 1971) by Gordon Thomas and Max Morgan Wills. Details of Palace life are recorded by Lucius Beebe and Charles Clegg in *San Francisco's Golden Era* (Berkeley, 1960). In *The City at the End of the Rainbow: San Francisco and Its Great Hotels* (New York, 1976), David Siefkin tells the story of the Palace and three other San Francisco hotels.

This chapter is based in part on my article, "The Splendid Caravansary," which appeared in AMERICAN HISTORY *Illustrated*, October 1974.

A RETREAT FOR THE NABOBS

Del Monte Lodge, Pebble Beach

The story of the builders of the Central and Southern Pacific railroads is told by Oscar Lewis in *The Big Four: The Story of Huntington, Stanford, Hopkins and Crocker, and of the Building of the Central Pacific* (New York, 1938). Del Monte in its early days is described by William Henry Bishop in "Southern California," *Harper's New Monthly Magazine* (October 1882), 713-728. Robert Louis Stevenson's comments are from his 1880 essay, "The Old Pacific Capital," reprinted in *From Scotland to Silverado* (Cambridge, Mass., 1966) edited by James D. Hart. Anecdotes of distinguished visitors to the Del Monte Hotel are collected in the *Memoirs* of Benjamin Franklin Wright (Monterey, Cal., 1936). The files of the *Monterey Peninsula Herald* and of *What's Doing on the Monterey Peninsula* (later *Game and Gossip*) have yielded numerous Del Monte references, among them Henry W. Rink's "Inside the Property," *What's Doing* (April 1947), 20-21, 32-33, and John Woolfenden's "Glamorous Gala Opened a Great Hotel," *Monterey Peninsula Herald, Weekend Magazine* (May 9, 1976), 10-15. A good description of Del Monte in the days of Samuel F. B. Morse is "Del Monte," *Fortune* (June 1940), 58-67, 104, 106-107.

WHERE TRADE WINDS BLOW

The Moana and the Royal Hawaiian, Honolulu

Mark Twain's Hawaiian experiences are chronicled by Walter Francis Frear in *Mark Twain and Hawaii* (Chicago, 1947). Robert Louis Stevenson's impressions of the islands are collected in his *Travels in Hawaii* edited and with an introduction by A. Grove Day (Honolulu, 1973).

Isabella Bird's description of the old Royal Hawaiian Hotel may be found in her *Six Months in the Sandwich Islands* (London, 1875; reprinted Honolulu, 1964). Charles Nordhoff's comments are from his *Northern California, Oregon, and the Sandwich Islands* (London, 1874). The Hawaiian experiences of Belle Strong (Isobel Field) are recorded in her autobiography, *This Life I've Loved* (New York, 1937). Some of Charles Warren Stoddard's most notable Hawaiian writings are his "Lazy

Letters from Low Latitudes," which appeared in the *Overland Monthly* (March 1884), 307-315, and *A Trip to Hawaii* (New edition, San Francisco, 1892).

Construction of the old Royal Hawaiian Hotel and the relation of the Hawaiian royal family to it are described by Ralph S. Kuykendall and A. Grove Day in *Hawaii: A History* (Revised edition, Englewood Cliffs, N. J., 1961) and by Ralph S. Kuykendall in *The Hawaiian Kingdom, Volume II, 1854-1874* (Honolulu, 1953). The story of Captain Heinrich (later Henri) Berger was told by Albert P. Taylor in "Henri Berger and Hawaiian Music," *Paradise of the Pacific Magazine* (May 1930), reprinted in *Honolulu Star-Bulletin* "Hawaii 185" *Progress Edition* (January 29, 1963), 6-7.

Construction of the liner *Malolo (Matsonia)* and of the new Royal Hawaiian Hotel are described in Clifford Gessler's *Tropic Landfall: The Port of Honolulu* (Garden City, N. Y., 1942). Joseph Feher's *Hawaii: A Pictorial History* (Honolulu, 1969) and Edward B. Scott's *The Saga of the Sandwich Islands* (Crystal Bay, Nevada, 1968) contain many passing references and pictures relating to the hotels.

QUEEN OF THE GLORY YEARS

Hotel del Coronado, Coronado

Marcie Buckley, official Historian of the Coronado, has surveyed the hotel's history in *The Crown City's Brightest Gem* (third edition, Coronado, 1975). The real estate boom and its effect on San Diego is described by Richard F. Pourade in *The Glory Years* (San Diego, 1964). John D. Spreckels' activities in San Diego are outlined by Glenn Chesney Quiett in his *They Built the West* (New York, 1934). Early descriptions of the hotel may be found in "Coronado Beach," *Harper's Weekly* (September 6, 1890), 699, and Charles Dudley Warner's "The Winter of Our Content," *Harper's New Monthly Magazine* (December 1890), 39-57.

According to local legend, Wallis Spencer and her future husband, the Prince of Wales, met at Coronado in 1920. The legend is supported by the recollections of Coronado old-timers, but not by the principals, and for that reason I have not repeated it. In her memoirs, *The Heart Has Its Reasons* (New York, 1956), the Duchess of Windsor recalls that she met Charlie Chaplin and John Barrymore at Coronado, "but not, as one popular story has it, the Prince of Wales." In *A King's Story* (New York, 1947) the duke recalled that he met Wallis in 1931. In his definitive biography of the duchess, *The Woman He Loved* (New York, 1974), Ralph G. Martin quotes Earl Winfield Spencer as saying that his first wife saw the prince at Coronado, but did not meet him there.

Other aspects of the hotel's history are examined by Burke Ormsby in "The Lady Who Lives By the Sea," *Journal of San Diego History* (January 1966), 3-13; Curtis Zahn in "The Coronado Carries On," *Westways* (January 1946), 10-11; Jerry MacMullen in "Tenting on the Old Camp Ground," *Westways* (September 1959, reprinted from June 1949), 10-11; and John C. Packard in "San Diego's Early Hotels," *Southern California Quarterly* (September 1968).

A MILE HIGH LEGEND

The Brown Palace, Denver

Construction of the hotel is described in "Iron and Steel in Large Buildings," *Scientific American* (May 21, 1892), 325. Jerome C. Smiley's *History of Denver* (Denver, 1903) describes the hotel as it was in its early days and outlines the life of Henry C. Brown. Brown's life is summarized in an obituary published in the *Denver Republican* (March 7, 1906). Brief accounts of the hotel's history are Caroline Bancroft's *The Brown Palace in Denver, Hotel of Plush, Power and Presidents* (Denver, 1955) and Lucius Beebe's "Denver's Brown Palace—A Western Legend," *House and Garden* (September 1956), 97-100, 161. Margaret Tobin Brown's story is told in Caroline Bancroft's *The Unsinkable Mrs. Brown* (Boulder, 1963). Evalyn Walsh McLean's own story is told in *Father Struck It Rich* (Boston, 1936), written by Mrs. McLean with Boyden Sparkes. The lives of Maggie Brown, "Baby" Doe Tabor, Meyer Guggenheim, and Evalyn Walsh McLean are woven into the broader history of Colorado by Phyllis Flanders Dorset in *The New Eldorado, The Story of Colorado's Gold and Silver Rushes* (New York, 1970).

A RIVIERA IN THE ROCKIES

The Broadmoor, Colorado Springs

Marshall Sprague's *One Hundred Plus: A Centennial History of Colorado Springs* (Colorado Springs, 1971) is the best general history of the city. Count Pourtales' Colorado experiences are recorded in his *Lessons Learned from Experience* (Denver, 1955). Marshall Sprague summarizes the Pourtales story in "The Milkman of Broadmoor," Chapter Nine of his *A Gallery of Dudes* (Boston, 1967).

Development of the Broadmoor Hotel is briefly traced by Helen M. Geiger in her booklet, *The Broadmoor Story* (Colorado Springs, 1918) and by William Thayer Tutt in his 1969 Newcomen Society lecture, reprinted as *The Broadmoor Story* (New York and Princeton, 1969).

Descriptions of Colorado Springs and Broadmoor in early days may be found in "Pike's Peak and Colorado Springs," *The Nation* (October 5, 1893), 245-246; Lewis Morris Iddings' "Life in the Altitudes: The Colorado Health Plateau," *Scribner's Magazine* (February 1896), 136 ff; Francis Walker's "Colorado Springs and Round About Pike's Peak," *New England Magazine* (October 1901), 236 ff; and Julian Street's "Colorado Springs and Cripple Creek," *Collier's* (November 21, 1914), 16 ff.

GUARDIAN OF THE STRAITS

Grand Hotel, Mackinac Island

The history of Mackinac Island is surveyed by Walter Havighurst in *Three Flags at the Straits, The Forts of Mackinac* (Englewood Cliffs, N.J., 1966), Meade C. Williams in *Early Mackinac* (New York, 1912), and Eugene T. Petersen in *Mackinac Island, Its History in Pictures* (Mackinac Island, 1973). A chronology of historical events and an early-day description of the island's natural features are contained in *Annals of Fort Mackinac* by Dwight H. Kelton (issued in several editions from 1885 on). A brief description of the island and hotel as they appeared in the early 1890s may be found in "The Fairy Isle of Mackinac" by William C. Richards, which appeared in the *Magazine of American History* for July 1891, at pages 22-35.

Washington Irving's description of Mackinac is from Volume I of his *Astoria* (Philadelphia, 1836). Captain Marryat's comments may be found in his *Diary in America* (London, 1839). William Cullen Bryant's *Letters of a Traveler* (New York, 1850) contain his references to Mackinac.

A brief but informative survey of the history of Grand Hotel is contained in W. Stewart Woodfill's pamphlet, *Grand Hotel, The Story of an Institution,* the text of an address delivered in 1969 before members of the Newcomen Society in North America (New York, 1969). An interesting profile of Woodfill is found in Norma Lee Browning's article, "Michigan's Island Innkeeper," which appeared in the *Saturday Evening Post* for June 4, 1960, at pages 38 ff.

FLAGLER'S FLORIDA

The Breakers, Palm Beach

"Florida's Overseas Railroad," *Florida Historical Quarterly* (April 1957), 287-302, by David L. Willing, tells the story of the railroad to Key West. A booklet titled *The Henry Morrison Flagler Museum* (Palm Beach, 1975) contains a brief sketch of Flagler's life and a complete description of his mansion, Whitehall. The architecture of the Breakers Hotel is described in "The Breakers, Palm Beach," *Architectural Forum* (May 1927), 453-456.

Contemporary journalists' views of Palm Beach and its hotels may be found in E. W. Howe's "The Real Palm Beach," *Saturday Evening Post* (April 17, 1920), 42 ff; "Palm Beach," *Fortune* (February 1936), 55 ff; "Two Great Resorts—A Candid Look," *Life* (January 28, 1958), 87-94; "Society's Last Outpost," *Look* (April 14, 1959), 31-32; Niven Busch's "Palm Beach: The Rarest Resort of Them All," *Holiday* (February 1969), 38 ff; and Rose Safran's "Very Special Resorts," *Holiday* (January/February 1974), 17-20.

Cleveland Amory's entertaining and informative *The Last Resorts* (New York, 1952) contains a good description of Palm Beach life and society in the first half of the twentieth century.

ON THE GREAT SKY TOP

Mohonk Mountain House, Lake Mohonk

Two histories of Mohonk, both available at the Mountain House, trace the interesting story of the Smileys and the resort from the 1860s through the 1970s. *A Short History of Mohonk* is a pamphlet publication issued at Lake Mohonk in 1957, 1970, and 1975. More complete is the hard-bound book by Frederick E. Partington titled *The Story of Mohonk,* originally published at Mohonk in 1911. Revised editions, with additional material by Daniel Smiley, Jr., and Albert K. Smiley, Jr., were published in 1932, 1950, 1962, and 1970. An early and fascinating description of the lake, Mountain House, and surrounding country is the *Guide Book to Mohonk Lake, Ulster County, N. Y.,* published at Lake Mohonk about 1890.

Recent descriptions of the resort are contained in John Egan's "Mohonk Mountain House," *American Home* (October 1971), 42 ff; Richard F. Snow's "Mohonk," *Americana* (September 1976), 2-6; and Arthur Sirdorfsky's "Mohonk Mountain House," *Travel* (December 1976), 32 ff.

A PARAGON OF GRANDEUR

The Plaza, New York City

Eve Brown's *The Plaza, Its Life and Times* (New York, 1967) is the best general history of the hotel. The history by Lucius Beebe written for the hotel's fortieth anniversary celebration in 1947 has been reprinted in *The Lucius Beebe Reader* (Garden City, New York, 1967), edited by Charles Clegg and Duncan Emrich.

The opening of the first Plaza Hotel is described in "A Handsome New Hotel," *New York Times* (September 30, 1890), 5. Conrad Hilton's story is told in his *Be My Guest* (Englewood Cliffs, New Jersey, 1957). Details of later Plaza history are recorded in "At the Plaza," *Newsweek* (October 21, 1957), 108; "Enhanced," *New Yorker* (September 9, 1961), 33-34; James Lavenson's "Think Strawberries," *Saturday Evening Post* (October 1974), 54-55; Robert Kiener's "The Plaza Renaissance . . . at last!" *Hospitality* (November 1975), L42-L43; and "Turn Backward, O Time!" *New Yorker* (February 23, 1976), 27-30.

GHOSTS OF PEACOCK ALLEY

The Waldorf-Astoria, New York City

The history of the Waldorf-Astoria has been more voluminously recorded than that of any other hotel in this book, if not in the United States.

Edward Hungerford's *The Story of the Waldorf-Astoria* (New York, 1925) traces the hotel's early history and tells the stories of William Waldorf Astor, John Jacob Astor IV, George Boldt, Lucius Boomer, and Coleman Du Pont. James Remington McCarthy's *Peacock Alley* (New York, 1931) covers much of the same ground, adding two chapters about the building of the new Waldorf. In two Waldorf volumes—*Peacocks on Parade* (New York, 1931) and *Old Waldorf Bar Days* (New York, 1931)—Albert Stevens Crockett chronicles a wealth of interesting hotel anecdotes.

Six generations of the Astor family are chronicled by Harvey O'Connor in his interesting and informative *The Astors* (New York, 1941). Oscar Tschirky's story is told in *Oscar of the Waldorf* (New York, 1943) by Karl Schriftgiesser. Thomas Ewing Dabney's *The Man Who Bought the Waldorf* (New York, 1950) traces Conrad Hilton's life through the Waldorf purchase. Hilton's memoirs, *Be My Guest* (Englewood Cliffs, N. J., 1957), add personal anecdotes and seven years to Dabney's chronicle.

Construction of the new Waldorf is detailed by Harry B. Lent in *The Waldorf-Astoria: A Brief Chronicle of a Unique Institution Now Entering Its Fifth Decade* (New York, 1934). Horace Sutton's entertaining *Confessions of a Grand Hotel: The Waldorf-Astoria* (New York, 1953) briefly traces the history of the old Waldorf and details that of the new.

ABOUT THE AUTHOR

Brian McGinty is the author of more than sixty articles on history, travel, law, and related subjects. His work has been reprinted in *The Craft of the Essay* (Harcourt Brace Jovanovich, 1977) and *Readings in American History* (Dushkin, 1978).

In 1974 McGinty edited a collector's edition of Robert Louis Stevenson's classic *Napa Wine,* and in 1975 his *Haraszthy at the Mint* was published as Volume 10 of the Famous California Trials series.

A graduate of the School of Law of the University of California, Berkeley, McGinty practices law in San Francisco.